JOHN FANTE

A LITERARY PORTRAIT

ESSAY SERIES 39

Guernica Editions gratefully acknowledges the support of the South
Central Conference on Christianity and Literature.
Guernica Editions gratefully acknowledges the support from Xavier
Review Press.

Canadä

Guernica Editions gratefully acknowledges the financial support of the
Government of Canada through the Book Publishing Industry
Development Program (BPIDP).

RICHARD COLLINS

JOHN FANTE

A LITERARY PORTRAIT

GUERNICA

TORONTO·BUFFALO·LANCASTER (U.K.)

2000

Antonio D'Alfonso, Editor.
Guernica Editions Inc.
P.O. Box 117, Station P, Toronto, (ON), Canada M5S 2S6
2250 Military Rd., Tonawanda, N.Y. 14150-6000 U.S.A.
Gazelle, Falcon House, Queen Square, Lancaster LA1 1RN U.K.

Legal Deposit — First Quarter
National Library of Canada
Library of Congress Catalog Card Number: 99-74141
Canadian Cataloguing in Publication Data
Collins, Richard
John Fante : a literary portrait
(Essay series ; 39)
Includes bibliographical references.
ISBN 1-55071-071-0
1. Fante, John, 1909-1983 – Criticism and interpretation.
I. Title. II. Series: Essay series (Toronto, Ont.) ; 39.
PS3511.A594Z56 1999   813'.54   C99-901462-5

Contents

Preface 9

Chapter 1: Introduction: Fante, Family and the Fiction of
Confession. 15

Chapter 2: The Road from Denver: 1909-1932 36

Chapter 3: Fante's Confessional: Stories or Plain Fiction . 51

Chapter 4: The View from Bunker Hill: 1932-1940 73

Chapter 5: The Apprenticeship of Arturo Bandini 96

Chapter 6: Bandini's Hunger 125

Chapter 7: Hollywood Hokum: 1940-1952 160

Chapter 8: Epiphanies of Incompetence 187

Chapter 9: Home Is Where the Hearth Is 219

Chapter 10: Rancho Fante, Point Dume: 1952-1983 244

Chapter 11: The Legacy of John Fante 263

Notes 274

Bibliography 287

For Leigh
good wife, evil companion

An appeal to the reader to catch the writer's spirit, to think with him, if one can or will — an expression no longer of fact but of his sense of it, his peculiar intuition of a world, prospective, or discerned below the faulty conditions of the present, in either case changed somewhat from the actual world.

Walter Pater, Appreciations

To feel that you have a destiny is a nuisance.
John Fante

KEY TO ABBREVIATIONS

Quotations from the works of John Fante refer to the Black Sparrow Press editions (Santa Barbara, 1980-1985; Santa Rosa, 1986-1991). References are in parentheses with page number and the following title abbreviations:

AD *Ask the Dust* (1980).
BG *The Brotherhood of the Grape* (1988).
BH *Dreams from Bunker Hill* (1982).
BY *1933 Was a Bad Year* (1985).
FL *Full of Life* (1987).
FM *Fante/Mencken: John Fante & H. L. Mencken: A Personal Correspondence,* 1932-1950 (1989).
PAD *Prologue to Ask the Dust* (1990).
RL *The Road to Los Angeles* (1985).
SL *Selected Letters, 1932-1981* (1991).
WB *Wait Until Spring, Bandini* (1983).
WR *West of Rome* (1986).
WY *The Wine of Youth: Selected Stories of John Fante* (1985).

Some letters referred to are not included in *Selected Letters, 1932-1981*. These are in the Carey McWilliams Collection, Special Collections Library of the University of California, Los Angeles.

Other sources are referred to parenthetically in the notes by author and date as listed in the Annotated Bibliography.

PREFACE

In his Preface to John Fante's *Ask the Dust*, Charles Bukowski called the story of John Fante's life and work "a story of terrible luck and a terrible fate and of a rare and natural courage. Some day it will be told but I feel that he doesn't want me to tell it here." I have tried to tell it here, not as Bukowski might have told it, nor perhaps as Fante would have liked it told. But I have tried to tell it in such a way that Fante's increasing number of readers will recognize the creator of Jimmy Toscana, Henry J. Molise, and Arturo Bandini.

When I began this book in the mid-1980s, I spoke of Fante as a "cult" writer. What I meant was that he had a certain select audience, or rather, an audience who thought of themselves as select. What I did *not* mean was that Fante was a figure of camp, like Ronald Firbank, say, whose prose is precious, obscure and virtually inaccessible. No one would mistake Fante for a figure of camp. His blend of bombast and lyricism, braggadocio and sentiment, makes Fante the least pretentious of authors — which is not to say that he does not have a sophisticated literary style, only that his lyric simplicity appears effortless, a highly crafted spontaneity that might be mistaken for naivety. In the style of a good, plain-speaking friend, Fante conveys his infectious delight and sorrow in life. It was no doubt this quality of naked honesty that was being sought when, in the early 1980s, ads starting showing up in the personals seeking other readers of John Fante. Few writers inspire that kind of

affection, that kind of trust. In short, what I meant by calling
Fante a "cult" writer was, quite simply, that he is the kind of
writer whose books tend to be pressed from one hand to
another, and when one reader of Fante meets another, they
nod in silent and secret understanding. Fante is one of those
writers who "belong" to readers. There is a special feeling of
benediction in believing that only "a few of us" are in on the
secret.

Since then, I have seen German translations of *Wait
Until Spring, Bandini* on book racks on the Greek island of
Samos, and French translations of *Ask the Dust* on the book-
stalls of Bucharest. More recently, a Polish student of mine
in Bulgaria has informed me with great excitement that a
Serbo-Croatian translation of *Ask the Dust* has just been
published in Zagreb. Meanwhile, in the bookshops of London, Fante is still shelved under the rubric of "Cult Writers."
Now that the world has come to know Fante, the select "few
of us," his so-called "cult," has grown to cover the globe.
Nevertheless, Fante is still pressed from hand to hand with
warm recommendations and secret smiles.

In May of 1995, a conference was held on John Fante
at California State University, Long Beach, not far from
where Fante published his first attempt at the short story in
the Long Beach City College literary magazine *Edda,* and
not long after that, received his first letter of acceptance from
Mencken's *American Mercury.* Most of the scholars and admirers who gathered to pay homage to John Fante from as
far away as Canada, France, Italy, and Romania, knew about
the second story but learned about the first. They learned
other things too. But it was not what was learned that was
most important, for it was the least academic of conferences,
if by that we mean the cold exchange of information and
theories and the advancement of careers. As the reporter for

the *Los Angeles Times Book Review* said, "At times, in fact, it seemed like a cross between an academic symposium and a family reunion."

More than once, in the midst of a personal recollection of Fante, the speakers were moved to tears. Fante's brother Tom, for example, had to pause while telling how John wasn't interested much in books as a kid, but only cared about baseball. Or his daughter Victoria, when my wife asked her at a reception over a glass of wine about the scene in *My Dog Stupid,* where Henry J. Molise enters his daughter Tina's room after she has left home and smells her pillow and touches all her things and thinks "oh shit" and starts to cry. Victoria recalled how her father used to come in and kiss her on the back of her neck when her friends were there: "I hated that," she said, with tears in her eyes. "He was so Italian!" Then, with the generosity characteristic of the Fante family, she changed the subject: "You've come from where? Romania! Mother, they've come all the way from Romania!"

The Fante family had waited all their lives for the success and recognition that they and Fante had always believed was just around the corner. Here it was, but too late for Fante himself to enjoy.

It wasn't just the family who were moved by the proceedings, or an old drinking companion like A. I. Bezzerides, who said, "that they're responding to him today, like he wouldn't believe, is fantastic. But why so fucking late?" It was the scholars, too. After his Keynote Address, Professor Jay Martin confessed that in all his years of giving hundreds of papers at conferences, this was only the second time he ever felt that he wasn't going to make it through to the conclusion because of the tears that were welling up in his throat.

A book is not exactly a personal ad, but it is an attempt at connection with like hearts and minds. This book is an attempt to locate readers of John Fante, however numerous and wherever they are, to share the common experience of Fante's fiction, to find out more about Fante's life, to better understand the connection beteeen his life and his fiction, and to form relationships, as they say in the ads, "possibly lasting." Throughout his life, Fante found consolation and inspiration in his family when he was unable to find what every writer desires, a faithful audience of readers, which is a kind of public family. When it came, he had little time to enjoy it. This book intends, somewhat belatedly, to extend and enlarge that family of friends. Fante had a healthy suspicion of critics and biographers, with their weird hypotheses and critical "hokum," and I suspect he might have had some choice words for me. I only regret that I won't be able to hear his honest opinion, delivered perhaps with all the brutal wit of Arturo Bandini on a rant, of this "literary portrait" of him. Such rough and eloquent honesty is just the kind of thing that inspires affection — and trust — among readers of fiction and personal ads.

In the process of writing this book I have formed several, I hope, lasting relationships with other readers of Fante. With friendship has come obligations, and I would like to pause here to thank everyone who helped to make it possible for me to finish this labor of love. First of all, I would like to thank all the participants of the John Fante Conference held May 4-6, 1995, at California State University, Long Beach, for sharing their knowledge and enthusiasm. I wish to thank especially the organizers, Stephen Cooper and David Fine, the Fante family, and Paul Yamamoto, as well as Kate Kordich, Gay Talese, Fred L. Gardaphé, but above all Professor Jay Martin, who has read this book in several manuscript versions over the years, and who has such a flare for titles.

It was Jay Martin who called an early version of this book "a literary portrait." I have adopted the phrase as the subtitle to the book, and have tried to live up to that venerable and difficult literary form. To put it another way, this book is, in Walter Pater's unfashionable term, an *appreciation*, "an appeal to the reader to catch the writer's spirit, to think with him, if one can or will — an expression no longer of fact but of his sense of it, his peculiar intuition of a world, prospective, or discerned below the faulty conditions of the present, in either case changed somewhat from the actual world." The book proceeds chronologically, with alternating chapters of "fact" and Fante's "sense of it," the life of Fante interspersed with the fictional lives of the Toscanas, Bandinis, and Molises. By this structure I have hoped to convey the intricate, inextricable texture of Fante's life and fiction.

I would also like to thank the editors of the following journals for permission to use material in several articles I've published over the years. An earlier version of Chapter 1 was delivered at the John Fante Conference as "Fante's Families" and appears in *John Fante: A Critical Gathering* (Madison, N.J.: Fairleigh Dickinson Univeristy Press, 1999), edited by Stephen Cooper and David Fine. Parts of Chapters 3 and 7 were published in *The Redneck Review of Literature,* 21 (Fall 1991) as "Of Wops, Dagos and Filipinos: John Fante and the Immigrant Experience." Part of Chapter 8 was published in *Aethlon: The Journal of Sport Literature,* 12:1 (Summer 1995) as "Stealing Home: John Fante and the Moral Dimension of Baseball."

Finally, I want to thank Antonio D'Alfonso for encouraging me to write the book I wanted to write, and to express what can't be expressed to my wife Leigh, without whom I could not have finished this labor of love.

Blagoevgrad, Bulgaria
New Year's Day, 1996

CHAPTER 1

INTRODUCTION

FANTE, FAMILY AND THE FICTION OF CONFESSION

> "You can't write your confession!" I wailed. "You have to tell it. In the confessional."
>
> John Fante in "My Father's God"

As the son of an Italian immigrant, and as one of the displaced in Depression California, John Fante knew what it was to be cut off from his roots in the past and alienated from society in the present. Fiction was his way of re-connecting. In the early story "The Odyssey of a Wop," Jimmy Toscana rejects his Catholic upbringing, his Italian-American heritage, and his own family, only to realize: "There's no sense in hammering your own corpse" (WY 41). The odyssey of John Fante led him away from family into bohemian rebellion and the lures of Hollywood fortune, even while literary fame remained elusive. But the way of his life and fiction always led him back to his parents and his children, the family providing the narrative strand that guides him through the retrospective maze of his entire autobiographical corpus.

For John Fante, family was the beginning and the end. In his work, family is the microcosm and the model for all community, but especially for the uprooted, whether immigrants from Europe or Asia, or migrants from the Midwest who, like him, found themselves alone in unfamiliar surroundings in California. Fante found his material in their dreams, which were his dreams of a family lost and found, even though other dreams of success and independence often came in conflict with the stability of the family and the tradition for which it stands. In the end, after the dreams have faded and the dreamers have failed, the family is there as consolation and reward after the epiphany of failure.

Fante found his impulse to write from a number of family structures, both actual and metaphorical, social and literary. The son of a bricklayer from the rocky Abruzzi, Fante grew up poor and Catholic in Denver and Boulder, attended a Jesuit high school, then in the early 1930s wandered west to seek his fame and fortune as a writer in Los Angeles. Fortune came more easily than fame, first as a short story writer, then as a screenwriter. Neither medium really suited him, though he was talented and successful at both. Short story writing was "pimping for the advertisers," and screen writing was only so much "hokum." Both were "money-makers" for what Fante considered his calling as a novelist. And the novels he wrote for the next fifty years are filled with fathers and sons, father confessors and confessing fathers, and confessional writers who happen to be fathers and sons.

In the early days in Long Beach and L.A., when Fante was sending off everything he wrote to H. L. Mencken, the editor of the *American Mercury* wrote back to say that Fante seemed to be obsessed with his family and that perhaps he should try his hand at some other subjects. "I have a feeling that you had better stop writing about your family. The subject seems to obsess you . . . Why don't you do some stories about other people?" (FM 37). With only a few exceptions, however, Fante followed his obsession. In the dynamics of a few families whose names end in vowels, Fante found all the characters and situations he needed to say what he had to say. Looking back on his first published novel, *Wait Until Spring, Bandini,* Fante wrote: "of this I am sure: all of the people of my writing life, all of my characters are to be found in this early work" (WB 8). The Toscanas of the early stories, like the Bandinis and the Molises of the novels, are essentially the same family, based on his own, and in some ways they are more accurate portrayals of the Fante family than the supposedly non-fiction novel *Full of Life.* All of Fante's narrators are his alter egos. All of them are fathers and sons, Catholics, Italian Americans, dreamers, writers, and fools.

All of Fante's families and their concerns are essentially the same, but I think we can see important distinctions between them that form a progression. In the Toscana stories Fante's obsession with family is developed from the kernel of his childhood experience into the most extended uses of the term family, including the formative influence of the metaphorical family of Catholicism with its Fathers, Sisters and Mothers Superior, and the equally formative influence of the Italian-American community with its heritage of cultural heroes from Dante and Columbus to Enrico Caruso and Joe DiMaggio. Fante felt the hegemony of these family structures, the subtle and not so subtle ways that they form and deform their members.

On the other hand, Fante found another, more fluid family structure in the community of writers, both living and dead. He discovered his roots in his literary ancestors and older contemporaries like Sherwood Anderson and Knut Hamsun, and he made contact with his mentor and literary father, H.L. Mencken. Through them, Fante discovered that art was a way of talking about all the family ties that had restricted him, a way of escaping from the material strictures of the Depression, and a way of figuring out his own place in the scheme of things in twentieth-century America.

In the four novels that make up The Saga of Arturo Bandini, for example, we see the young writer in four distinct stages of development: the formative influences of family, religion and ethnic heritage before the desire to write becomes conscious (Wait Until Spring, Bandini); the rough beginnings of self-expression and the breaking of ties with all formative influences except the literary (The Road to Los Angeles); the first successes of a writing career, and the ensuing realization that there is more to life than literature (Ask the Dust); and the seductions of early success, which in Arturo's case lead into the detour of screen writing and the illusory freedom of financial independence (Dreams from Bunker Hill). The first two novels are of starting out and breaking away, while the latter two express Fante's best hopes and bohemian beginnings in and around Bunker Hill in the 1930s. In these novels, Fante shifts his emphasis away from the family and heritage to the young writer's necessary alienation from these structures. Bandini tries, through the braggadocio of his art, to establish his independence from each of these family ties and their coercions to compromise. Ultimately, such attempts at escape turn out to be futile, but the works of art remain as exemplary attempts at absolute freedom.

In these novels, too, Fante freely transforms his alter ego, according to the life of the fiction, without regard to facts established in previous books in the series.[1] Arturo grows up in California or Colorado, his father is deceased or still living, his siblings are a single sister or several brothers, his middle name changes from Gabriel to Dominic, and so on.[2] Other details of character and situation change from book to book, but Arturo's basic profile remains the same. Arturo Bandini is the bridge between the sensitive but rebellious altar boy Jimmy Toscana and the disillusioned middle-aged screenwriter and family man Henry Molise. Arturo is both the incorrigible altar boy of *Wait Until Spring, Bandini* and the less than successful screenwriter and aspiring novelist in *Dreams from Bunker Hill*. Bandini is never, however, the doting son, the uxorious husband, or the self-sacrificing father. He is always the eternal adolescent, the incurable idealist, and, above all, the archetypal struggling artist, as his name implies.

Fante chose the family names Toscana and Molise for their associations with the Italian regions of Tuscany and Molise, locating them solidly in the Italian landscape. Guido Toscana, for example, puffs his trademark Toscanelli cigar. But Bandini's name is singular, unattached. It is significant that the conductor Arturo Toscanini was a household name when Fante was growing up, and a cultural idol of Italian Americans. Not only does Bandini share Toscanini's first name (the last name linking him to Jimmy Toscana), Arturo conveniently connotes (at least to American ears) an "author." Fante may also have been drawing upon the Italian verb *bandire* (to proclaim, to announce, to publish) with the name Bandini, since Arturo does proclaim and announce at the top of his lungs his intention to publish, and so becomes a kind of *banditore*, or public crier. But as Arturo would be the first to admit, he is also a *bandito*, an outlaw, an outcast "banished" from society, a loner whose message is a cry from the lunatic fringe.

In the Molise sequence of novels Fante confesses how the early ambitions of Arturo Bandini didn't pan out, how he betrayed first his family and then his own dreams, and concludes by pleading for absolution and reconciliation with his family, usually at the expense of the independence that was so hard won and that had seemed so important in his youth. Each of the Molise novels hinges upon a sort of epiphany, what I call an "epiphany of incompetence," an "epiphany of fallibility," or an "epiphany of failure." Young Dominic Molise of *1933 Was a Bad Year*, for example, finds out that the dreams of one generation inevitably conflict with those of the next, for as he says, "we were a house full of dreamers" (BY 36). He wants to go to Catalina Island for a tryout with the Cubs; his father wants him to lay brick, ruin his hands, pitch on Sundays, and go into the bricklaying business. Since the dreams of fathers and sons are, archetypically, incompatible and irreconcilable, one must give up his dream to allow the other to pursue his. Sometimes it is the father who makes the sacrifice, sometimes the son, and sometimes, as in *1933 Was a Bad Year*'s O. Henry-style variation, both.

This thematic progression from obsession to alienation to reconciliation is paralleled by Fante's attitude toward the art of fiction: from simple story-telling as a calling and a career in the beginning, to a hunger for achieving novelistic form and critical fame, to writing less as a career than as a constant call to confession for its own sake. Always the concern is with the shifting border realm between truth and lies, "stories and plain fiction," autobiography and confession. From the beginning, story-telling and confession are bound together for Fante into a single paradox about the nature of narrative. In the oral culture of Fante's youth among the Italian immigrants in North Denver, story-telling was a received art, a learned pretext that used traditional forms, borrowed or formulaic, to connect one's voice to the community — not, in that sense, so very unlike the formulaic ritual of the confessional.

I suspect that Fante's familiarity with these two forms of narrative, the oral tale of his Italian-American upbringing and the confessional of the Church, was no small part of what made movie-writing or scenario-pitching so easy for Fante. Borrowed formulas were second nature to him, and easily applicable to the genres of the Western, the gangster film, or, more to his taste, the domestic or romantic comedy. Fante made use of these conventions throughout his career as a screenwriter, and he in turn used screenplay devices for certain effects in his fiction (the quick character sketch, the snappy true-to-life dialogue, the rags-to-riches-to-rags turns of fortune, the tear-jerking conclusion).

For instance, in the opening story of *Dago Red*, "A Kidnaping in the Family," we see Jimmy Toscana getting his mother to deny the actual events of her courtship and to tell it the way it was supposed to be. She collaborates with her son, detail by detail, on what amounts to the scenario for a romantic Western, and to do so she has to distort the facts of her own history to suit her son's imagination. Jimmy Toscana is too young, idealistic and unconsciously Oedipal to see that the real-life romance of the once-dashing, once-young, cigar-chewing, wine-drinking, aria-singing Guido Toscana in pursuit of the "rebel" Maria Scarpi who would rather have been a nun, is better, more vivid, and yet more accurate and true to the facts than the empty formula of the Western. But Fante is mature enough to see this, and conscious enough of the forms he is playing upon, to make us see it too.

Because Fante knew very well what made a movie scenario, as well as how this differed from his "literary" fiction, he often shaped a short story to fit his market, cynically sending off inferior work to *Collier's*, *Good Housekeeping* or *Woman's Home Companion*. This is especially true of the stories from the 1940s and early 1950s, when Fante was most deeply involved in making it as a screenwriter. Significantly, he often abandons the family material in these lesser stories, as he did in his screenplays, for protagonists with Anglo-Saxon surnames.[3] For the most part, Fante reserved his family material for his serious fiction, as though it were somehow sacred. These days we hear a lot of cant about "family values" of the canned and intolerant variety that Fante would no doubt have called "hokum" and then found a story and a market to place it in that appealed to just such values. Fante knew, however, that "family values" are a difficult matter, perhaps the most difficult matter, to write about — precisely because the family invites knee-jerk (and tear-jerk) formulas.

The closer Fante gets to his family material the more problematic the conflicts become, and the more he must reconcile the artistic balancing act between truth and fiction, confession and the artful lie. All of Fante's young narrators tell stories. More accurately, they are tellers of tall tales. From Plato to Mark Twain, Nietzsche and Oscar Wilde, the art of lying as the essence of story-telling has been well-established. The Italian literary tradition is even more pertinent in Fante's case, since Benvenuto Cellini and Giovanni Casanova confused autobiographical narrative with the most outrageous lies in their literary confessions.[4]

While religious confession is not identical to literary confession, they are similar enough to make the comparison between them a logical, indeed irresistible theme for any

Catholic writer who happens to deal in the autobiographical. The literary confession has this, at least, in common with the religious confession: each is a way of being absolved of sins, lies among them, while — and through — telling stories full of drama and conflict. Only the most incriminating and salacious details are expected to be narrated, and must be narrated in full and regularly, preferably once a week. As Jimmy Toscana says in "The Road to Hell": "When you go to Confession you must tell everything" (WY 111). Fante's young alter egos are not only thieves and blasphemers, they are also experienced liars. And while they usually tell the truth in the confessional of the Church, some of them recognize that lying is a good finger exercise for their ambitions of becoming maestro fiction writers. For an autobiographical writer, "everything" includes the process of how the story came to be: thus the frequent metafictional component of Fante's work.

The importance of confession, and the relationship of the spoken to the written word, is most apparent in Fante's last published story, "My Father's God," which appeared in *Italian Americana* in 1975, long after Fante had given up the short story form and its financial rewards. "My Father's God" has none of the "pimping for the advertisers" cynicism that Fante associated with his short fiction. Although the family name is not given, the story appears to be, logically and chronologically, a by-product of (or study for) the novel Fante had been working on since the 1950s, *The Brotherhood of the Grape,* and therefore part of the Molise sequence. In this story, as in that novel, Fante makes a valiant last effort to come to terms with his difficult father, who died in 1950. "My Father's God" is, arguably, Fante's finest short story.

The story concerns the "the tedious struggle" (WY 185) for the soul of the narrator's father, who has his own ideas

on what religion and praying and confession are all about. "
'God's everywhere, so why do I have to see Him in a
church? He's right here too, in this house, this room. He's in
my hand. Look.' He opened and closed his fist. 'He's right
in there. In my eyes, my mouth, my ears, my blood. So
what's the sense of walking eight blocks through the snow,
when all I got to do is sit right here with God in my own
house' " (WY 189-90). The son offers to stay home and pray
with his father, but Papa snaps, "Nobody prays here but
me" (WY 190). When a new priest arrives, a Sicilian "All-
American halfback from Boston College" (WY 185), it is
difficult to give odds on which "father" will win the struggle
for Papa's soul. Father Ramponi is "a bull of a man, with
wide, crushed nostrils out of which black hairs flared," but
his voice is "small and sibilant, surprisingly sweet and un-
certain" (WY 187). After the two men consume several gal-
lons of Prohibition dago red from Papa's cellar, they strike a
deal. Since Papa is adamant that he will not enter the confessional, Father Ramponi agrees to receive Papa's confession in writing.

The narrator's bricklayer father briefly turns writer to
compose his confession. Papa labors over the manuscript for
a week of late nights, filling "a jumbo school tablet" with
thirty years of sin. The son lodges a protest against this
deviation from the normal procedure: "'You can't *write* your
confession!' I wailed. 'You have to *tell* it. In the confessional.'"

The father replies that no one will "get me in that box!"
(WY 195). Over his protests, the son is made to deliver the
manuscript to the priest. "Why should I be forced to walk
the streets with it? They weren't my sins, they were his, so
let him carry them to the priest" (WY 195). Still, he carries his
father's burden.

Father Ramponi arrives at the house with the manuscript, and says that Papa has deceived him. Papa stands firm. "It's all there, Father. I didn't forget a thing" (WY 197). Then Father Ramponi must make a confession: he does not speak Italian. "Or read it. Or write it. Or understand it." Papa is stunned; it's unbelievable. Not read Italian! "'The pope speaks Italian,' my father said. 'The cardinals, they speak Italian. The saints speak Italian. Even God speaks Italian. But you, Father Bruno Ramponi, don't speak Italian'" (WY 197). Papa has unwittingly bested the representative of the Church, and the representative knows it. By conceding defeat to the peasant from the Abruzzi, the Jesuit from Boston College admits that teology is once again bested by humanity.

Still, a deal's a deal. So the priest orders Nick to burn the manuscript and gives him absolution in the middle of the kitchen floor, as though his house were a church, after all. Before leaving, Father Ramponi says that next time he expects to see Papa at Mass and in the confessional. Papa is coy: "We'll see, Father" and "I'll try and make it, Father." Papa has got everything he wanted: he has made his house into a place of worship, he has confessed without entering the confessional, he has been absolved and blessed, all on his terms and on his turf. After Father Ramponi leaves, Papa stands in the middle of his house and raises a glass of dago red heavenward to his Italian-speaking God and drinks.

This scene is crucial for the immigrant writer's pride and sense of self in America. Far from being handicapped by his "ignorance" of the American language, Nick is doubly knowing (gnostic), doubly enabled, because, unlike the Americanized Father Ramponi, Nick is bilingual. Not only is he able to get by in English, Nick is in a sense closer than Father Ramponi to God, who may speak English, but most definitely "speaks Italian." The father's written confession is his triumph over the mediation of the Church, a direct communication with his God, accomplished without the demeaning gesture of putting himself "in the box." If confession is an encouragement to tell the truth, the father's confession has served its purpose, for as Oscar Wilde said, "There is a luxury in self-reproach. When we blame ourselves we feel that no one else has a right to blame us. It is the confession, not the priest, that gives us absolution."[5] If confession is an expression of faith, Papa's confession is again valid, even if Father Ramponi is unable to validate it. Not only does Nick escape the confines of the confessional, he also escapes the indignity of the exposure of both the spoken and the written confession. The son's biggest fear when delivering the story was that one of the older boys might filch it: "I was in a panic as I imagined the confession being passed around, being read in the lavatory, touching off raucous laughter spilling into the halls, the streets, as the whole town laughed at my father's sins" (WY 196). As it turns out, this was an unfounded fear, since any one of the boys in his "school full of thieves" was unlikely to be conversant in Italian, either. We never see what is in the manuscript, but we can assume that Nick has told the whole truth in his narrative of thirty years of sin, without any of the temptations of literary flourishes, tall tales or lies. We have the tantalizing sense that the story is not only true but also complete, that, as Papa says, "it's all there, over thirty years, the bad things in a man's life" (WY 197).

Although Fante was not bilingual, he too was doubly enabled in having at his disposal both a literary tradition (Italian, British and American) and an oral tradition (Italian, Catholic, familial). The two traditions do not always perfectly mesh, but they can and often must be freely translated (if not exactly transposed or transliterated) by the generation that finds itself with both traditions at its disposal. Incorporating the oral tradition into the written is one way for the ethnic writer to come to terms with his heritage while asserting his identity as an American. As Fred L. Gardaphé has claimed, for the "American-born children" of immigrants, "literacy became synonymous with 'going American.'"[6] Form may determine content, but content also determines form. The subject matter of the Italian-American writer — character, setting, conflict and plot — chart what this "going American" means, while the style — the storytelling form that draws on oral resources — reflects where the characters are "coming from" in "going American." The importance of this dynamic concerning ethnic narrative becomes clear when we acknowledge that the great discovery of the narrator in "My Father's God" is that one can, under certain circumstances, deviate from the orthodox procedure, and tell one's confession in writing.

It is the father's triumph that no one reads his confession. The writer, on the other hand, triumphs only if his confessions are "passed around" and "being read," even if only in the lavatory, "touching off raucous laughter spilling into the halls, the streets" and "the whole town." In the confessional of literature, it is necessary to speak (through writing) and to be heard. In this sense, the father is more of a nonconformist and more radically protestant than his son, in that he deals directly with his God and bypasses the mediation of the Church. For Fante, literature replaced Church and religion, without losing their functions. The great writers became his pantheon of gods, and Mencken his father figure, like a confessor, to whom he took all his early errors and aspirations. Like a priest, the editor mediates between the writer and his public, and if the writer's

confessions are worthy or artful enough, the editor publishes them for readers, that silent community of confessors,
who give or withhold absolution in the present, and for the
presiding god of literature, Posterity, who passes judgment
on the immortality of the author over the ages.

Autobiography cannot be read without considering it
as metafiction, which is perhaps why the theory of autobiography has developed significantly only in the last twenty
years.[7] It always comments on its own composition; is always its own critique and revelation. When Fante felt himself posing, indulging in "smart-aleckery," playing "the wise
guy, the white-haired boy," he would stop himself because
he knew he was "playing a trick" on no one but himself. "I
know when I am honest and when I am cheating," he said,
and when he was cheating he would "rather go to jail than
have people read the book, because there is no truth in it. I
don't mean autobiographical fact, I mean something else. I
don't know what you would call it, but it's different from
autobiography, yet it's very much like it" (SL 56-7). What his
hero Knut Hamsun called it, and what Fante was perhaps
trying to describe, was "unselfish inwardness."[8] In Fante's
confessional — whether we think of it as that of Rome or
Rousseau — the point of the autobiographical narrative is to
reflect on one's life with candor and self-conscious earnest-
ness.[9] In the process, one must admit to *telling* distortions,
both in the sense of admitting to distorting the truth, and in
the sense of the distortions betraying or telling on themselves. "It's that feeling you get when you begin to write
something you really love," said Fante, still trying to describe his sense of confessional truth. "I don't think I have
made this very clear, but the best I can say is that when you
write in this vein that I speak of, you have a very keen
satisfaction in what you're doing. You don't worry about

plots and dramatic sequences. They come quite naturally. You simply write and write, and lo! By God, there's a story, and a swell story. I know that feeling. If I don't have it, I write like the white-haired boy. Fuck him!" (SL 57).

The truth of the telling, in the final analysis, can be felt only in the sincerity of the teller. This, I believe, is the key to Fante's success as a writer in the 1930s, and his even greater success in the 1980s and 1990s, and why he floundered in the dangerous decades of hypocrisy and idealism in between. Fante was impressed neither with the "Word-Culture" of modernism, in Bukowski's phrase, nor with the extension of that obsession in the word games of postmodernism. Fante is that other kind of postmodernist, engaged less with the *experimental* mediations of literary style and form than with the *experiential* immediacies of life. Like Henry Miller, Edward Dahlberg and Knut Hamsun, Fante does not hide behind literature but uses it in a more relevant and rebellious endeavor, to expose himself, to find a way to tell about all of his experience, and, more, to confess even that which has been experienced only in the imagination, in a state of "unselfish inwardness." In Fante's case, this flight from the complexities of "literariness" has to do with the failure of the romance of literature. In this way, he is representative of his times, the 1930s, 1980s and 1990s. The compensation and reward for the failure of life-long dreams, whether to achieve stardom in the sports pages or the literary reviews, is a greater appreciation of life as it is, the texture of life that was glimpsed, for example, in the courtship of Jimmy Toscana's mother by the cigar-chewing, wine-drinking, aria-singing Guido Toscana who saw the beauty of life (and of his future wife) better with a little wine in his belly.

Fante knows this secret, the secret of the tragic "broth-erhood of the grape." He is willing to play the fool in all his books because it is only the fool who persists in his folly who becomes wise. One reviewer of *Full of Life* said that Fante managed to escape "the horrors of cuteness" in the "cliché-ridden territory" of domestic comedy.[10] It is not so much that Fante escapes the clichés, but that he is so aware of them that he confronts the kitsch head-on. Since kitsch is all-pervasive, it is self-deception to think that we can escape it; indeed, such self-deception is itself the most self-congratulatory and insidious form of kitsch.[11] The best we can do, without sacrificing spontaneity and true sentiment, is to be aware of the kitsch we succumb to. As screenwriter and short-story writer, Fante knew the territory of kitsch inside-out. He was also wise enough to know that the domestic clichés could no more be avoided than one's family, religion, heritage, or self. Indeed, to do so is to betray oneself; or, as he says in "The Odyssey of a Wop," to batter one's own corpse.

If *Full of Life* represents Fante's flirtation with and exploitation of kitsch in his popular fiction, the other books in the Molise cycle of novels, *1933 Was a Bad Year, My Dog Stupid* and *The Brotherhood of the Grape,* show his summary rejection of kitsch. The difference is between a book "written for money" and those written out of purely artistic and personal motives. As Joyce Fante has pointed out, *Full of Life*'s sunny portrait of a couple in the midst of post-war affluence was, ironically, perhaps Fante's most dishonest book, bearing the least resemblance to the real-life turmoil they were undergoing.[12] While the John Fante in the book dotes on his wife and the baby to come, the John Fante who wrote the book was staying out all night drinking and gam-bling and demanding that his wife have an abortion. The irony is that the publisher, Little, Brown, wanted the book to be marketed as non-fiction, prompting Fante to change the characters' names from Molise to Fante.[13] Writing to Mencken, Fante confessed: "I must admit that I made one rather embarrassing compromise along the way. The book is fiction, pure and simple. Little, Brown felt that as fiction it would not sell. They wondered if I would object to using my own name for the hero. I went along. Now, by virtue of this absurd change in names, the book is no longer fiction but fact" (FM 137).

Fante admitted it was a dishonest book and "not a very good novel" compared to his more important works, which he compared to boils: "I wrote [Wait Until Spring, Bandini] because it was a boil that had to be lanced. Most of my short stories were smaller boils. Ask the Dust was a painful boil. It had to be bled and cleansed. Full of Life was written for money. It is not a very good novel. My Dog Stupid is another boil. I lanced it" (SL 294). But Full of Life was a band-aid over a boil, a cover-up. It was, however, his most financially rewarding book. This is less an irony than a fact of publishing life as Fante had come to know it. Fante's most honest book, in his opinion, was The Road to Los Angeles, "fearfully honest," and never found a publisher in his lifetime. When it was rejected by Knopf, Fante vowed never again to write with such "candor" or "unrestraint": "it's a poor policy to be honest" and "much better to be artistic." He concluded that if he wanted to be "a famous writer" he had better look at literature through the eyes of the publishers "and forget whatever I feel" (SL 130-31). The result was the outrageous and wildly successful lie, Full of Life.

Fante atoned for the dishonesty of Full of Life with the biting comedy and brutal authenticity of the other three Molise novels. In these books Fante does his best to come to terms once and for all with the coercions of the family, first

from the point of view of the son who betrays the father in
1933 Was a Bad Year, then from the point of view of the father
who is betrayed by his sons in *My Dog Stupid* and *The
Brotherhood of the Grape.* At the same time he is able, at last, to
reconcile his own identity with that of his father, who he
said was the inspiration for all of his best work: "My best
efforts in all my books have been directed toward my father,
his problems, failures and successes" (SL 231).

"Dreamers, we were a house full of dreamers," says
Dominic Molise in *1933 Was a Bad Year* (BY 36). This is true
of all of Fante's families. Like all immigrants, Guido Toscana
is a dreamer by definition. Like all writers, so is Arturo
Bandini, in addition to being painfully self-conscious and
grandiosely ambitious. In each of the Molise novels, the
father's dream of having at least one of his children join him
in the bricklaying trade is pitted against the son's dream to
play baseball (in *1933 Was a Bad Year*) or to have a level floor
(in *Full of Life*), or to win the Nobel Prize for literature (in *The
Brotherhood of the Grape*). In *My Dog Stupid,* the tables are
turned, and it is the narrator-father who dreams of going to
Italy to escape the burdens of his family. In each book,
however, the dreams of the father must be given up for
those of the son.

Henry J. Molise, in *My Dog Stupid,* feels unappreciated
by his wife and kids. Driving up the Coast Highway in his
Porsche 356, the wind in his hair, Henry imagines himself
the carefree writer, sipping cappuccino in a Roman piazza,
a brunette by his side for a change. He sells his beloved
Porsche, symbol of what little independence he has
achieved, to buy a ticket on Al Italia. But when Stupid, the
stray dog he has adopted and come to identify with, runs
away, he promises his son Jamie to get the dog back. He has
to use the money for his Roman escape to ransom the dog

back, but as he says, "What's Rome if you have to live with the betrayal of your own son? What's Paris, or New York, or any place in the world? My duty is clear. God knows I have my faults, but I won't be accused of disloyalty to my children" (WY 135). Having recognized his own "selfishness and unreasonableness," Henry J. Molise's epiphany of incompetence is a revelation that frees him from his dreams as much as it shackles him to his duty.

In *1933 Was a Bad Year*, Dominic Molise steals his father's cement mixer to finance his trip to Catalina Island to try out with the Cubs, but he can't go through with it because he is confronted by his grandfather's ghost. In the end it is the father, Nick Molise who makes the sacrifice for his son, even after the son has betrayed him by stealing the mixer. But whereas Dominic feels he has to go through with his trip to Catalina because of the father's sacrifice, Henry J. Molise has already been having second thoughts about his trip to Rome, even before the serendipity of the dog's disappearance brings Molise back to "the only reality" of his family and himself. Romantic and picturesque as his dream is, it pales beside the reality of the Molise family. What he would really find in Rome, he realizes, are European discomforts and the Italians' disdain for him as an Italian American, one of the "cowards who had fled the beautiful national poverty" (WY 134). His epiphany marks the failure of a dream as a projected image of himself, but it also marks the success of the heart, the point at which he sacrifices his selfish dream for that of the family. When Odysseus returned home to Ithaca, he was recognized by his nurse; when Henry J. Molise returns home in Fante's own Odyssey of a Wop, he recognizes himself in his dog Stupid.

When Molise ransoms the dog, he is freeing himself. But there is a complication. Stupid has fallen in love with a pig, who reminds Molise of his mother: "She gave off comfortable bourgeois vibrations of stability and faith in the Holy Ghost. She was my mother all over again" (WY 142). Unable to betray the memory of his mother, Molise buys the pig, indirectly paying his back his mother — karmically and comically — for her sacrifices. In the end, Henry J. Molise cries not for the abdication of his dream, which is inevitable, but for his own human family, his wife, and himself, who in turn, given the nature of things, will have to abdicate their dreams as well.

Kenneth Burke in *Attitudes Toward History* has a wonderful passage about the comic attitude toward the inevitable human failures pressed upon us by history and what we can salvage from the failures of our ability to act (or we could also say, our inability to act) according to our will. What we salvage, what Fante salvages, is a bittersweet sense of comic fulfillment, which of course tends toward farce, that comic enactment of the tragic. "The progress of humane enlightenment," says Burke, "can go no further than in picturing people not as *vicious,* but as *mistaken.* When you add that people are *necessarily* mistaken, that all people are exposed to situations in which they must act as fools, that EVERY insight contains its own special kind of blindness, you complete the comic circle, returning again to the lesson of humility that underlies great tragedy."[14]

It is the lesson of humility that we find over and over again in Fante, from the tough-kid Altar Boy voice of Jimmy Toscana in the earliest stories, through the Bohemian braggadocio of the Bandini novels, to the mature Mitty-like confession of folly in the Molise novels. At every step Fante never lost sight of what he owed to his family, and he paid them back in the best way he could: by picturing them not as vicious but as mistaken, himself among them, and himself necessarily mistaken along with them. This is a joyous epiphany, comic and courageous. The real tragedy, it seems to me, is that it has taken so long for publishers, readers and critics to recognize the value and extent of "the progress of humane enlightenment" in the work of John Fante.

CHAPTER 2

THE ROAD FROM DENVER

1909-1932

But however braggadocio I am superficially I am softer than
a babe's skull . . .

John Fante in 1934

"I was born in Denver, Colorado, in 1911, in a macaroni
factory, which is just the right place for a man of my genealogy to get his first slap" (FM 29). So begins one of John
Fante's many self-portraits, this one in a 1932 letter to H. L.
Mencken. It is a typical Fante cocktail in the tradition of
Cellini, Casanova and Mark Twain: one part humor, one
part fiction, and a dash of fact. Actually, John Thomas Fante
was born in Denver on April 8, 1909 — not 1911 and not in
a macaroni factory. He was the eldest son of Nicholas Peter
Fante, an immigrant bricklayer who had come from the
rocky landscape of the Abruzzi to the Rocky Mountains in
search of the American dream. Nick Fante would pass on
many qualities to his son, including his short, stocky physique, his impulsive temperament, his adoration and fear of
women, and his passion for wine, gambling and building
things that last. He would also pass on his disappointment
in the American dream and diabetic tendencies. Nick Fante
was "so happy" at his son's birth, John Fante claimed, that

he "got drunk and stayed that way for a week" and continued to celebrate in the same way on and off for the next twenty-one years (FM 20).

His mother, Mary Capolungo, was born of Italian parents in Chicago, which John Fante said made him "just as much of an American as is necessary" (FM 29). Mary Fante's loyalties, like her husband's, were equally divided between a devotion to her earthy, irascible husband, her children, and the God of the Roman Catholic Church. Living under the constant surveillance of his mother's religiosity, John chafed and complained and tugged at the bit. Shocked at his reading such titles as Gamaliel Bradford's *Bare Souls* or *Darwin*, she would censor his reading material: "My mother nearly fainted when she saw Darwin's picture in the frontispiece," Fante explained to Mencken. "He looks exactly as she suspects a monkey-man to look. There's no use trying to explain that Darwin was a humble, sweet fellow" (FM 34).

Fante tells the story of his parents' stormy courtship in "A Kidnaping in the Family." Maria Scarpi is a beautiful girl "who wanted to become a nun instead of a wife" (WY 14). There is a change in her plans when she is sighted at the Saint Rocco parade on the North Side of Denver by Guido Toscana and stalked by this brash young man who "snarled with importance" twice as hard as necessary because he was not a big man. Guido is arrogant and "gay with white wine, but he saw beauty much clearer that way" (WY 15), and he courts Maria by blowing cigar smoke under her hat. When she flees in horror at his forwardness, he follows her home and installs himself outside the house like a guard dog. Maria's mother calls him a drunken pig and tells him to go back to the drunken pigs he came from, but Maria begs her not to yell because the neighbors will think she's crazy. To Guido, her reproach is a song of love and "her voice was that little girl in the throat of Enrico Caruso" (WY 16). He asks her to marry him as he begins to sing *"Mena, Me!"* in the street: "Give a kiss. One kiss. You must do this!" The young narrator of the story describes his future mother, Maria Scarpi, as "not much for sharp wits, a soft-hearted girl who wanted to become a nun and pray for the sins of the world," noting that she was no match for his singing father as she stared down from the window, "transfixed" (WY 17) by the man who would ruin her dream of becoming a nun.

The marriage was not always happy. Nick Fante worked hard to build the vision he had for his wife and children in America, and he played hard when the vision failed to materialize. In his youth Nick Fante had wanted to be a singer, but "had to work like a dog from the age of twelve, and it embittered his whole life. It made a brute of him in many ways" (FM 63). When his investments in gold mines did not pan out, Nick Fante gambled to recover his capital, making a quick buck at cards or pool. When work, or the lack of it, and the burdens of supporting a growing family got the better of him, he sought solace in wine and other women.

The young Fante took these domestic tensions to heart, and when he began to write, his mother's religious devotion and his father's disappointments and marital infidelities would provide the recurring dramatic conflicts of his fiction.

Growing up in Denver, John Fante saw little of his Italian ancestry outside the tense yet fiercely affectionate atmosphere of his home. The Fantes moved to the fringe of the fashionable East Side, where they were isolated from other Italian families, most of whom had settled on the middle-class North Side, where John was born in a basement apartment below a pasta factory. But when relatives came to visit at holidays, funerals and weddings, Fante heard the oral tales and family legends passed down through generations. These would form the basis of such stories as "A Wife for Dino Rossi" and "One of Us."

What did it mean to be an *Italian* American? Singled out as "the Italian kid," the son of a man who smelled of Toscanelli cigars, garlic, red wine and brick dust, and a mother redolent of votive candles, incense and old world superstition, Fante wondered what this hybrid identity of his really meant. In spite of his red hair and freckled face, Fante was too poor and too Italian to blend in with the sons and daughters of the affluent Swedish and English immigrants in the neighborhood, and too Catholic for any but the Irish. His heritage was a dilemma and a burden. Like other writers of his generation, Jo Pagano and Pietro Di Donato, whose names ended in a tell-tale vowel, Fante would write much of his fiction to answer these questions and to explore the meaning of his dual identity. Again and again Fante would confess his early, childish rejection of his *italianatà* to atone for this betrayal of his people, and to resolve the dilemma of the "hyphenate" writer in American literature.[1]

Fante was capable of feeling pride as well as resentment for his heritage. He was, after all, descended from "the greatest Wop who ever lived," Cristoforo Colombo, patron saint of all Italian Americans (WY 135). On the other hand, he was the son of a Dago, a dirty Wop, terms which even to his parents could mean either "the essence of poverty, squalor, filth" (WY 135) or the grandeur that was Rome. When Fante discovered that his surname sounded French, he allowed himself to be called Frenchy, which "feels fine" (WY 135), but then he hears of a famous "fellow named Dante," an Italian, and he hates him "as if he were alive and walking through the classrooms, pointing a finger at me.

One day I find his picture in a dictionary. I look at it and tell myself that never have I seen an uglier bastard" (WY 135).

All of Fante's childhood aspirations and obsessions, even the monosyllabic bite of his tough-guy slang, were American. His first love was baseball, he was a crack short-stop, had an arm that was a gift from God, and he dreamed of playing in the big leagues like Joe DiMaggio. He idolized the Hollywood glamor queens and the local suburban prin-cesses. He vowed to make wads of money, drive flashy cars and marry an heiress to a house in suburbia. Yet these things seemed impossible. He was poor, Italian, and lived in a bad climate for a baseball player. Later, when he gave up playing baseball for writing books, he knew he was in for another kind of poverty and struggle, the kind that was justified by the devotion to his art. As it turned out, he never made the Hall of Fame, but neither did he have to endure poverty for long. Fante eventually married his suburban heiress and made enough money in Hollywood to park cars for each of their very American children in front of their sprawling house in Malibu that he called Rancho Fante. But he had to struggle his entire life for recognition as an artist.

In 1920, when Fante was "still a little squirt" of seven or eleven, the family moved to Boulder, Colorado.[2] At the Sacred Heart School of Jesus the nuns recognized his talent with words and encouraged him to write. "During the en-suing eight years I achieved high marks in baseball, basket-ball and football, and my life was not cluttered with books or scholarship" (DB 55-6). This period was a time that Fante would look back on with longing and affection. As he wrote to his mother from Los Angeles in 1935, "I think I can truthfully say that there was nothing lacking in my boy-hood" (SL 110). He recalled most vividly the snow-bound Colorado winters when his father was unable to lay brick and the family was thrown together, sheltered from the harsher elements of financial worries and thwarted dreams, for which winter became a symbol, notably in *Wait Until Spring, Bandini* and *1933 Was a Bad Year*. It was a warm and generous and passionate household, especially around the holiday season, "with everyone yelling at once, and everyone finally getting all he could eat with plenty left over for the dog, the cat, and the chickens" (SL 110). In his fiction Fante returned obsessively to this setting, as though it were some paradise lost.

Fante returned to Denver to spend four years as a day student at Regis College, a Jesuit boarding school, where he played baseball for the Regis Clovers. As an inveterate prankster collecting "bitter memories of a devilish boyhood" (SL 87), Fante made friends easily, one of whom would someday become president of St. Louis University, Paul Reinert, S.J. The Jesuits won his heart on the baseball diamond and his head in the classroom. He was impressed by their intellectual discipline, if not wholly convinced by their doctrine, but he was impressionable and he took their teaching to heart, even though he would always rebel against the Church with the earthy ambivalence of his father and the pseudo-intellectual vigor encouraged by his precocious reading of Voltaire, Nietzsche, Spengler, and of course Mencken.

On his own Fante discovered the literature that would inform his views on life and literature. He devoured Russian and French authors, especially Dostoevsky and Maupassant, and idolized the great American realists, Theodore Dreiser, Jack London and Sinclair Lewis. In the first bloom of enthusiastic reading, he tried to emulate them, suffering along with Dostoevsky, blaspheming with Nietzsche, pontificating with Spengler, and dooming and glooming and misogynizing with Schopenhauer. But in the end it was Sherwood Anderson, Dostoevsky, Knut Hamsun and Mencken who made the most lasting impressions, with whom he identified, and who gave him the inspiration and encouragement to write. In Mencken's case, adolescent emulation went beyond "mental and conversational gymnastics" and turned into aping and idolatrous accessorizing, as Fante admitted. "It extended to smoking cigars, wearing high shoes, parting my hair in the middle, and staring intently out of one eye at the speaker." All of which, Fante confessed to Mencken, was "more pathetic than stupid" (FM 57).

Among the modern Italian writers he was drawn to D'Annunzio, Pirandello and later to the Ignazio Silone of *Bread and Wine*. Among the classic Italian writers he avoided the earnest and finger-pointing Dante in favor of those great old Italian liars, Casanova and Cellini, in whose works Fante discovered a precedent for his kind of fiction — stuffed with experience and full of life, autobiography without a too-fastidious regard for fact, fiction compounded with confession, yet ultimately, as he claimed with some exaggeration in the preface to his first published novel, with "nothing of myself" (WB 8).

If books gave Fante pleasure and solace, women seemed only to complicate his life. Fante always admitted to having a misogynistic streak that had more to do with his father's infidelities to his mother and his own Catholic upbringing than with his superficial reading of Schopenhauer. "I have strong prejudices, which I feed," he told Mencken. "For example, I will not read books by women or Catholic priests" (FM 30). Women were threats, a force larger than life, whether they were the Madonna that his mother worshiped or the seductive matinee goddesses of the cinema.

Yet from this ambivalent response to women arose a passion of purpose that ignites all of Fante's work. No matter how arrogant or erudite his fictional personae, they always come around to the Fantesque *ne plus ultra*: one atom of female flesh, one gesture of female love and understanding is worth all the books in all the libraries. As the idealistic and idolatrous blasphemer and masturbator Arturo Bandini puts it in *The Road to Los Angeles*, "I would rather have the beauty of Hazel's fingernails to ten million volumes by Oswald Spengler" (RL 107). The function of love in the human comedy was, for Fante, to overcome prejudices taught by religion and society and literature, and to affirm the value of life: "You kiss me," Arturo cries out to the ill-fated Rosa Pinelli in *Wait Until Spring, Bandini*, "and I'll make history!" (WB 49).

After leaving Regis College, Fante entered the University of Colorado but dropped out when, as he confided to Mencken, he was unable to study because he was distracted by "the overflowing voluptuousness of everything feminine after four years of confinement with the Jesuits" (FM 30). He claims that he fell in love with his English teacher and tried to seduce her by getting her to explain Sherwood Anderson's "I Want to Know Why," a story about a boy's curiosity about sex.[3] Such, he says, was the "Jesuitical technique of making love" (FM 30). Elsewhere, Fante claimed (less convincingly) that he fell in love on the first day of the semester with a girl who drove his deprived Catholic senses wild. When she quit college to enter business school in Boulder, he followed suit. When she then gave that up and moved to the flatlands of eastern Colorado, he tagged along after her, only to find that she had married the Sheriff of Holyoke. He returned to Boulder and the university, but his heart was not in the curriculum.[4]

Soon after leaving the University of Colorado, Fante left Colorado for California. Whether he had at this time any clear intention of becoming either a writer or a shortstop is not clear. How exactly he got from Colorado to California has, like other facts of Fante's life, merged long ago with the legend. One version of the events leading up to his sudden departure is recounted in *1933 Was a Bad Year*, in which a boy leaves home to try out for the Chicago Cubs at their training camp on Catalina Island. To friends and interviewers Fante gave other versions that contain puzzling elisions of narrative and suspicious flourishes of style. One night in the spring of 1930, so one story goes, without saying good-bye and with $1.33 in loose change in his pocket, Fante left Boulder with his friend Ralph Burdick, heading for Catalina Island and a tryout with the Cubs. Thumbing rides and hopping trains got them as far as San Francisco, where the money ran out. Working at odd jobs, Fante saved enough money to proceed down the coast alone to Wilmington and the Los Angeles Harbor. In another version, told thirty years laters, Fante said he took the train to Los Angeles instead of New York because the ticket was cheaper.[6] Whatever the real story, it seems that after the fiasco of college (and perhaps a fickle romance) Fante felt disenchanted with his prospects in his home state, intellectual and otherwise, and decided to strike out for new territory.[7]

Meanwhile, Fante's father had abandoned his mother for another woman, leaving the family in "smithereens" and without "a kopek" (FM 30). Mary Fante moved to Wilmington to be near her brothers and to join her son, who embarked on a year-long series of temporary jobs (twenty-four, he told Mencken) in an effort to support his mother, his sister Josephine, and his brothers Tom and Pete. He worked in grocery stores, gas stations and hotels. The closest he got to Catalina or a tryout with the Cubs was working as a stevedore for the boats shuttling to the Island. For six months he worked alongside Japanese, Mexican and Filipino immigrants in the fish canneries, an experience vividly and hilariously depicted in *The Road to Los Angeles*. In this, Fante's first novel, the father is, significantly, absent. The novel begins: "I had a lot of jobs in Los Angeles Harbor because our family was poor and my father was dead" (RL 9). Fante's feelings for his father ran deep, and his fiction was one way of dealing with them; in this case, meting out justice and getting revenge, an eye for an eye, neglect for neglect, a fictional death for the father's real betrayal.

Nick Fante returned from his tryst to find his family in California and his son John in his place as head of the family. The repentant father took the family north to Roseville, near Sacramento in the Central Valley, where the family would remain together until Nick Fante's death in 1950. The reconciliation was complete, but it could not heal the wounds opened up by the father's betrayal of the family. These events became central to John Fante's life and fiction, straining his relations with his father, whom he resembled in so many ways, and supplying him with much of his best and most difficult material for his work.

With his family settled in Roseville, John Fante was free to begin his writing career in earnest. Still hedging his bets, he made one last attempt at formal education by enrolling in English classes at Long Beach City College in the Fall of 1931. He lived with relatives and later a professor, doing chores in exchange for room and board. He stuck it out for almost a year, before dropping out to take a gamble on his talent as a writer.

At Long Beach City College, Fante was caricatured in the student newspaper, and was remembered for his wit years later by other members of the campus literary society. In the 1970s, when he was one of a long and mostly undistinguished list of nominees into the Long Beach City College Hall of Fame, Fante wrote a letter accepting the honor and acknowledging the encouragement he received from his English teacher, Florence Carpenter. It was she who got him started on the typewriter, which he thereafter used religiously for almost all his manuscripts and correspondence. One day she asked him: "What do you have against a typewriter?" Stung, Fante got a job as a copy boy at the Long Beach *Independent Press-Telegram* just so he could teach himself how to type after hours. One of Fante's stories was accepted and published by the college literary magazine. A wholly ordinary and amateurish story about love and suicide, "Eleven-Thirty" would be impossible to identify as the work of John Fante if it didn't have his name under the title. The story bears some embryonic resemblance to one of Villiers de l'Isle Adam's *Cruel Tales*, which was just the sort of thing Fante had been reading at the University of Colorado, along with Joris-Karl Huysmans and the verses of Rupert Brooke and Ernest Dowson, before discovering H. L. Mencken and the *American Mercury*.

It is impossible to know exactly what turned the Fante of "Eleven-Thirty" into the Fante of "Altar Boy," published in the *American Mercury* a few short months later. Fante had probably written his first serious attempts at fiction the previous year, either as a freshman at the University of Colorado, or soon after he left the university. In *Dreams from Bunker Hill*, Fante describes how he spent time at the library looking at the pictures in magazines until one day he went to the bookshelves and pulled out *Winesburg, Ohio*. "I read another Anderson. I read and I read, and I was heartsick and lonely and in love with a book, many books, until it came naturally, and I sat there with a pencil and a long tablet, and tried to write, until I felt I could not go on because the words would not come as they did in Anderson" (DB 57). Literary taste always outruns literary ability, and it no doubt took some time to digest the lessons of Mencken's hard-headed belief in the American language, in straight talk as a guide to clear thinking, which was just the right antidote to the heavy chunks of philosophy Fante had consumed without fully digesting. And after the verses of Brooke and Dowson, the prose of Mencken must have seemed meaty and wholesome.

But it takes more than literary influence to make a writer. As Arturo Bandini laments in *Ask the Dust*, how could he write without having lived? "That's your trouble: your ignorance of life. Why, my God, man, do you realize you've never had any experience with a woman?" (AD, 18). In Long Beach, John Fante had his first adult affair, with Helen Purcell, a high school music teacher, who despised jazz and adored Schubert and Wagner. As Fante crows to Mencken, "I have a girl, and I love her, and she loves me, and we are both little pigs for the music of Richard Wagner" (FM 31). The model for Mrs. Helen Brownell, Arturo Bandini's fifty-five year old widowed landlady and love interest in *Dreams from Bunker Hill*, Helen Purcell was about thirty-four and twice-married (once widowed, once divorced). When his mother expressed anxiety that Fante might marry "the widow," he told her not to worry, "All young men have got to be sidetracked by at least one" (SL 71), and "she is too old for me to marry. I prefer to tell her I love her and enjoy her as much as I can as a free man" (SL 73). Fante obviously reveled in the attentions of a mature woman, but there was little cause for his mother's fears, especially in later years

when Fante still saw Helen from time to time after her brief
and disastrous third marriage.

In Long Beach, too, Fante began what was to become
a long correspondence with H. L. Mencken, the hero he was
never to meet. With all the arrogance and ambition of the
tyro, the aspiring writer sent Mencken lengthy missives full
of the books he was reading and the people he met, his
casual observations and his consuming obsessions, his family problems and his great expectations (to take over the
editorship of the *American Mercury*). He asked Mencken for
advice on life and writing, and Mencken responded with
tact and grace, encouraging the young writer's ambitions
and advising him on how to deal with his father. In effect,
Fante adopted Mencken as his literary father. Often these
fan letters to the Great Debunker would include a short
story, which in the beginning Mencken would politely re-
ject. It didn't matter to Fante; even the rejections were
gospel.

Then one day in the Spring of 1932 there came in the
mail a check for his story "Altar Boy." This was what he had
been waiting for: a sign from the gods that he was a writer.

"Altar Boy" was Fante's first success at capturing the
voice that would, with variations and subtleties still to come,
allow him to say all he had to say. Fante himself defined his
essential voice in 1934 when he contrasted himself with
another young writer, who was not sufficiently "audacious"
or "bombastic," "with no capacity for bluff and bluster, and
that is so essential unless you're a Cabell or Rupert Brooke .
. . But however braggadocio I am superficially I am softer
than a babe's skull" (SL 83). Having discovered his voice, his
altar boy braggadocio, Fante set himself down at the typewriter and pounded out more of these short stories, thinly-
disguised memoirs about an Italian kid growing up in Colo-

rado, educated by nuns, plagued by guilt, and oppressed by his parents' old world ignorance and superstition. He sent everything he wrote to Mencken as soon as he could stuff an envelope, which eventually prompted Mencken to point out that one magazine could not possibly print all that one writer produced. Having Mencken authenticate Jimmy Toscana as Fante's first genuine alter ego was the turning point in Fante's life as an artist. Thus began what Ross Wills calls, "the long, exasperating metamorphosis from letter-writer to conscious story-teller" (SL 333).

Fante celebrated by going on a shopping spree, buying two suits and forty dollars worth of neckties at Bullock's. In *Ask the Dust* Arturo Bandini purchases a whole wardrobe of clothes at the May Company and lays in stocks of cigarettes, candy, enough writing supplies for an office, a first-aid kit (!), and the obligatory pair of Southern California sunglasses, no doubt to protect himself from ardent admirers. Fante returns to the scene in *Dreams from Bunker Hill*, in which a less flamboyant Bandini buys a single suit, "several pairs of shorts and T-shirts, a dozen pairs of socks, a few neckties and finally an irresistible glorious fedora" (DB 10) — not at a department store but at the Goodwill, and for a mere twenty dollars. The later version has the modest ring of truth mellowed in retrospect, not only because it reflects Fante's lifelong concern about money, but also because of the "irresistible" note of the "glorious fedora," since Fante was equally capable of wasting money, either on self-indulgent luxuries or, more dangerously, on gambling.

In any case, it seems that after the acceptance of "Altar Boy," Fante sat down at the typewriter dressed to kill. As he tried to pound out the stories that were to make his name, they wouldn't flow the way his letters had. He was homesick and the writing was bad. To make matters worse, one night while he was out with Helen Purcell, a burglar absconded with his zany neckties and glorious fedora, and then returned to add injury to insult by stealing what was left of his writing capital. Fante wrote to Mencken that with nothing better to do and nothing in his pockets, he was going to hop a train to see his parents in Roseville. He poured his homesickness into a story in which he described what he would find there: the comforting familiarity, old affections and old complaints, the dinner conversation degenerating into bickering, the flaring of old feuds with his brother and father. He posted the story with the letter and hit the road, hitch-hiking to Roseville. A reply was waiting for him when he got there. Mencken wanted to re-title the story and publish it as "Home, Sweet Home."

Fante shot back a thousand-word autobiographical sketch to "correct" the author's note that had accompanied his first story in the *American Mercury*, which had concluded: "He began studies for the priesthood, but discovering no vocation, abandoned them. He lives in Long Beach, Calif." (FM 28). While it is true that Fante never studied for the priesthood, his "correction" begins with a falsehood: "I was born in Denver, in 1911, in a macaroni factory . . ."

CHAPTER 3

FANTE'S CONFESSIONAL: STORIES OR PLAIN FICTION

DAGO RED

> When you go to Confession you must tell everything.
> Jimmy Toscana in "The Road to Hell"

The individual stories collected in *Dago Red* (1940) show Fante practicing the basic elements of his craft, testing his voice for its tonal capabilities, and organizing his experience for its unifying themes. All the themes that appear later in the novels are tested here: an obsession with family, the Church, and the fate of the immigrant in America, as well as the writer's compulsion to absolve himself of his past sins against all three through the confessional of fiction. None of these conflicts exists in isolation, and in the best of the stories — "A Kidnaping in the Family," "Altar Boy," "The Odyssey of a Wop," and "Hail Mary" — Fante shows how each of these conflicts aggravate the others, giving the collection as a whole a coherence that bears comparison to other more famous collections best seen in terms of their unity, such as Anderson's *Winesburg, Ohio,* Joyce's *Dubliners,* or Hemingway's *In Our Time.*[1]

Like Fante's other child alter egos, Jimmy Toscana is a liar, a blasphemer and a thief, but he is a little criminal, more dangerous to himself than to anybody else, and a visit to the confessional usually leaves him feeling like a free man. His voice has a range that extends from Two-Gun Toscana, the Death Kid, who carves his moniker on the walls of a jail cell, and who knows he'll get a licking from his father for stealing a sackful of carbide to blow the corks out of bottles, but he pretends not to care because "I am plenty tough" (WY 67, 69), to the nameless narrator and supplicant of "Hail Mary," who asks the Virgin to please send him some money because he once knocked the teeth out of Willie Cox for calling her a name.

In this chapter I shall discuss four pairs of stories from *Dago Red* that seem representative of Fante's themes in the short fiction.[2] The first two pairs are set in Colorado, in Jimmy's childhood, and focus on family and religion. For example, "A Kidnaping in the Family" (1936) and "A Nun No More" (1940; not included in *Dago Red*) reveal Fante's obsession with his mother and the Virgin Mary that verges on fetishism and Oedipal fixation and resolves itself in an affirmation of earthly life. The focus of "Altar Boy" (1932) and "The Road to Hell" (1937) shifts to Fante's preoccupation with theft and the necessity of confession, which suggests the conflict of a writer's grappling with the truth of words in dealing with his Catholic shame. The second two pairs of stories are the final four stories of *Dago Red,* which are all set in California, after Jimmy has left home and is trying to make it as a writer. "The Odyssey of a Wop" (1933) and "Home, Sweet Home" (1932) deal directly with the self-lacerating denial and attempted abandonment of Fante's Italian-American heritage, and his nostalgic longing for a return home. The previously unpublished stories that conclude the volume, "The Wrath of God" and "Hail Mary," round out the volume as a sort of metafictional coda, with

Jimmy Toscana in the chrysalis stage of becoming Arturo Bandini of *Ask the Dust*, published the year before. Elements of these stories suggest that they were studies for the novel (the earthquake scene in "The Wrath of God," and the supplicant writer in his hotel room praying for his rent money in "Hail Mary"). While Fante allowed some stories to be dropped from the original *Dago Red* line-up, he insisted that these two stories stay: "They are the measure of my faith and they belong" (SL 167). Presumably, Fante means his faith in himself as a writer, as much as his faith in the Catholic Church, since they paint a fairly accurate portrait of John Fante (even more than of Arturo Bandini) on the verge of becoming a novelist.

1. Maculate Conception: "A Kidnaping in the Family" and "A Nun No More"

"There was an old trunk in my mother's bedroom" (WY 11). So begins the opening story in *Dago Red*. Out of this trunk comes the whole history of the Toscana family, a cornucopia and a Pandora's box for the narrator Jimmy. The history comes in bits and pieces, scraps of fabric and paper, wedding linen and legal documents. To young Jimmy Toscana it is ancient and sacred, like the Torah containing the scrolls of Moses, secretive and suggestive. "It was the oldest trunk I ever saw. It was one of those trunks with a round lid like a fat man's belly" (WY 11). This image of the fat man's belly full of wedding gifts and birth certificates is striking in its blend of male and female characteristics, evoking a mythical archetype of the original androgynous God pregnant with creation. That it is in his mother Maria's bedroom (which is also his father Guido's) evokes Biblical associations with the Holy Family. At fourteen, Jimmy is curious about the mystery of his conception. To penetrate the mystery he must violate the temple, discover the key "hidden under a corner of the rug" and open the trunk that his mother "wouldn't permit anyone to open" (WY 11). What he finds is the lost arcana, the secret knowledge of his genealogy, his book of Genesis.

At the very bottom of the trunk is a box of family pictures, and when Jimmy opens it he releases a chaos into his notion of the family order. He especially falls in love with one picture, "which my fingers ached to clutch and my eyes longed to see when I found my mother that way — it was a picture of her taken a week before she married my father" (WY 11). This image of his virgin mother becomes an icon for him, and he takes it to the bank of a creek, sets it on a stone for an altar, and prays to it. He becomes bitter with the shock of mortality because now his mother is a haggard at the kitchen sink, her arms "limp and white like dry clay from toil, her hair thin and dry against her head, and her eyes sunken and large and sad in their sockets" (WY 11). He denies that this mortal woman is his mother and curses the cruelty of time, not only because of what time has done to her, but because he is denied being able to know her in her glory: "Why couldn't I remember anything about her? Why did I have to be so young when I was born?" (WY 12).

At fourteen Jimmy Toscana is himself on the brink of change, awakening to the changes in his own body that are the biological answer to time and mortality — sex. And so he vows that "if I ever saw my mother as beautiful as she was in the picture I would immediately ask her to marry me. She had never refused me anything, and I felt she would not refuse me as a husband" (WY 12). He realizes that there is a hitch to this Oedipal plan of attack, namely the Catholic ban on divorce. But he is willing to wait for his father's death. A typical Fante alter ego, Jimmy ignores common sense and imposes a legalistic logic upon the situation, searching his catechism and prayer book "for a law which stated that mothers could not marry their sons. I was satisfied to find nothing on the subject" (WY 12), opening the way for his courtship of his mother through her picture. He takes the picture and shows it to his father, expecting him to "shout with excitement." Instead, the man reading the paper and smoking a cigar examines the treasure "as though it were a bug, or something; a piece of stale cake, or something" (WY 12). Jimmy inexplicably loses interest in the picture. "Something happened at that moment and the picture was never so wonderful again. It became another picture — just a picture" (WY 13), and he never opens the trunk again.

He does, however, continue to unravel the mystery of his conception, first from what he knows of the family history, then more directly by interrogating his mother. Not satisfied with her mundane story of her courtship, he bullies her into elaborating on the details until the story no longer resembles the reality of a drunken, boorish, cigar-smoking immigrant winning the hand of a second-generation Italian girl who "wanted to become a nun instead of a wife" (WY 14). His mother's story is: "Your father courted me, and after a few months we were married. That's all." Jimmy refuses to believe it: "I didn't like it that way. I hated it. I wouldn't have it" (WY 19). In his imagination, the courtship becomes a Western romance straight out of the American cinema, complete with her being kidnaped by an outlaw on a black horse, who wields a pearl-handled six-shooter and keeps her prisoner in a mountain hideout until she consents to marry him. At first his mother clings to the truth, tired and clutching a broom, until she puts the broom down and enters into the fantasy and the fatigue melts from her face.

"'Yes!' she said. 'He did kidnap me! He came one night when I was asleep and took me away'" (WY 19). She is, in effect, restored to her former glory when she is seduced by her son's fiction.

What is most touching about "A Kidnaping in the Family" is not the mother's complicity in her son's distortion of the truth (she had never refused him anything); it is the narrator's implicit realization that the real beauty of the courtship was in the rough lyricism of the way it actually happened. Jimmy Toscana's romantic recycling of the cinematic myth of the Wild West denies his immigrant heritage by substituting a formula that is inadequate to express the transitory beauty of life. The narrator can understand what Jimmy can not: that "Guido was gay with white wine, but he saw beauty much clearer that way" (WY 15), and that "To Guido Toscana her voice was that little girl in the throat of Enrico Caruso" (WY 16). The sheer determination of Guido's desire is what won him the hand of Jimmy's virgin mother, that and a serenade with an Italian love song that he sings now only when he is shaving.

Jimmy's denial of the true story of his parents' courtship blinds him to the lyricism of reality. The older and wiser narrator's recognition of what little Jimmy has missed, however, is an acceptance of the truth and beauty of reality over myth. It is also a reconciliation with the present through an examination of the past. Just as the mother allows Jimmy to overcome his Oedipal fixation by letting him reconstruct the story of her courtship — to court her himself, fictionally — so the fiction of the story itself allows the narrator to overcome his denial of his father and his father's heritage, and, paradoxically, to accept the value of reality over myth. Also, just as the mother puts away her ambition to become a nun in favor of marrying in the real world, so Jimmy puts away his hopes of recovering the virgin mother he found in the trunk.

"A Nun No More" (1940) is little more than a retelling of the courtship in "A Kidnaping in the Family." The narrator's mother is again thwarted in her ambition to become a nun by marrying an earthly man with a trowel and a red mustache, a wine-drinking bricklayer, because he makes her laugh. She gives up a heavenly redemption for the redemption of earthy laughter. Yet compared to "A Kidnaping in the Family," the story has no dramatic conflict, partly because it lacks the energizing Oedipal strain of the young Jimmy's competition with his father, and partly because it lacks the narrator's informing participation in the son's viewpoint. The religious motif, however, is the same in both stories, which conclude that earthly love is superior to the heavenly variety. A nun, the narrator explains, "can't get married or have fun. Your husband is Jesus" (WY 182). To the extent that Jimmy in the earlier story worships his virgin mother Maria, he is a kind of Jesus, superior to his earthly father Guido (not Giuseppe or Joseph, but just another Italian Guy). By giving up the Church, Maria gives up her rightful glory of being married like Mary to God, or like a nun to Jesus, and in accepting the hand of her husband gives up the hand of her son. Thus the mystery of Jimmy Toscana's conception, which is no more immaculate than that of his ageing mother, is solved in these two stories of the courtship of his mother. The implication in the resolution to both stories is the narrator's, and Fante's, acceptance of earthly life, with all its rough lyricism and tragic beauty.

2. Sin and Braggadocio: "Altar Boy" and
   "The Road to Hell"

"Altar Boy" was the first story Fante published in a major
journal and the first appearance of Jimmy Toscana, *Dago
Red*'s confessional voice.[3] Very much a child of the times,
Jimmy Toscana talks the "tough-guy" talk of the 1930s. His
voice is almost a parody of that popular posture. "Worms
Kelley was my partner. Worms hated Maguire like the dickens, and so did everybody else, but Worms hated him most
because Maguire was a snitch baby, and he had a suck with
the nuns" (WY 42). Here the tough guy is a not-so-tough kid,
battling not the evils of crime or social injustice, but the
oppression of a doting mother and well-meaning nuns and
priests. "I was standing there wishing Father Andrew was a
man instead of a priest, and more my size, so I could knock
the hell out of him, and get even" (WY 39). When his father
beats him for putting ink in the priest's communion wine,
he takes it "like a real guy. The reason is, I knew he was my
father, and he would stop hitting before he hurt me too
serious. He kept saying he was going to kill me, but he is my
father, and he does not scare me with that stuff" (WY 44).
What makes this bluff attitude so endearing is not that we
admire Jimmy Toscana for his street sense, as we might
Dashiell Hammett's Ned Beaumont, for instance, but that he
admires himself so much. He may be made to confess to his
crimes, but he always gets away with them anyway, feeling
better for having confessed.

More than this, the tough-kid voice is a transparent
disguise, endearing because, just as we always suspected,
tough guys are not so tough after all. Beneath the hard
surface of their talk is a soft creature made of chivalry,
romance and sentiment, a "babe's skull" beneath the hard-

shell "braggadocio." The Altar Boy, for all his talk of whomping on priests and taunting nuns, for all his talk of praying to the Madonna just so he can "get out of school a lot on account of her" (WY 45), is a true believer in a Catholic heaven, a Catholic hell, and a Catholic earth.

In "The Road to Hell," Sister Mary Joseph instructs the class on the nature of Temptation by telling a parable about a boy who steals a baseball glove, something that all the boys in the class can relate to. Theft leads to lying, and one lie leads to a multitude, which in turn lead the boy in the parable to lie to the priest at confession. "Concealing a sin in the Confessional is bad enough and a mortal sin, but actually to go to Holy Communion afterward is the worst sin possible — a sacrilege" (WY 115). The boy on "the road to hell" is turned to stone. The boys in the class claim not to believe a word of it — "It's a lot of baloney" and "a lot of bunk" (WY 117) — yet next time they go on a swiping spree at the local hardware store they leave with their sweaters empty of loot.

When the Altar Boy and his cronies steal fountain pens from a drugstore, he gets "scared to death" (WY 48), not for fear of being caught, nor even of going to hell, but because he knows he will confess it to Father Andrew and Father Andrew will get sore. "I wanted to run. I am not goofy, and a fountain-pen does not scare me, but I wanted to run away. I did not want to go to Confession, because the last time I confessed stealing migs, and Father Andrew got sore. I mean he talked real loud. If I told him I swiped a five-dollar pen, I bet he would yell. The holy people outside would hear him" (WY 48). This concern for what others will think of him reveals the real reason behind the pose of the tough kid in the first place; he is so concerned about what others will think of him that he is willing to shape his entire speech and manner to a role that has very little to do with his real feelings. The pose is both a warning not to come too close and a challenge to pierce the armor. It is the shield that reveals his vulnerability, the mask that betrays his sincerity.

The Altar Boy is incorrigible to the end. When he finally confesses the theft to Father Joseph, who does not have the goods on him as Father Andrew does, he leaves the confessional "whistling hymns like I always do after Confession" (WY 49). He has still got the fountain pen and the system all figured out. "I would keep it. I would tell my mother I found it. It was a lie, but a lie is only a venial sin. You do not go to Hell if you have a venial sin on your soul. You go to Purgatory. Then you go to Heaven" (WY 50). What's a little Purgatory to a tough kid willing to take the rap? What Jimmy conveniently and only momentarily forgets is the cycle of lying that puts one on the "the road to hell."

Although these stories of growing up Catholic are most directly concerned with the nature of confession, Fante's fictional method demands that painful truths be confronted head on. Fante knew from reading Mencken that a writer must free himself from religious superstition and social prejudice in order to see himself clearly in relation to his experience and environment, even when this meant admitting that he is in fact in thrall to the very familial or social strictures that he had rejected. For a Catholic, the nature of truth should be clear: it is what must be told always, above all in the confessional. For a writer of fiction, truth is relative: the facts may be changed as long as the essential truth is somehow embodied. Such truth can be painful when dredging up the deep Oedipal fixations of "A Kidnaping in the Family," admitting to the sin and braggadocio of "Altar Boy" and "The Road to Hell," or confronting one's rejection of — and the resulting nostalgia for — one's own heritage in "The Odyssey of a Wop" and "Home, Sweet Home."

3. Escape and Return: "The Odyssey of a Wop" and "Home, Sweet Home"

In November 1933, Fante wrote to Mencken that he was "contemplating" a book-length essay to be written "in a deliberately Menckenian manner," a kind of *Prejudices* on the character of Italian Americans. He would call it *Violent Death* and it would "make a lot of noise." It would be "an iconoclastic, sociological treatment of Italian Americans. In it, I shall attempt to prove that the Italians in the United States are not only unprincipled murderers but also a stupid gang of lost yokels whose social significance is not in their ability to be good citizens, but bloody clowns: a ludicrous and unsocial people who have forsaken poverty and accepted harlotry" (FM 58-60). Mencken's reply — "Write it in your own way, whatever that way may happen to be" (FM 61) — is a paradigm of wisdom because he seems to have recognized that Fante had, by the end of his letter describing the book, talked himself out of writing it: "But in the *Prejudices* the material was written around Americans in general, which included Italians. In the book I plan, concentration upon the stupidities of a few ignorant immigrants would offhand seem very unfair." He also noted his lack of experience with Italians anywhere but in the West, and his inability to speak Italian. Still, he thought it might be worth it if he could "so anger these ignorant people that they'll take notice of me first, and then themselves" (FM 60).[4]

In fact, Fante had already written up the material in his own way, and his way was fiction. Published in the *American*

Mercury in September, two months before his letter to Mencken, "The Odyssey of a Wop" bore no resemblance to the "thoroughly vicious, albeit humorous and intolerant book" Fante described to Mencken (FM 61). By telling the inside story of his own experience as an Italian American, Fante could not help but write with increasing sympathy and understanding of the immigrant experience, just as he came to a better understanding of his religion and his family through writing about them.[5] When he submitted the story to Mencken in July 1933, Fante introduced it by saying that the story was "an old one" that had been "dressed up a bit and shorn of some of its hysteria" (FM 52).

The odyssey is that of Jimmy Toscana who "comes home" to his Italian heritage only by leaving his family in Colorado to become a writer in California. It begins with Jimmy Toscana recalling stories of how his father bit off an Irishman's ear for calling Jimmy's grandfather a Wop. He is confused, though, because he has heard Dago and Wop used among his own people as terms of both intimacy and insult, as either "the essence of poverty, squalor, filth," or the fact that they are proud descendants of Christopher Columbus, "the greatest Wop who ever lived," as his father says, adding: "So is Enrico Caruso" (WY 135). In school Jimmy finds that his name sounds French, although it rhymes with Dante, an autobiographical transparency that shows John Fante behind Jimmy Toscana's mask. "Thus I begin to loathe my heritage" (WY 137), but Jimmy also takes pride in defending it, just like his father defending his grandfather's honor, pride being mixed with shame.

For a writer, discovering the existence and efficacy of fighting words like Wop and Dago is exhilarating. "Now school days become fighting days . . . This is fun; I am getting somewhere now, so come on, you guys, I dare you to call me a Wop!" The violence is a bonding point between father and son. "Sadly happy days! My father gives me pointers: how to hold my fist, how to guard my head" (WY 138-9). Yet this violence is also turned inward against his heritage, his family, and finally himself. When Jimmy brings friends to his house, he is ashamed because the place "looks so Italian" and tells his father "to cut out being a Wop and be an American once in a while." His father's response is physical, beating him with a razor strop, while Jimmy's response is verbal: "A Wop, that's what my father is! Nowhere is there an American father who beats his son this way." In any case, the violence is reciprocal. At the root of the problem is language, constantly tagging him as an outsider with ethnic slurs and surnames, or betraying him with accents and the old-world tongue. His grandmother, "hopelessly a Wop," speaks with a thick accent: "When, in her simple way, she confronts a friend of mine and says, her old eyes smiling: 'You lika go to Seester scola?' my heart roars. *Mannaggia!* I'm disgraced; now they all know that I'm an Italian" (WY 139). Or she speaks Italian to him in front of his friends, to which he pretends ignorance and smirks.

This denial of his heritage continues into parochial school: in the classroom, on the football field, and in the kitchen, where he works to defray his tuition. When Jimmy rebuffs the Italian chef's friendly overtures, they become sworn enemies, Jimmy resorting to physical violence, like his father, by threatening the chef with a knife, while the chef retreats into words, calling Jimmy a Wop. When Jimmy becomes the captain of the school's winning football team, he is proud of being one of "the Wop Wonders" in the backfield, but when a group of students cheer them with the nickname, he quits in disgust. He turns out to be "a bad Latinist," failing his exams on purpose, but "the Jesuits are wise fellows" who see through his ploy and taunt him into passing the course: "The language is in your blood," they say, and "you're a darned poor Wop." His fighting spirit roused, he studies in earnest, finding that Latin is "a lot like the Italian my grandmother taught me" (WY 142-3).

During registration, even before he gets into a classroom, he avoids the eyes of the other Italian boys, resisting "an irresistible amalgamation, a suffusive consanguinity" in their gaze, and looks away, ashamed. But the Jesuit fathers recognize him: "Another Wop! . . . You speak Italian?" At the entrance to the school, his father reads the Latin inscription *Religioni et Bonis Artibus* "with an Italian inflection," and Jimmy Toscana weeps with poignant ambivalence for this man who "looks exactly like a Wop . . . exactly like one of those immigrants carrying a blanket. You can't be my father!" (WY 140-1). At this point, he is ashamed of his father and his heritage, his own flesh and blood, but he is not yet sufficiently ashamed of his shame.

It is not until Jimmy goes to Los Angeles that he "comes home" to his heritage. Far from his family and lonely, he is speaking Italian with Rocco Saccone, a *paesano* of his father's, in Rocco's restaurant in the Italian quarter, basking in the familiar sounds and smells of his childhood, when he recognizes himself in Rocco's brother-in-law, "a skunk" who is "ashamed of his own flesh and blood . . . Ashamed of being Italian" (WY 145). It is then, "quietly, without trumpets and thunder," that Jimmy comes to his senses. Like the Jesuit chef, he feels like beating this Wop who won't admit to being a Wop, and tells Rocco to "get rid of him." But then he relents, forgiving the skunk, since "There's no sense in hammering your own corpse" (WY 146).

Leaving home brings Jimmy to terms with his Italian heritage in "The Odyssey of a Wop"; returning brings him to terms with his family in "Home, Sweet Home."

"I am singing now, for soon I shall be home." Thus begins a wanderer's lyrical paean to the family scene he expects to greet him on his return. Because it is about expectation, the story is told in the future tense. Knowing what to expect, Jimmy anticipates no surprises. In the security of the habitual life of the family, past and future are seen as identical. Conflicts will rise and fall like the three acts of a well-known drama, according to a set dynamic with each family member in his or her established role: embattled patriarch, nurturing mother, petulant sister, bratty little brother. Jimmy, of course, will observe it all like a stranger, a prodigal son returned to the fold, experiencing déjà vu.

More than any other member of the family it is Jimmy's father who represents his own future. As they eat and drink together, they will think the same thoughts, "for we are of the same flesh and bone, and the stuff of my brain and spine is the stuff of his, and so we will think the same things together, and each will know that the other is thinking the same things" (WY 148). At this point the narrative shifts to the past tense, and to their memory of "another welcome spread" that turned into a brawl, "and we were like two animals, and I knocked my father to the floor, and he fell with a thud" and there was "only the beastly whining and snarling," after which all Jimmy can say is, "Ah, God, forgive my father and me!" (WY 148-9). To avoid repeating such a confrontation, Jimmy returns to using the future tense, where he "will not look into the eyes" of his father after he has gulped his "electrifying wine" (WY 149).

Instead of facing such battles, the family will take refuge in the habitual: eating the same spaghetti, telling the same stories, laughing at the same jokes, even taunting one another according to a script learned long ago. To depart from these patterns is to invite disaster, for such habits insure us of what to expect in the future tense. The narrator is well aware of his ploy. He expects to have arguments, but in the euphoria of an expectant nostalgia they develop gently and dissipate in affection. When he paraphrases Swinburne by thanking "whatever gods there be" for "the triumph of the meal" and the mother who made it, his sister will accuse him of being an atheist, and he will correct her: "Atheist? When I use the plural? You mean polytheist." She will protest his use of a word she doesn't know, and he will answer: "'Look it up, squirrel eyes.' And that will bring smiles" (WY 154-5). Inevitably, the taunting is taken too far, the script is exceeded, and the reality of conflict enters again. "That will be the end of our joy" (WY 151).

Since he identifies so closely with his father, Jimmy must reclaim his identity by bragging about his success to his father, who is out of work.

> I am younger than my father: my hopes scream to the skies. His have dwindled to despair. I know my father sees me at fifty-two, and I at fifty-two am my father. What I will say will please him and yet sadden him . . . I will say: "Well, in a few days there'll be a check in the mail for me." I will say this to my father about the manuscript I am now writing (WY 153).

It is said partly to make his father envious, but mostly to show his father that he has not yet "dwindled to despair" and that his "hopes scream to the skies" (WY 153). Later his father, "as he sometimes does," will say: "Ah, well, better days are coming." Jimmy will recall what Nietzsche knew, that hope is "the first sign of defeat," and he will wish he were back with his girl Claudia in Los Angeles and not in "this goddamned, godforsaken, one-horse town" (WY 157). In other words, he will wish to be back at his desk with his own sign of defeat, his hope in his writing. More specifically, he will wish he is where he is now, writing "the manuscript I am now writing."

4. Apocalypse and Atonement: "The Wrath of God" and "Hail Mary"

The last four stories of *Dago Red* show the struggling young writer Jimmy Toscana living on his own, away from home, trying to get some perspective on the conflicts of his boyhood. Each story enacts a reconciliation: "The Odyssey of a Wop" with his ethnic heritage; "Home, Sweet Home" with his family; "The Wrath of God" with his religion, and "Hail Mary" with all three strains of conflict subdued by the single dominant chord of his one ambition: to become a writer. Writing about these subjects, Jimmy Toscana finds at last a way out of the role of the rebellious Altar Boy, and into the role of Artist. In other words, "Hail Mary" serves as Fante's metapoetic coda to his apprenticeship as a writer of fictional confessions.

"The Wrath of God" is based on Fante's experience of the Long Beach earthquake of 1933, an event treated at greater length and to more dramatic effect in *Ask the Dust*. The scene here, however, although unspecified, appears to be Venice, where Fante actually was at the time, several miles north of the earthquake's center.[6]

Jimmy is living with a woman "who I liked to believe had lured me from my Faith. Ever since I was a kid who served at Mass I had wanted a sinful woman, someone to lure me like a siren. Now I was tiring of it" (WY 160). When the tremors start, like Arturo Bandini, Jimmy takes the natural catastrophe to be a personal message from God about his living in sin. Unlike the more irrational Bandini, however, Jimmy refuses to take the fleeting notion seriously. Instead, he uses his Jesuitical training to attribute it all to "coincidence; Aquinas would call it that, and so would Augustine, and St. Ignatius, and Father Driscoll," he tells himself, "and so must you" (WY 162-3).

At the end of the story, after his mistress has left him amidst the apocalyptic ruins and the dead and wounded, he runs into this Father Driscoll, an extraordinarily well-read priest, who uses the opportunity to invite Jimmy back to the Church. The coincidence of this chance meeting, so soon after Jimmy has thought of the priest in connection with coincidence, suggests that Father Driscoll's appearance may be a hallucination, but it hardly matters, since the earthquake itself may as well be a surreal projection of Jimmy's psychic state. The earthquake brings Jimmy no great revelation, as it does Arturo, only to a gentle reconciliation with the Church. As Jimmy watches the Protestants react to the earthquake by singing around a bonfire on the beach "like savages crawling back to their pristine altars," he appreciates the common sense of the Catholic Church, as well as its sense of aesthetics. "I said, not for me this voodooism, not for me this slobbering at the feet of catastrophe; my Church fostered this civilization and if God wills that an earthquake destroy it I will at least refrain from singing hymns and acting like a Holy Roller" (WY 163).

The only indication that Jimmy's is above all a writer's dilemma is Father Driscoll's off-hand and good-humored reproach: "'You better get smart," he said, "you fifth-rate Huysmans!" (WY 166). By mentioning the Belgian decadent writer Joris-Karl Huysmans, author of the satanic *Là-Bas* and the bible of aestheticism *À Rebours,* Father Driscoll is making a flattering but pointed comparison. Huysmans was, in Mario Praz's view, one of the "literary neo-Catholics" described by Anatole France as sensualists for whom religious observance heightens the supreme voluptuousness of sin.[7] In *Ask the Dust,* too, Arturo Bandini compares himself to the defiant Huysmans: "all the gods have deserted me, and like Huysmans I stand alone, my fists clenched, tears in my eyes" (AD 27). This stance makes a fine contrast to that of Papa in "My Father's God," saluting his God in his kitchen with a smile and a glass of wine. Father Driscoll does not approve of Huysmans any more than he does Jimmy's living in sin, but he does offer intelligence, tolerance and patience in his good-natured warning for Jimmy to "get smart." As he leaves, Father Driscoll slaps Jimmy on the back and says, "So long, sucker. Look out for the girls" (WY 166), leaving Jimmy feeling that "soon my slate would be clean again" and "grateful that my Church was above all a good sport" (WY 167), suggesting that he fully intends to go to confession.

The final story in *Dago Red* affirms Jimmy Toscana's faith in the Virgin Mary, and in his own fiction of confession, if not in the rituals of the Church as a whole. "Hail Mary" is a writer's prayer to the Virgin to help him pay his overdue rent. There is a slump in Hollywood and the landlady is slipping pieces of paper under the door, so all he asks is a small favor — or rather the return of a favor, for once upon a time he defended her honor by bloodying the nose of one Willie Cox who called the Holy Virgin "a whore like all Catlickers" (WY 171). All Jimmy asks in return for his chivalry is that the Virgin send a little luck his way, because "I know that I cannot bloody the nose of a Slump in Hollywood or knock the teeth out of my landlady's mouth" (WY 173).

Before he finishes his prayer Jimmy realizes that she has miraculously helped him already, simply by being there, "an unending pattern of celestial blue" (WY 172), the "sad and mystical" Catholic girl par excellence (WY 161), his Madonna and Muse. By inspiring him to write this "prayer," and by reminding him about how she inspired him to knock Willie Cox's teeth out, she has supplied first the impetus and then the material for the story he is now writing. "Holy Mary, Mother of God, I was going to ask a favor, I was going to ask boldly about that rent. I see it is not necessary now. I see that you have not deserted me. For in a little while I shall slip this into an envelope and send it off" (WY 173).

As the final story of the collection, "Hail Mary" takes on a metapoetic resonance. We can take the unnamed narrator to be either Jimmy Toscana or John Fante, or Arturo Bandini for that matter. He is both the Altar Boy and the artist who has grown up to become the Altar Boy's creator, who is thanking the Virgin and the Catholic Church for the memories of his experiences with religion (not precisely religious experiences) that have gone into the making of *Dago Red*. "Hail Mary" is Fante's confession and contrition, a dedication and a consecration of his work to the various elements of his upbringing, a repayment of his fiction's debt to his heritage, which, like his rent, he knows is long overdue.

5. Conclusion

Sometimes truth cannot be told, or must be deferred or told in highly ambiguous or euphemistic terms. For example, Fante gives two different versions of his first confession, once in *Dago Red* and again in *Dreams from Bunker Hill,* half a century later. It may be useful to compare the two versions to see the difficulty Fante had in approaching the truth of confession truthfully in his fiction.

In "First Communion" (1933), Jimmy Toscana rehearses how he is going to tell the priest that he has "used bad words six times" (WY 31). In his confession class there is an "ugly little girl" named Catherine "who grew up to be a nun." She cries constantly in class, causing Jimmy to wonder what she could possibly have to cry about, since she is a paragon of faith and devotion. "I imagined her in the act of committing a sin. I took her out of the church pew and transposed her to the filling-station grounds, my favorite hang-out. I leaned her against the filling-station wall, put a cigarette butt in her mouth, and made her swear, say the six wicked words" (WY 32).

In *Dreams from Bunker Hill,* which Fante said was "more accurate" than his previous work, Arturo Bandini is five years old when he sees his cousin Catherine standing in his aunt's bathroom, "stark naked except for her mother's high-heeled shoes, a full-fledged woman of eight years." Feeling "the confusion of my cousin's electric beauty pouring into me," he masturbates to her iconic image. He carries the burden of his sin, "like a criminal, a skulking, snot-nosed, freckle-faced, inscrutable criminal for four years thereafter, until sagging beneath the weight of my cross, I dragged myself into my first confession and told the priest the truth of my bestial life. He gave me absolution and I flung away the heavy cross and walked out into the sunlight, a free soul again" (DB 55). The two versions are virtually the same, except that the masturbation (which is Arturo's specialty) and family connection are repressed in

Jimmy's version and transformed into a preoccuation with "bad words" and how to express his sin of having said them.

Fante began his first Bandini novel, *The Road to Los Angeles*, about the time that "First Communion" was written. In a key scene, Arturo Bandini is asked by the owner of a diner: "What do you write? Stories? Or plain fiction?" This may be merely the question of a naive reader splitting illusory hairs, but Bandini takes it seriously. "Both," he answers. "I'm ambidextrous" (RL 28). If we take "stories" to mean the craft of fiction, in which truth must be confabulated with fiction to catch the spirit as well as the letter of lived events, and "plain fiction" to mean outright lies, then ambidexterity would imply that Bandini is capable of both. But such a double capability would also imply that he is not yet up to the demands of either, and has not quite incorporated the two. Eventually, Fante was, however, able to write stories that were a form of meditation in which to confess his sins against his family, his heritage, his religion, and his own best intentions, molding the "stories" and "plain fiction" told in the confessional of fiction into the alchemy of his meditative art.

CHAPTER 4

THE VIEW FROM BUNKER HILL

1932-1940

Outwardly, characteristically, everywhere but in print I am
something of a charlatan.

John Fante in 1933

On Monday, August 7, 1933, the *Los Angeles Herald Express*
ran a feature with the blaring headline:

BUS BOY DURING DAY, AT NIGHT HE'S AUTHOR.

Next to the story is a photograph of the "Literary Dish
Juggler," with the caption: "John Fante, 22-year-old author
and bus boy, waits on Coral Hatton, who is casting admiring
glances."

After moving from Long Beach to downtown Los Angeles, Fante had taken a job as a bus boy at Marcus' Bar and
Grille on the ground floor of the Fay Building at Third and
Hill for five dollars a week plus meals. Upstairs on the
seventh floor Fante moonlighted as "editor-in-chief of a
crooked literary agency" in the offices of an "old Frenchman
with a goatee" by the name of Jean C. de Kolty, Manuscript
Advisor and Literary Agent (SL 306).

The newspaper article was de Kolty's idea, a publicity stunt orchestrated to drum up interest for his business. Fante agreed to the idea because he thought it would be good for his career. De Kolty tipped off the newspapers about the brilliant fellow who "Would Rather Be Good Dish Carrier Than Bad Writer," as a subtitle in the story said. Coral Hatton, who is beaming at Fante as he balances tray and sandwich plate, was actually a waitress in the bar. To complete the sham, Fante had again given his date of birth as 1911, as he had to Mencken and for the same reason: to make himself appear more precocious by two years. It was his first taste of celebrity, or as Arturo Bandini says in *Dreams from Bunker Hill,* his "first collision with fame" (DB 9). Fante was all of twenty-four.

The feature did less for his career than for his ego. As late as 1978, Fante still fondly recalled: "It was a happy time for several weeks after my picture appeared . . . I used to strut around in that cafe, an apron around my waist, signing autographs and lending profundity to my remarks. Everybody liked me . . . and regarded me as the coming whiz" (SL 306). As Fante realized, the stunt would have done him more good if he had had a book to promote, but that would take another five years of hard work.

Meanwhile, he was John Fante of the Editorial and Sales Dept., according to the letterhead on which he wrote to his mother in February, 1933: "My name at the letterhead doesn't mean anything. De Kolty asked me if he could put it there, and I gave my consent. Sometimes I work here, but there isn't any business" (SL 46). Fante clearly disparaged the work he did for de Kolty, who appears as the goateed con artist Gustave Du Mont in *Dreams from Bunker Hill.*

Fante appreciated the use of the quiet office, high above the traffic, and the access to typewriter, paper and stamps, but he considered the job of cutting and slashing hopelessly illiterate manuscripts the futile drudgery that it was. His attitude was, perhaps, not unlike that of some graduate students in creative writing, who nowadays find themselves teaching composition. Like them, Fante may even have learned something about how not to write from the manuscripts' negative example.

All the while, Fante kept writing. He had moved downtown from Long Beach to take a two-dollar room in the old Alta Vista Hotel (the Alta Loma in *Ask the Dust*) on Bunker Hill, which had already long ceased to be the city's chic hill-top apartment district. Here in the heart, or tenderloin, of Los Angeles, he felt he could at last become a writer. It was a "time of dream and reverie" (AD 15), a time "to hunger and dream with eyes awake" (AD 41). Here he conceived of his life-long alter ego, Arturo Bandini, and drank in the sights and sounds of Los Angeles. In David Thomson's words, "though he was unknown and strapped for his rent money, he had the fierce, self-dramatizing appetite for words and experience of someone who had felt his nature as a writer early enough to live with every disappointment."[1] He was rich when he sold a story and poor again just as soon as he could get rid of the proceeds. Often, however, after splurging on cookies and glorious fedoras, he would send the remainder to his mother in Roseville to pay off the family's grocery bill.

By night Fante haunted the downtown speakeasies, dance halls and all-night theaters, where according to his sometimes friend Ross Wills, he picked up a menagerie of "outcasts, defeated, defrauded, and lost human beings" and took them home to the tiny Bunker Hill room for "a communal life-story telling contest," egging them on as he "listened and commented sympathetically" (SL 333). When he sold a story, sometimes Fante would redistribute the wealth among these comrades, his own version of a literary coterie, whose stories had no market but his sympathetic ear.

If we are to believe Ross Wills in his suspiciously vivid portrait of Fante, published in 1941 and reprinted in the *Selected Letters*, Fante was pure spontaneous fun and games, and something of an idiot savant. At various points Wills compares Fante to "a small, hungry boy," "a healthy puppy" and "a young chimpanzee that had just been set free in the jungle" (SL 330). Later Fante would claim that it was this, his former friend's "idiotic sophomoric" characterization of him, that prejudiced the Guggenheim committee against his application for a grant, even though Mencken recommended him as "a more likely young man" than any of that year's candidates, with the exception of Henry Miller (SL 190; FM 159).[2]

Whatever the accuracy of Wills' portrait — both Fante and his wife Joyce denied the truth of it with different degrees of resentment — it has long since passed into the Fante legend, partly because it was virtually the only available biographical source for several decades.[3] Ross Wills defended the portrait by claiming that some of it was told him by Fante himself and that the anecdotes in any case were "like" him. It may be significant in this context to mention that Ross Wills was completely deaf and that any stories "told" to him by Fante would have been put in writing, and these helped along — inspired, as it were — by several drinks. "I spent many a night in bars writing my thoughts to Ross. He enjoyed the practice. He liked people around him handing him notes, the more the better, but it did get tiresome" (SL 306). Thus John Fante's "telling" was not the testimony of a sober man in an interview but of an

aspiring spinner of yarns elaborating on dull fact with a
healthy, professional disrespect.

Some of what Wills conveys as fact may therefore be
doubted, but with that in mind, I think we can rely on the
spirit of the portrait for a sense of what it was like to be
around Fante in the Bunker Hill years. For example, Wills
overstates (rather than lies about) the editorial liberties
Mencken took with Fante's letters: "Mencken had found
buried in his last long letter an excellent short story, had cut
it out and called it 'Altar Boy'" (SL 332). Untrue. Mencken
did change the title of "Home, Sweet Home," but the stories
Fante submitted were quite separate, crafted creations, not
accidents culled from his letters as Wills would have us
believe. But Wills is right about Mencken's influence in
shaping Fante's voice by encouraging him to trust his natural speaking (or letter-writing) voice over any so-called literary one. Not that there was ever much danger of Fante
becoming stuffy; when he erred it was on the side of superfluous candor. Perhaps the same can be said of Wills and his
portrait of Fante, since it remains valuable insofar as Fante
himself played up the myth of the precocious naif.

The two met at the beginning of 1933 when Fante
appeared in Wills' office at MGM (where Wills was head
script-reader) with a letter of introduction from Carey
McWilliams. "I hesitated," writes Wills, "for in those days
every young writer who came to Los Angeles — and they
came! — made a bee-line to Carey's law office where he,
already a well-known author, was asked for various favors,
mainly for aid in getting jobs in the movies" so they could
write the Great American Novel (SL 329). But Wills had read
"Altar Boy" in the *American Mercury* and decided to take a
look at the author of this "striking story."

And there he was. He couldn't have been overlooked. He was not sitting on the bench meekly waiting. Not he. Characteristically, as I would later discover, he was boldly leaning over the desk of the pretty receptionist, pouring out upon her flustered head a veritable waterfall of urgent poetic words...A bouncey, sawed-off runt, quick-bitten finger nails on his stubby hands, he was arrayed in old sneakers and big, baggy gray pants that threatened to drop from his hips and meet the point where their extra length had been rolled up to his sock tops. Underneath a patched, bright green, pinch-back coat with too-short sleeves, he wore an old purple V-neck sweater (SL 329).

Far from being the typical Italian-looking kid that Wills expected to find, John Fante turned out to have "a mop of sandy-reddish hair" and "as impudent a freckled face as might ever have come out of any small American town" (SL 329). (It was the red hair of Jimmy Toscana, as much as the color of his father's wine, that went into the title of Fante's collected stories *Dago Red*.) If Fante were not "Huck Finn's direct descendant, he was Huck's first cousin's direct descendant . . . For John Fante looks less characteristically Italian than any Italian I ever knew, and as characteristically American as any American one might find" (SL 329-30). Echoing this impression, Carey McWilliams, another of this trio of "evil companions,"[4] would describe Fante fifty years later: "John is as American as Huckleberry Finn" (SL 291).

With the help of McWilliams and Wills, and the blessing of Mencken, Fante had little trouble breaking into Hollywood and partaking of the fortunes of its writers. Soon he was making $300 a week as a studio hack, having come a long way from his combined earnings as literary dish juggler and de Kolty's editorial plenipotentiary. Fante's imagination went to work before he did. Already he was spinning tales to tell the folks back in Denver about the stars he worked with, or the starlets he bedded. He also began to spend his earnings, buying a used Plymouth. It was not exactly the LaSalles or Marmons he had lusted after in his teens, nor the Dusenbergs of the stars, but it was a car and it seemed to validate him as a true Californian, a real American, upwardly and horizontally mobile.

Casting himself in the role of Fante's guardian, Wills gave Fante contacts, explained his contracts, and generally gave him the low down on the business in Hollywood. At one point Wills claims to have acted as Fante's banker, encouraging him to squirrel away much of his windfall if he was serious about holing up in a cabin in the Sierras and writing the long-deferred novel. Having persuaded his prodigal friend that he could soon save enough money to write for a year, Wills convinced Fante to turn his checks over to him and to keep for himself only a modest allowance to live on. Wills even invited Fante to move in with him in Culver City to be closer to the studios and further away from his Bunker Hill cronies, who had begun to seek him out in his success.[5]

At the end of two months, Fante was astounded to find that he had $1200 in the bank. At Fante's request Wills brought the bankroll to him in a wad of ten and twenty dollar rolls. On his way to the mountain cabin Fante wanted to spend a week in Denver to strut his Hollywood success. But first he had to go shopping so that his homecoming could be made in style. It took both Wills and McWilliams, acting as valets and "evil companions," to get him outfitted in "vast, gunboatish yellow shoes . . . ; a stunning deep-purple shirt with a green-and-white necktie; and a three-button, cross-striped, double-breasted suit of a quite indescribable color combination" (SL 335). Over this he draped a Harpo Marx overcoat, an inch thick and dragging the ground, a new Stetson, and (a last-minute flourish by McWilliams) an ochre cane bought on impulse on the way to the midnight train. In this get-up John Fante was ready for his triumphal homecoming.

For two weeks his home town rolled out the red carpet for what the local newspaper called "one of Denver's most distinguished sons, the famous young author and motion picture producer." But, claims Wills, one by one his possessions disappeared, the cane, the Stetson, the Harpo overcoat, and he woke up one morning with a hangover, broke. Like a character in one of his own novels (the one he was to have written in the cabin had he got there), he sold his luggage to a bell hop to pay his bill and skipped town, making it back as far as Roseville. From here he sent a collect cable to Wills: "Wire me twenty-five. Anxious to get back. Got million dollar movie idea" (SL 336).

Later he told Wills that while hitchhiking on the edge of Sacramento, he counted two dollars in his pocket, which made him sixty-seven cents richer than he was when he had left Colorado a few years before to seek his fortune in California. He fell down rolling with laughter in a ditch and holding his sides, until a motorist stopped to ask if he were okay, then told him to hop in.

This scenario is a good example of Wills at his best as a caricaturist, if not a portraitist. Although Fante did return to Denver with a prodigal splash (in 1934, not 1932) and was hailed in the local newspapers in a romantic light, he was considerably more careful with money than Wills makes him out to be, and he almost certainly did not return to California broke and half-naked. He returned via his parents' house in Roseville by train; he did not hitchhike. Even the comic departure from L.A., as described by Wills, is in question since he wrote to McWilliams from the train, "Left

Los Angeles tonight on impulse" (SL 87), as though McWilliams knew nothing about it. But it makes for high comedy as Wills tells it, especially the transparent comparison with Harpo Marx: Wills was a Hollywood writer, after all.

So was Fante. The studio work came easy and the living was easier. When his father was out of work, he could pay off the family's grocery bills up in Roseville. The Italian kid from Denver could buy all the goofy ties that burglars could steal, and he could range through the marketplace of all the chrome-plated American status symbols he could drive. The shortstop from Regis High could also indulge his catholic taste for women, playing the infield for all the hard-hit American princesses that came his way, although as he confessed to Carey McWilliams, his similarity to Casanova was slight: "like most scribblers, most of my fucking is done on paper."[6]

Movie hackwork was lucrative; it was not the dream. When he wasn't playing pinball or collaborating on scripts, Fante stayed home and exorcized the stories that haunted him from his past. He began a novel called *Pater Doloroso*, for which he had received an advance from Mencken's publisher, Viking. He was unable to work his "hodge-podge" of material into a novel, and it was rejected, but he was able to cull a number of Colorado stories from the material. At a time when a short story writer could still make a living, Fante had no trouble publishing his bittersweet stories about baseball, work, religion, sin and death in such magazines as the *Atlantic Monthly, Harper's Bazaar, Scribner's,* and of course the *American Mercury,* where he placed eight stories from 1932 to 1937. Mencken left the magazine in 1933, but as he predicted, this did not dry up Fante's favorite showcase. There would always be a market, it seemed, for

Fante and his flair for the mad moments of human awkwardness told with gentle humor and rough honesty.

After giving up on *Pater Doloroso* Fante lost no time in getting to work on what would become *The Road to Los Angeles*, which he bragged to Mencken would be "a colossal affair . . . a modern Huckleberry Finn" (FM 71). Fante had got another advance, but he was unable to finish the novel in the projected seven months. It was 1936 before he was able to complete the novel. On Bastille Day he wrote to McWilliams:

> *The Road to Los Angeles* is finished and boy! I'm pleased . . . Some of the stuff will singe the hair off a wolf's rear. It may be too strong; i.e., lacking in "good" taste. But that doesn't bother me (SL 129).

It bothered Bernie Smith at Knopf, however, who thought it "horrible." Acting on Knopf's behalf while the publisher was away, Smith said in his letter of rejection that he was, in Fante's paraphrase, "sorry and bitterly disappointed that the writer of such brilliant short stories in the Mercury should do such a job as that particular novel" (SL 129).

As the new novel was declined by one publisher after another, Fante became disillusioned. "What embitters me a bit is this — I wrote that book with such fearful honesty. I really sweated out the candor in it. I shall never again write with such unrestraint — all of which goes to prove that it's a poor policy to be honest and that it is much better to be artistic" (SL 130). As a true disciple of Mencken, he allowed the critics their due. "Of course it may be that the book is simply bad. In that case I have no complaint, except the feeling that somebody, including myself, has been kidding me" (SL 130). He had faith in the book as an honest piece of work, "not a masterpiece or anything like that — but a good, solid piece of writing"; yet he realized that if he wanted to become "a famous writer," he "had better look at literature" through the eyes of the publishers and "forget whatever I feel" (SL 130-31). In his pique he threatened to "recall it and burn it" so that he could go on to something else. Luckily, he chose simply to file it, where it was found among other rejected manuscripts and published in 1985, two years after his death.

The Road to Los Angeles shelved, Fante marshaled his resources and went to work on another novel. For all the thematic coherence of the stories that were to make up *Dago Red,* the short form could not give him the satisfaction of a novel, nor did it create the kind of unity he needed to see take shape in an extended chronological narrative. Because the short story was too dependent upon the support of advertisers, it tended to corrupt and shackle a writer, and although it allowed him to tell fragments of his own story, it was only a step away from the restraints of screen writing. Only the novel could give him the freedom he needed to say all he had to say.

So John Fante, unpublished novelist, again sat down to reflect on the material in the manuscript of *Pater Doloroso.* He thought about his troubled relationship with his father, a poor man who earned his living with a trowel when he could and with a pool cue when he had to. He thought of his religiose mother, how she martyred herself to this earthly man while she dreamed of saints and eternal life.

And, with a healthy dose of Catholic guilt, Fante thought about how he himself, intellectually arrogant, ashamed of his father's ignorance and his Italian heritage, had not made life any easier for this man from the rocky Abruzzi, whose youthful dreams of improving himself and making his family proud had come to nothing in the rocky heartland of America. Then he sat down to face the white sheet of paper in the machine and, envisioning his father cursing the elements, he began to write: "He came along, kicking the deep snow. He was a disgusted man. His name was Svevo Bandini" (WB 11).

So the new Bandini novel, a "prequel" to *The Road to Los Angeles*, began to take shape. It would be called *Wait Until Spring, Bandini* because Arturo hated the snow that kept him off the baseball diamond and his father out of work. It would be set in Rocklin (Boulder), Colorado, and would focus not on the braggadocio of the Arturo Bandini of *The Road to Los Angeles*, whom the publishers didn't seem to like, but on Svevo, Arturo's rebellious, embattled father, whom the publishers seemed to love. Fante would dredge up old guilts and old resentments about his father, who had left his mother briefly for another woman in 1930, but he would tell it all with tenderness as well as truthfulness. The result would be a gentler depiction of the Bandini family, a tender and truthful portrait of Arturo's childhood, like that of Jimmy Toscana, who was loved by readers and publishers alike. The novel would also be a token of love to his mother and a peace offering from a prodigal son to a prodigal father, dedicated "to my mother, Mary Fante, with love and devotion; and to my father, Nick Fante, with love and admiration" (WB 7).

But before beginning *Wait Until Spring, Bandini*, Fante felt it necessary to sort out his love life. With his usual ambivalence about women, Fante seemed to be of two minds about marriage. On the one hand, he would write to his mother in March, 1934, in connection with Helen Purcell, that he was "not the marrying kind" and that marriage was "a bad environment for a writer" because it "changes a man's point of view. He ceases to be free. He ceases to think for himself. What he does thereafter is done for two people and not for one. His worries increase and so do his debts. He gets fat, and his ambitions are not so strong. I am against marriage for myself" (SL 73-4).

Two years later, however, in March 1936, Fante was singing another tune about marriage, this time in connection with another woman with whom he was living, Marie Baray. A twenty-three year old artist's model, who later became his model for Camilla Lopez in *Ask the Dust*, Marie had nursed him through a long illness, and it is possible that Fante was "seriously considering getting married" to her, partly out of gratitude. He also noted her virtues as "a wonderful housekeeper and an extraordinarily fine cook," as well as someone who would produce healthy children (SL 119). In December 1935, several months before writing this brief in favor of marriage, in which he seems to be trying to convince himself, Fante had written of Marie in another tone entirely: "She wants to marry me and I tell her that some day soon we shall certainly become man and wife, but I'm afraid I am not sincere when I tell her that" (SL 112).

In other words, Fante may have been ready to get married, but not necessarily to Marie Baray. It seems that Fante was looking to marriage to put some order in his chaotic life and improve his ability to work. Again to his mother Fante writes: "if I got married I would have to settle down and work . . . I haven't worked very hard in my life, and I rather like it this way, taking it easy, working on my stories whenever I feel like it, and doing as I please. It's a fine life, and rather easy for a man who gets broke, but having been sick, I have come to the conclusion that a family is a good thing, and I want one. The next year will tell the tale" (SL 119).

His prediction about the next year would prove prophetic.

But if what Fante was looking for in a wife was order and discipline, then Marie Baray, "a highly excitable girl, easily frightened" (SL 112), was probably the wrong woman. Writing to Keith Baker in 1940, Fante states: "The love story in *Ask the Dust* is almost true in that I once had an infatuation with the girl in the novel, and she is, in my opinion, as fascinating and interesting in real life as I attempted to make her in the book. Today she is down on Spring Street in Los Angeles, working in the same bar I described in the novel, having returned there from the insane asylum, the desert, and points north" (SL 185). In 1979, Fante identified the model of *Ask the Dust* as what almost appears to be another woman: "You see, the theme running through *Ask the Dust* is very subtle, and it might escape some people because I never screwed this girl. The love affair in that book is a true love affair. There's only one thing missing. I didn't mention it because I don't think I could have handled it and that was the fact that the girl, Camilla, was a lesbian."[7] Fante goes on to say that he did not know this until after he had given her a copy of the published book. She was pleased, he said, by the portrait of her, even though it was "not true," but she did not really appreciate the merits of the book because "she was a wildcat. She was ignorant, illiterate."[8] If any of this is true, then Marie Baray was definitely the wrong woman in whom to seek shelter and stability.

Fante's sudden departure for Roseville, soon after his letter to his mother saying he was about to marry Marie Baray, can be explained only partly by his desire to get away from screen writing and close to the material for the book he wanted to write, or to have the time and freedom to write it. It seems reasonable to assume that there was some more

personal reason. If Marie had suffered a breakdown or disappeared, or if Fante had been living with a woman he
could not sleep with, this would explain Fante's sudden
silence — and later obfuscation — on the subject of Marie
Baray and any planned marriage, as well as his subsequent
flight to Roseville. [9]

In Roseville, however, as he worked on the novel, the
subjects of love, lust and marriage still plagued him. "I am
hotter than hell these days," he wrote to Carey McWilliams,
"and it's futile trying to work off sex vitality playing golf. I
feel like chewing these walls. The only menace I find in
poverty is that I can't fuck enough. I am not in favor of
Capitalism or Communism, but Clitorism" (SL 134). Ideally,
the problem of "sex vitality" could be solved only through
marriage, but marriage seemed possible only if he could
solve the nagging problem of poverty. "What the hell is
there to say to the modern American girl who is unwittingly
a whore seeking top dough in the marriage racket?" (SL
134). Fante could have solved his financial problems, however, by staying in Hollywood. More important, it seems,
was the immediate problem of finishing his novel. More
than anything else, marriage in the abstract seemed like a
good encouragement to settle down and get to work.

Meanwhile, Fante was looking for new ways to support his writing, such as a Houghton-Mifflin Foundation
Fellowship or a Guggenheim grant to Italy on the strength
of his Italian-American stories, but none of these projects
panned out. While it is interesting to speculate what effect a
trip to Italy would have had on him this early in his career,
it is also difficult to imagine Fante in the role of expatriate.
When he finally got to Italy in the late 1950s, it was under
the auspices of Hollywood money, and by that time Fante's
appreciation of America and its comforts was too deeply

ingrained for him to romanticize his Italian heritage. For the moment, he would have to be satisfied with the Italians he had at home.

Living with his parents in Roseville meant living close to the subjects and conflicts of the work in hand — sometimes too close. Life with Nick and Mary Fante too often resembled a slapstick sketch out of James Thurber to be conducive to serious writing, but it was fine for comedy in his letters to McWilliams:

> This is hot country. We're temporarily crowded now that I've arrived, and my two brothers and I sleep in one bed. Awful conditions. Last night I gave up and slept on the floor. About 2 a.m. my father, highly soused, and with no need of a light, staggered through the room toward what he believed was his own room, and stepped on my neck. It tripped him up, and he ended matters by sitting on my head. However, he was so tight he never knew the difference, so I got up, rolled him in the blankets, and piled in with my mother. The only reason she knew it was I, and not my father, I leave to your imagination. Then, highly suspicious, she turned on the light and found me asleep beside her. Meanwhile, my father had wakened, pulled my brother from bed, and piled in himself. When the dawn came, he and my mother were asleep in the boys' bedroom, my two brothers were asleep in hers, and I, alas, had retired to the bathtub. Even that wasn't the end, because my father entered the bathroom about six, saw me there, and turned on the water. I got up at 6; dressed, and, my body refreshed, sat down and wrote 40,000 words of glorious prose. (You can believe the last if you feel like it.) (SL 122-23)

Living close to his material could be an advantage, but even when the excitement died down it was sometimes difficult to get the perspective needed to write about his parents in their own house.

Here's a situation for you. A man sits in a room writing a story
about his mother. There are episodes in that story which
have to do with the secretest events in that mother's life. And
in the room this guy writes. And in the next room sits this
guy's mother with a rosary in her hand. And what is she
doing, but praying for the success of that story. Jesus Christ!
If you only knew what that does to a man. It makes him feel
that his guts are hanging out. I have had enough of it. I am
moving back to Los Angeles.[10]

As an antidote to his experience in Hollywood, and perhaps
to the domestic chaos, Fante was rediscovering the Greek
classics. "By God, *that's* literature! The Apologia of Socrates
is the finest thing ever written, and for every modern two-
bit idea in the world, you'll find fifty gems in old Socrates . .
. Every modern novel, philosophy, credo, has its even
greater source in the Dialogues" (SL 125). There is more
enthusiasm here than insight, but Fante could be expected
to relish Socrates' Defense for its unrepentant noncon-
formity as well as its bemused and melancholy tolerance of
human stupidity.

In January 1937 Fante, who was now writing a column
with his own byline for the Roseville *Tribune*, met Joyce
Smart, a Stanford graduate working as an editor. She had
read and "adored" Fante's stories in the *American Mercury*,
where she was soon to publish a poem herself. "Accordingly," recalled Joyce in 1989, "I arranged for someone to
introduce us."[11] Her family, which had been in California
since the Gold Rush, did not approve, hoping for a better
catch. A wounded Fante wrote: "My Stanfordite's mother is
against me and the marriage. If we get hitched my spouse
will be disinherited from what must be a fortune, since the
threat is uttered with the most awful imprecations. Unfortu-
nately the other daughter married a friend of the Vander-
bilts, which makes it tough on a mere scribbler."[12] Less than

a month after writing this, and after only six months of a
largely clandestine courtship, Fante decided that since he
was twenty-seven, and Joyce was twenty-two, they didn't
need the consent of her parents. With ten dollars borrowed
from Fante's parents, and a car borrowed from Joyce's parents, the couple drove to Reno, where they were secretly
married, July 31, 1937. When Joyce's parents heard the
news, they did indeed disinherit her, but relented after less
than a year.[13]

From 1932, which marks the beginning of his writing
career with the appearance of "Altar Boy," to 1936, when he
left for Roseville, Fante had lived a hand-to-mouth existence
in rooms, cheap hotels and friends' couches, all over the Los
Angeles area, not just in Bunker Hill, but everywhere from
Long Beach to Hollywood, with sojourns in Terminal Island
and Venice Beach. When he returned to Los Angeles a
married man in 1937, "the lean days of determination" were
coming to an end, and Fante was soon to publish not just
one book, but three in quick succession. In a series of little
apartments in the Wilshire district, John worked on *Wait
Until Spring, Bandini* and *Ask the Dust*, while they lived on
the $94 a month Joyce was making working for the Writer's
Project of the Works Projects Administration, contributing
to the WPA Guide to Los Angeles.[14] In March 1938, when
Fante informed Mencken of his marriage, Mencken replied
on stationery bordered in black: "I send you my most sincere
congratulations, but have only condolences for your poor
wife. She will discover soon enough that living with a literary gent is a dreadful experience. I hope that she is never
tempted to load your victuals with roach powder" (FM 119).
Fante's prophecy that marriage would enable him to work
came true, and the next three years saw the appearance of

as many books, the first significant fruits of his loves and their labors.

Wait Until Spring, Bandini appeared in 1938, followed by *Ask the Dust* in 1939. Sales were not brisk. One reason given by the publisher, Stackpole Sons, was that their advertising budget had been decimated by a copyright lawsuit over their unauthorized publication of *Mein Kampf*, in which they argued that Hitler was a stateless author who deserved no royalties. The lukewarm sales of the novels made their appearance all the more disheartening to Fante. Was this the result of eight years of apprenticeship? Still, the two Bandini novels and the stories collected in *Dago Red* — which even today largely constitute the basis of Fante's reputation — gave Fante much to show for in the way of literary achievement at the close of the decade.

The reviews, however, were encouraging. John Chamberlain in *Scribner's* compared Fante predictably to James T. Farrell: "But Fante believes in the quintessentializing, 'poetic' technique, while Farrell uses a mixture of the naturalistic and the grotesque" (SL 151).

In a similar vein E. B. Garside compared Fante to Saroyan, calling his prose "a kind of poetry" that "breathes in life from a whirligig American existence." He singled out *Ask the Dust* as particularly powerful: "*Ask the Dust* realizes to the full the quizzical wonder inherent in Saroyan's fragmentary writings, and recognizes the cruelty of man's lot besides . . . Fante must have lived this out at some time." The review concludes with high expectations for the young writer: "now that he has written his *Werther*, let us hope fervently he can go on to another *Faust*." [15]

More recently, Gary Krist has picked up the same analogy, knowingly or not, ironically linking Fante's fiction to his life: "For a writer of serious fiction, selling a book to

the movies is a bargain with definite Faustian overtones."[16]
It might be said that if Fante lived out his *Werther* in his
Bunker Hill years, he lived out his *Faust* in the Hollywood
years to come.

Other critics were more guarded, particularly with
regard to the morality of *Ask the Dust*. H. L. Binsse called it
"a strange novel, one which is most emphatically not recommended for reading by the young, or even by the old
who dislike sordid pictures of immorality."[17] While the *New
Yorker* approved of the story of the Bandini family as "real
and consequential," the magazine's praise of *Ask the Dust*
was tepid: "told in a well-managed, colloquial prose, but
doesn't add up to much. Not as interesting as Mr. Fante's
Wait Until Spring, Bandini."

These brief reviews seem to have missed the point.
While complimenting Fante on his prose and (seemingly)
the Bandini family for being poor Italians in Colorado, there
is no hint of the tragicomic romp with a family of eccentrics
violently at odds and in love with life, wine, God and each
other. Neither is there mention of its vivid supporting cast,
such as the glass-eyed nun who disdains baseball only to
proclaim, "Football's my game." Nor do they give a sense of
the mad and memorable, naive and vulnerable Arturo
Bandini, obsessed with literature, baseball and the female
sex. *Ask the Dust is* treated as though the reviewer had
expected Depression-era realism and didn't know what to
make of the book's brilliant comic absurdity. The problem
seems to have been with the egoistic and pseudo-intellectual Bandini.

The critics had no such problems with the return of
Jimmy Toscana in *Dago Red,* published by Viking Press in
1940.[19] The eccentricities of the Toscana family were seen as
the oddities of humble people with big hearts and simple

minds. Yet the Bandini and Toscana families are, in their confused passion and emotional largess, otherwise identical. It is the Arturo Bandini of *Ask the Dust* who was a new and unclassified breed. The critics applauded Fante in *Dago Red* for his return to simple subjects told in a more conventional tone. *Time* magazine greeted the collection with enthusiasm: "perhaps 1940's best book of short stories: the sort many people wish that William Saroyan, with a grip on himself at last, would write." Fante received further encouragement as a short story writer when "A Nun No More," originally published by the *Virginia Quarterly Review*, was included in *The Best Short Stories of 1941*.

The appearance of *Dago Red* thus marked the end of John Fante's apprenticeship as a fiction writer. He had come a long way from being the literary dish juggler and author of "Altar Boy." It would be twelve years before the next volume by John Fante, *Full of Life* (1952), saw print, and forty-two years before the next installment in The Saga of Arturo Bandini, *Dreams from Bunker Hill* (1982). Both books would feature a screenwriter as the narrator, since Fante in these decades was occupied more with writing for the movies than for himself.

All told, the time John Fante spent in and around Bunker Hill did not amount to more than two or three years, yet the spaces in which our identities are formed have very little to do with the blocks on the calendar. As Gaston Bachelard has shown in relation to the poetic image, an identity like that of Bandini, the alter ego formed by Fante during his Bunker Hill years and retained for over half a century, "is not an echo of the past. On the contrary, through the brilliance of an image, the distant past resounds with echoes, and it is hard to know at what depth these echoes will reverberate and die away." For such an image "has an entity and a dynamism of its own." Such an identity is much more susceptible to the contours of those spaces where our consciousness is most active, where "the *onset of the image* in an individual consciousness" occurs.[20] In Fante's words, it is where we "hunger and dream with eyes awake" (AD 41). Writing to Keith Baker in 1940, Fante admitted: "You want to know if I am Arturo Bandini, and I say that I am — particularly the Arturo in *Ask the Dust*" (SL 184-5).

John Fante's identity as a writer was formed not in the first years of his marriage while he was writing *Ask the Dust (1938-39)*, but during the "lean days of determination" (AD 17), when he, like Bandini, was imagining himself into becoming a writer, as he looked out of the window of the Alta Vista — or Alta Loma — Hotel, looking for inspiration and seeing his own image in the dust-choked palm tree and writing: "palm tree, palm tree, palm tree, a battle to the death between the palm tree and me" (AD 17). Fante's marriage, in fact, brought an end to the bohemian life that was symbolized by the view from his two-dollar room in the old Alta Vista Hotel. But Bunker Hill would always be the dusty blossom of that "sad flower in the sand" (AD 13), Los Angeles, the city that Fante said in later years had "changed so much they should give it a new name."[21] Joyce Fante described the city as it was when Fante would have seen it, with all his ambition intact: "In the Downtown of those days, there was no smog, the air was clear, it was much less congested, and the huge waves of population from the South hadn't arrived yet. Bunker Hill was clean and cheap and comfortable. It was a great place to be young and poor."[22] It was this Bunker Hill that would always be the high point of Fante's early career, the hey-day of his apprenticeship, synonymous with his beginnings, best intentions, and first successes as a writer, just as home would always be the Boulder of his boyhood before the break-up of the family and the move to California. It was California, however, where John Fante joined "the uprooted ones," became one with "the new Californians," and could say, with Arturo Bandini, "These were my countrymen" (AD 45).

CHAPTER 5

THE APPRENTICESHIP OF ARTURO BANDINI

WAIT UNTIL SPRING, BANDINI
AND THE ROAD TO LOS ANGELES

> ... All of these people of my writing life, all of my characters can be found in this early work. Nothing of myself is there any more ...
>
> John Fante, Preface to *Wait Until Spring, Bandini*

1. Nothing of Myself: *Wait Until Spring, Bandini*

Like the mercurial Socrates, whom Fante admired as a great novelistic character, and like the figures of classical myth, Arturo Bandini is a hero with a thousand faces, mutable and unfettered by realistic considerations of any strict continuity of character or personal history. Like Quixote, Shandy, Werther, and Candide, all of whom he at times resembles, Arturo Bandini embodies an archetypal tendency in all of us. We identify with his naive vulnerability and his foolish arrogance, which is to say his humanity. This is perhaps what Charles Bukowski meant by the Bandini *"magic,"* and why, during a quarrel with the woman he was living with when he first read Bandini, he could scream: "Don't call me a son of a bitch! *I am Bandini, Arturo Bandini!*" (AD 6). At such moments, when we are caught with our eccentricities down around our knees, we are all Arturo Bandini.

Certainly there is much of Fante in Arturo Bandini. No single passage more succinctly sums up Fante's early conflicts than Arturo's self-portrait as an anti-realist in *Wait Until Spring, Bandini*:

> His name was Arturo, but he hated it and wanted to be called John. His last name was Bandini, and he wanted it to be Jones. His mother and father were Italians, but he wanted to be an American. His father was a bricklayer, but he wanted to be a pitcher for the Chicago Cubs. They lived in Rocklin, Colorado, population ten thousand, but he wanted to live in Denver, thirty miles away. His face was freckled, but he wanted it to be clear. He went to a Catholic school, but he wanted to go to a public school. He had a girl named Rosa, but she hated him. He was an altar boy, but he was a devil and hated altar boys. He wanted to be a good boy, but he was afraid to be a good boy because he was afraid his friends would call him a good boy. He was Arturo and he loved his father, but he lived in dread of the day when he would grow up and be able to lick his father. He worshipped his father, but he thought his mother was a sissy and a fool (WB 33-4).

The four major conflicts of the early stories — family, religion, heritage, and ambition — are here repeated in a detailed outline. This profile of Arturo, a composition in counterpoint between what he is and what he would like to be, shows that the essence of Arturo Bandini is contradiction. It is the one characteristic that remains constant throughout the Bandini novels.

In his 1983 preface to *Wait Until Spring, Bandini*, Fante wrote: "I cannot bring myself to look back, to open this first novel and read it again. I am fearful, I cannot bear being exposed by my own work. I am sure I shall never read this book again." When he wrote these lines, Fante was blind and would never again be able to read this or any other book, though he might have books read to him. No wonder, then, that he concentrates on the fragmentary sounds of "melodious memory" to "mesmerize" him in the dim light of a "half dream," such as "the memory of old bedrooms, and the sound of my mother's slippers walking to the kitchen" (WB 8). *Wait Until Spring, Bandini* introduces not only Arturo, but all of the Bandini family. Indeed, Fante went a step further: "All of the people of my writing life, all of my characters are to be found in this early work. Nothing of myself is there any more" (WB 8). This is an overstatement, of course, but to the extent that family dominates his work, and that the Bandinis are essentially the same family as the Toscanas, the Molises and the Fantes, it is a sincere and self-conscious reflection of the supreme importance of family in his work.

Two other assertions in this preface deserve comment because they may appear disingenuous: "I cannot bear being exposed by my own work" and "Nothing of myself is there any more." Fante is constantly "exposed" in the confessional of his fiction. But the function of confession takes place on two levels, whether in Augustine, Rousseau or Fante: first, to admit one's failings to a confessor (priest or reader), who may or may not grant absolution; more importantly, to admit one's failings to oneself. That Fante's work exposes him to his reading public is unavoidable, but that is not what he is afraid of (otherwise why let the book be republished?). What he is afraid of is being his own confessor, hearing, once again, his own confession in the form of *Wait Until Spring, Bandini*, and thereby being exposed to himself. The John Fante of 1983 was not, after all, the John Fante of 1938, despite his having written a new novel

(*Dreams from Bunker Hill*) from Arturo's point of view. Like Fante himself, Arturo was constantly changing. Thus, "Nothing of myself is there any more."

For all its confessional character, *Wait Until Spring, Bandini* is the only Fante novel narrated in the third person. The omniscient narrator moves in and out of the consciousness of Svevo, Maria and Arturo Bandini to show their individual reactions to their poverty in the midst of a Colorado winter. Maria gets through it by fingering the beads of her snow white rosary until "she was no longer Maria, American or Italian, poor or rich," and rises to "her quiet flight out of the world" into the "land of all-possessing" (WB 75). As Arturo says, his mother had "too much God in her" (WB 165). Svevo and Arturo are different than Maria; each of them is the Bandini of the title, subject to earthly weather, who must "wait until Spring." For Svevo the end of winter will mean self-respect, work, food on the table, shoes and clothing for his family. For Arturo it means self-fulfillment, baseball season, warming up the pitching arm, a beginning of fame and fortune and a future away from his family. During the long white wait of winter, Arturo goes to school and ponders the differences between mortal and venial sins, goes to the movies and fantasizes about his girl, Rosa Pinelli. Svevo smokes his Toscanelli cigars, plays poker at the Imperial Poolhall, drinks with his friend Rocco Saccone, and takes up with another woman, the rich widow Effie Hildegarde.

One reason for Fante's shift to the third person point of view is that he was discouraged by Knopf's rejection of *The Road to Los Angeles*, which he told in the cynical voice of Arturo at his most eccentric. By returning to the more conventional antics and motifs of the Toscana stories, Fante hoped to satisfy readers' expectations. Like Jimmy in "A Kidnaping in the Family," Arturo Bandini is the naughty altar boy fascinated by his mother's picture and obsessed with Oedipal fantasies tinged with Madonna worship. Maria Bandini's maiden name is Toscana. The novel has other echoes of the stories in *Dago Red*, as well. It opens with Svevo cursing the snow ("A Bricklayer in the Snow"), centers on the father's betrayal of the mother (hinted at in "A Wife for Dino Rossi"), and concludes with the death and funeral of Rosa Pinelli (reminiscent of "One of Us").[1]

More than any publishing consideration, however, Fante needed the third person point of view to deal with the subject of the father's infidelity. In *The Road to Los Angeles* Fante had taken the writer's easy revenge in killing off his father for deserting the family. In *Wait Until Spring, Bandini* he resurrects the father in order to do something more difficult, namely to confront the old man's infidelity as the focus of the plot, allowing him to tone down Arturo's brasher idiosyncrasies. Paradoxically, the objective point of view also allowed Fante to get closer to the autobiographical truth by avoiding the narrow scope of the immature son and gaining some distance on a painful experience in order to begin to come to terms with his cantankerous father and their troubling relationship.

We meet Svevo Bandini on his way home, kicking the snow and cursing: "*Dio cane. Dio cane.*" God is a dog, God is a dog. He is poor and disgusted by his poverty, not because he must wear cardboard from a macaroni box inside his shoes, but because he is unable to support his passionate and religious wife and his ungrateful children.

One of these children is Arturo, who has left his sled on the front walk. Svevo slips on the sled, lands in the snow, and curses the "little bastard" and God. The entire material world seems to be against him, the snow, the unpaid for house, his son's sled, his own shoe laces. He kicks the snow, wants to dynamite the house, tears the sled to pieces, breaks his shoe laces. *Dio cane! Diavolo!* Even the cards at the Imperial Poolhall have turned against him, taking his last ten dollars. Even his own son, Arturo, has turned against him by leaving his sled in his path, not to mention breaking a window by pushing his brother's head through it. "He's like you, Svevo," says Maria. "You were a bad boy too . . . You didn't have any brothers, Svevo. But you pushed your father down the steps and broke his arm" (WB 20).

With such a life, it surprises no one when Svevo spends ten days away from home, seven of them with the rich widow Effie Hildegarde. No one, that is, except Svevo, who is taken by surprise when he, a peasant, is seduced by a rich woman. Arturo, however, understands completely: "He could understand his father. A man had to do something: never having anything was too monotonous" (WB 165). He is proud of his father's escapade, and protective of his secret. The ambivalent identity between father and son, poignantly expressed in the violent confrontation remembered in "Home, Sweet Home" and elsewhere, haunts much of Fante's fiction, but there is no violence here. The distanced perspective seems to have softened Fante's treatment of his own father's betrayal, since Arturo's response is sympathetic. On the other hand, it is natural that Arturo forgive his father for betraying his mother, since Arturo betrays her himself by stealing the cameo his father had given his mother on their first anniversary, only to give it to Rosa Pinelli as a Christmas present. When Rosa rejects it, correctly guessing that it is probably stolen, he throws it over a rooftop.

Indeed, Fante's treatment of Maria Bandini is harsher here than anywhere else. This might be attributed to the resolution of the Oedipal fixation that Arturo is going through, or (with less justification) to Fante's admitted misogynistic streak. In any case, she is portrayed as a fool, a haggard, and a weakling when she is not lashing out in bestial fury. When Svevo returns on Christmas Eve, for example, a hundred dollars in his fist and kangaroo-leather shoes on his feet, Maria scratches his eyes and throws the money in the stove. Svevo staggers out and blots his face with "the linen of the sky" (WB 162), the omnipresent hated snow. Instead of sticking up for his betrayed mother, Arturo sympathizes with his father and cheers his father's escape back to the widow Hildegarde: "Ah, give it to her Papa! Me and you, Papa, because I know how you feel." The snow stained with his father's blood prompts a pledge of masculine solidarity: "Papa's blood, my blood." Returning to the house, Arturo tears the rosary out of his mother's hands and pulls it to pieces, as she watches, "martyrlike"; then he throws the snow white beads into the blood-spattered snow (WB 164-5). Looking at his mother, Arturo admits that "if *he* could choose between Maria and Effie Hildegarde, it would be Effie every time" because when "Italian women got to a certain age their legs thinned and their bellies widened, their breasts fell and they lost sparkle."[2] Arturo realizes that Rosa Pinelli is also Italian and hopes she dies before she goes downhill like his mother. "So give it to her Papa! I'm for you, old boy. Some day I'll be doing it too, I'll be right there some day with a honey like her, and she won't be the kind that scratches my face, and she won't be the kind that calls me a little thief" (WB 165-6).

In the ten days that Svevo was gone and in the weeks that pass after he is driven away, Arturo takes his father's place in the house, stoking the fires, getting his brothers off to school, protecting his mother, and even sharing her bed. His father's absence fulfills an Oedipal fantasy, allowing him to discover that it is not his mother he wants, but a girl of his own. When Arturo and his brothers return home from school, they find their mother stretched out on the bed "like a dead woman," or down in the cellar "kneeling over that barrel of wine Papa had vowed not to open until it was ten years old" (WB 228), or in the coal shed among her husband's tools, clutching Svevo's trowel (WB 135). Her invasion of the coal shed particularly infuriates him: "His mother had no right in this place. It was as though she had discovered him there, committing a boy-sin, that place, identically where he had sat those times" (WB 136). This reference to masturbation reminds him of his Oedipal fascination for a picture of her, sixteen years younger, he once found in a trunk: "O that picture! . . . — a picture of a large-eyed girl in a wide hat, smiling with so many small teeth, a beauty of a girl standing under the apple tree in Grandma Toscana's backyard. Oh, Mamma, to kiss you then! Oh, Mamma, why did you change?" (WB 141). When he returns to the picture in the trunk now, he feels "a sense of evil degrading him," as he wonders what it was like "to have felt the cradle of that beautiful womb" (WB 142). Earlier he had felt "the sticky sensation of evil" in the sound of certain words, including the word in the prayer: "Hail Mary full of grace, the Lord is with thee and blessed art thou among women, and blessed is the fruit of thy womb. The word shook him like thunder. Fruit of thy womb. Another sin was born" (WB 114). It is when he puts the picture away (apparently for the last time) that he steals the cameo for a girl his own age, Rosa. This theft symbolizes the resolution of his Oedipal conflict: by throwing his mother over for Rosa, he takes on his father's role in courtship, but the object of his desire is no longer his mother. Always before he had wanted his mother to be beautiful for him; now he wants her to be beautiful only so that she might lure his father back, and so restore the symmetry of the family order.

Maria too indulges in symbolic gestures. One day Arturo comes home to find all his father's clothes washed and hanging on the line, "stiff and frozen" as though his sin had been cleansed, his passion chilled, and he hung there in effigy. Maria also kills the rooster Tony, her favorite, who, like Svevo, had a "jaunty thick comb" and "fine strutting plumes" and a "mighty swagger." She feeds Tony to her children, but she doesn't touch him. "Reminiscences of Tony: what a rooster he had been! They mused over his long reign in the chicken yard: they remembered him *when*" (WB 231).

Arturo recognizes that it is up to him to bring his mother back from the walking death (or madness) into which she has descended, by finding his father and bringing him back. He remembers a time when he had gone to find his father at the Imperial Poolhall, and his father had come: "Then he put his fingers around my throat not hard but meaning it, and he said: don't do that again . . . In his life he had got but three beatings. Only three, but they had been violent, terrifying, unforgettable" (WB 235-6). Yet the time has come to stick up for his mother by confronting his father on his own turf and reminding him of his responsibilities at home.

When Arturo finds the widow Hildegarde's house, he cannot deny his admiration for his father, nor his identification with him: "The sight of the cottage . . . made him very proud of his father. His father was a lowdown dog and all those things, but he was in that cottage now, and it certainly proved something. You couldn't be very lowdown if you could move in on something like that. You're quite a guy, Papa. You're killing Mamma, but you're wonderful. You and me both. Because someday I'll be doing it too, and her name is Rosa Pinelli" (WB 236). When he sees a pile of stone in the yard, he is disappointed and disillusioned: "His father wasn't living with the richest woman in town. Hell, he was only working for her" (WB 237). As Arturo is leaving in disgust, however, his father appears at the door, the ember of his Toscanelli cigar "like a red marble at his mouth," and all his admiration returns. "Arturo shuddered with delight. Holy Jumping Judas, but he looked swell! . . . like Helmer the banker and President Roosevelt. He looked like the King of England" (WB 237). He reproaches himself for having thought of bringing his father home from "the splendor of that new world," back to the burdens of a "martyrlike" wife and children, because Arturo, for one, is willing to suffer for the vision of his father in his sinful glory.

One look at his mother when he returns home, however, "and he hated his father again." Arturo lies to her, fueling her hope by telling her that he had seen his father and his father wanted to come home. Ironically, it is not really a lie. Svevo does want to come home, but he is too proud to admit it. Meanwhile, Rosa Pinelli dies of pneumonia, putting an end to Arturo's own erotic fantasy. As he grieves, his mother invites him into her bed to comfort him, and his "very fingers seemed to burst into tears as he slipped beside her and lost himself in the soothing warmth of her arms" (WB 248).

The day Rosa is buried is a pretty day, and Spring is in the air. Arturo adopts a stray dog he calls Jumbo, and Maria mysteriously announces that Svevo is coming home. How does she know? She just knows. Arturo takes Jumbo along to Hildegarde Road where he finds his father at work, and tells him, "She wants you home. She told me. Spaghetti for dinner. That isn't being mad" (WB 260), playing perhaps on the two meanings of "mad." Svevo is coy, but a tear trickles down his cheek. It is not until the widow Hildegarde tries to run Jumbo off her grounds and calls Arturo a contemptible little monster that Svevo begins to side with Arturo and even the unfamiliar dog. Then she goes a step too far: "'You peasants!' the Widow said. 'You foreigners! You're all alike, you and your dogs and all of you'" (WB 265). Svevo spits in her face and calls her an animal and a whore: "'Bruta animale!' he said. 'Puttana!'" Then he turns to Arturo: "Let's go home." As they walk home together, talking of the coming Spring, they feel the snowflakes coming down. The waiting isn't over yet, but the false Spring is, which is a good sign. It's back to reality for both of them, or rather all three, including the dog.[3]

In the beginning of the novel, Svevo confused God with a dog. In the course of the novel he becomes a "low-down dog." In the end it is a dog who brings him to his senses. Jumbo works as a *deus ex machina*, a catalyst to show Svevo (and Arturo) what an animal the widow Hildegarde is, despite the trappings of gentility. The dog also brings Svevo home to Maria, who is, like the winter, warming up to him. But it will take some time for the family to heal, just as Spring is yet to arrive, despite signs of thawing.

2. The Rage of Arturo: *The Road to Los Angeles*

The Road to Los Angeles, the second volume in The Saga of Arturo Bandini, was the first to be written and the last to be published. Written with what Fante called brutal honesty and candor, this novel continues to be the one book that his readers have the most trouble accepting. Even while writing the book, Fante suspected that this might be the case. On

Bastille Day, 1936, only days after completing the manuscript, Fante wrote to McWilliams: "Some of the stuff will singe the hair off a wolf's rear. It may be too strong; i.e., lacking in 'good' taste. But that doesn't bother me. If literature needs blood and pain its appetites shall be sated by 'The Road to Los Angeles'" (SL 129). These brave words by a twenty-five year old first novelist might seem more appropriate to describe the *Iliad* than *The Road to Los Angeles*, but there is a comparison to be made between the two books, if only in terms of a travesty, and between the rage of Achilles and the rage of Arturo.

During his years with the Jesuits at Regis College, Fante would have become well-acquainted with Homer, to whom he alludes in the titles of two stories, "The Odyssey of a Wop" and "Helen, Thy Beauty Is to Me—." He considered using the former for the title of *Dago Red*, but decided against it in the end because it sounded "too much like Christ carrying a cross up a hill" (SL 167). In any case, the mock-epic tone of *The Road to Los Angeles*, its episodic structure and travesty of several epic conventions, in addition to the many similarities between Arturo Bandini and Achilles, suggest that if Fante saw Jimmy Toscana's journey to Los Angeles in search of himself as an *Odyssey*, he may well have seen Arturo Bandini's battles with the mundane world as an *Iliad*.

The rage of Arturo Bandini is a premeditated provocation, but when the book was rejected Fante acknowledged that he had made a strategic error in being too relentlessly truthful about Arturo's many faults. Writing to McWilliams in the tone of an editor admonishing himself, Fante wrote of the book: "Its peculiarly vicious quality exasperates rather than interests the reader" (SL 131). At a time when social consciousness was in vogue, and a book's sociology was as important as its artistic merit, *The Road to Los Angeles*, with its picaresque satire of a young writer in rebellion against everything that was fashionable and politically correct, must have gone distastefully against the grain.[4] Knopf had granted the contract for the novel on the basis of the sweetly lyrical, if unsentimental stories about Jimmy Toscana. The rawness of the novel Fante delivered instead must have come as a shock. Here was the Altar Boy without the altar, lyricism but in an anti-lyrical sort of way.

The key to the novel, and to its unacceptability, both then and now, is that Fante's candor in this work was ahead of its time, which is ironic, considering that the working title for the novel was "In My Time." That Fante can still be misread, however, is shown by a recent reviewer's wrong-headed and politically correct reading of the book. "We are, I suppose, intended to interpret [Bandini's] behavior as a result of social, economic forces clashing within an artistic heart and mind. Such a motif is valid, of course, in line with other 1930s novels about immigrant families (Henry Roth's *Call It Sleep* and James T. Farrell's *Studs Lonigan* trilogy), but the rage in Fante's novels is unrelieved, too pure one might say, so that he allows no aesthetic or psychological distance for the reader."[6] The critical suppositions being made here are several, obvious, and as inapplicable to Fante as they are to Homer (if for different reasons). In discussing similar objections to the character of Achilles as "a fully created character whose motives and action form an intelligible unity," Bernard Knox explains Homer in terms that can be applied as well to Fante: "In the creation of character Homer spares us the rich, sometimes superfluous, detail we have come to associate with that word in modern fiction; he gives us only what is necessary to his purpose. Similarly, in his presentation of motivation, he is economical in the extreme.

Homer shows us character and motivation not by editorial explanation but through speech and action. And he also invokes the response of an audience familiar with heroic poetry and formulaic diction, counting on their capacity to recognize significant omissions, contrasts, variations and juxtapositions."[7] Misurella's comparison of Fante with the sprawling novels of Roth and Farrell, his inability to recognize the mock-epic, satiric and picaresque elements of Fante's novel, and his insistence on a formulaic reading of 1930s novels according to social and economic determinants, not to mention his miserable lack of a sense of humor, show perhaps better than anything else why *The Road to Los Angeles* remains Fante's most misunderstood novel among what Arturo calls the reading species *Boobus Americanus*.

The Road to Los Angeles depicts a consciousness in flight from family, employers, and himself. Like Achilles, Arturo Bandini is in flight from his own fate. The violently outspoken Arturo would like to run off to Los Angeles (only twelve miles away) to begin his career as a writer, but he spins his wheels in Wilmington, California, planning impossible titles he'll never write in imitation of Spengler, Schopenhauer and Nietzsche, and preparing his Nobel Prize acceptance speech. Bandini's gods are the great writers and philosophers, who have given him the gifts of books and words, which are his shield and weapons. Unlike Achilles, whose vulnerability resides in his heel, Arturo is a heel and vulnerable all over. He tests the range of his voice, which is his weapon, but his range is not long or wide. He is master of the lyric insult, the poetic slander, the creative racial slur, the name-calling epithet, and the periodic imprecation. He speaks in tirades of insult or affection to the world in all its forms, animal, vegetable or mineral, as though he were a pantheist, and communicates with the supernatural world, as well. At the slightest provocation he might launch into a prayer to his favorite dead writer or a curse against his mother or sister or employer; a sportscaster-like commentary on an imaginary exploit or contemplated revenge; or a biography of his own yet-to-be-lived life, usually told in the third person. Occasionally, like the voice of the adolescent he is, his shrill tirades crack, deepen, and achieve the rough texture of vulgar poetry.

It is true that *The Road to Los Angeles* has no real development of plot or character, only an episodic elaboration of the picaro Arturo as he finds his direction revealed in the title. A genius manqué alienated from his environment, Bandini is a bundle of impulsive contradictions that tend to cancel themselves out and end in inertia. He is a Nietzschean atheist who lives with his religious mother and sister, a socialist anarchist who must toe the production line to earn a living for his family, an intellectual who labors among illiterates whom he despises, a writer whose only work with words is to label the tins of fish in the cannery. The episodes that reveal Bandini's character are raw, nervous, visceral, and psychologically exact. Bandini's only creative acts are acts of destruction, creatively carried out, but all in words. The situations are permutations on coercion, humiliation, and revenge in connection with his family, employers, co-workers, and the rest of the animate and inanimate world. His driving force is escape from these situations, in his imagination or in reality, and everything he does is an effort to prove himself better than the world which at every turn humiliates and defeats him. As in any picaresque novel, there is no progress, peripety or resolution, only an abrupt conclusion with a final, curtain-closing departure.

But *The Road to Los Angeles* can be understood fully only in relation to its satiric and mock-epic dimensions, since this is where the tone and force of the novel expose the weaknesses of Arturo Bandini with the brutal candor of an overheard confession. In comparing Fante's book to the *Iliad*, I probably should point out that I am not trying to validate the novel's worth but only to better understand what Fante was doing by invoking these echoes of a masterpiece, which was first and foremost to make readers laugh at Arturo (and themselves), and only secondarily to rage with him.

Rage is, of course, the first word and controling epithet we associate with Achilles, and it is equally applicable to Arturo, who, in the second paragraph of the novel is seen digging a ditch with "fury" (RL 9). Like Achilles, Arturo sees himself as a hero who will tolerate no insult from mere mortals. When the autocratic Agamemnon tells Achilles, "You are nothing to me" (1. 213), it is no more insulting and no more provocative of his wrath, than when Arturo's mother tells him, "You are nothing but a boy who's read too many books" (RL 17). For Achilles, a peaceful existence is something he spurns, and if his fate is to die in obscurity in his homeland or to die in glory on the battlefield, he will eventually choose the latter. Like Achilles, Arturo postpones his fate because, as a hero, he must be given the glory that is his due, and seen as a central and essential part of the battle. But Arturo's talent is not recognized by anyone he knows, from his mother and sister and Uncle Frank to the endless series of employers and co-workers he must lower himself to associate with. Like Arturo's dead father, Achilles' father Peleus is relatively unimportant, except that "a single son he fathered, doomed at birth, / cut off in the spring of life" (24. 630-2). And like Achilles who avoided the draft in drag,

Arturo is made to live among women, postponing his destiny.

In the most famous (or infamous) scene from the novel, Arturo slaughters a civilization of crabs on a jetty of rocks, first with stones, then with a BB gun, working himself up into a fascist delusion of erotic grandeur: "I was Dictator Bandini, Ironman of Crabland. This was another Blood Purge for the good of the Fatherland." He court martials and executes the survivors, including one "brave crabess," a "princess," whom he shoots in the face. He orders a stone placed where "this ravishing heroine" had fallen "during the bloody June days of the Bandini government" (RL 34). Another wounded crabess, "an exquisite creature, reddish and pink," offers herself to him, the Fuhrer Bandini: "There beneath the bridge in the darkness I ravaged her while she pleaded for mercy. Still laughing I took her out and shot her to pieces, apologizing for my brutality" (RL 34). The crab scene is brutal, uncompromising satire and brilliant farce, a surreal lampoon of Il Duce Mussolini, whom Fante hated as "the destroyer of a gifted and cultured people" (SL 337). Yet it is unlikely that a public primed by the earnest editorializing of a Dos Passos were ready to recognize that there is a little fascist adolescent in all of us and so in the crazed idealist Arturo Bandini. When one considers that such titles as *Lamb in His Bosom* by Caroline Miller and *Honey in the Horn* by Harold L. David were winning the Pulitzer Prize in the years that Fante was trying to place *The Road to Los Angeles*, and that it would have been up against *Gone With the Wind* if it were published in 1936, one wonders how Fante could have had the audacity to imagine that anyne in America could appreciate Arturo Bandini, Fuhrer of Crabland.

The slaughter of the crabs, however, is best seen not in the contemporary light of the Nazi threat, but in terms of the mock-epic echoes from the *Iliad* that make Bandini's pretensions to glory so absurd.

Homer's poem opens:

> Rage — Goddess, sing the rage of Peleus' son Achilles,
> murderous, doomed, that cost the Achaeans countless losses,
> hurling down to the House of Death so many sturdy souls,
> great fighters' souls, but made their bodies carrion,
> feasts for the dogs and birds,
> and the will of Zeus was moving toward its end (1. 1-6).

When Arturo goes among the dead crabs, congratulating himself on his victory and them on their brave struggle, we can almost hear in his bookish tone the rustling of Homer's pages: "I went among the dead and spoke to them consolingly, for even though they were my enemies I was for all that a man of nobility and I respected them and admired them for the valiant struggle they had offered my legions. 'Death has arrived for you,' I said. 'Goodbye, dear enemies. You were brave in fighting and braver in death'" (RL 35). Like Achilles, humiliation has turned Arturo into a violent man, who has isolated himself from the world. Aristotle said in the *Politics* that, "The man who is incapable of working in common, or who in his self-sufficiency has no need of others, is no part of the community, like a beast, or a god."[8] Achilles finally breaks out of his "self-imposed prison of godlike unrelenting fury,"[9] but not without slaughtering masses of enemies smaller and more insignificant than himself.

But most of Arturo's violence is done on paper, or more often, in his head, with words. The gods gave Achilles invulnerability and the shield of Hephaestus. Arturo's gods, who are the philosophers and great writers, gave him books and words. But unlike Achilles, Arturo doesn't know how to use his gifts. In his humiliation and alienation, he tries to define himself and the world primarily by negation and nay-saying. Epithets, imprecations and insults are directed at the world to distinguish himself from *them,* who threaten to engulf his identity in what he sees as their mediocrity and stupidity. And so he spends most of his time calling people (and things) names, turning his fellow man into animals and insects: stupid ants, bourgeois ants, rats, uncultured rats, rodents, pigs, alley rats, dock rats, boiled rats, pole-cats, evil-tongued rats, skunks, skunk-faced rats, jackals, weasels, donkeys, gutless sheep, monsters and Christian dogs. They come in several varieties of fool: nitwits, yokels, imbeciles, boobs, cretins, dolts, anthropoids, ignoramuses, gigantic frauds, looming lugs, clod-hopping poltroons, etc. There are species of numskulls native to America: Comstock trulls, Boobus Americanus, bourgeois Babbits, American boors, "Victims of Comstockery and the American system, bastard slaves of the Robber Barons" (RL 45), boobs of limited vocabulary, etc. Some of his wordier epithets have a social or political bias: capitalistic proletarian bourgeois, goddamn Mexican peon of a boot-licking bourgeois proletarian capitalist, tool of the bourgeoisie, whore of modern capitalism, ablative absolute, dynasty of slaves, monstrous travesty on the dignity that is man's primordial antecedent, etc. And a whole class of unclassifiable creations all his own: neuroses, fungus mouths, bucolic rainspouts, etc.

Arturo's most vehement imprecations are aimed at his sister Mona, partly because she aspires to be a nun. She is an "intense moron" (RL 145), a "frustrated, inhibited, driveling, drooling half-nun!" (RL 24), a "God-intoxicated nun" (RL 111), and "A nun, a god-lover! What barbarism!" (RL 17). But there are other reasons for his extreme reaction to her. For one thing, she may not know what all the words he uses mean, but she understands that neither does Arturo. Often he doesn't have the slightest idea of what he is talking about. More importantly, there is a sexual struggle going on here. Not only does Arturo call her a "Catholic ignoramus" and a "filthy Comstock," as well as a "clod-hopping celibate" and a "sanctimonious, retch-provoking she-nun of a bitch-infested nausea-provoking nun of a vile boobish baboon of a brummagen Catholic heritage," he calls her, for no good reason, a "slut": "You nunny slutty slut out of the belly of the Roman harlot" (RL 140-1). This verbal violence against his sister, always sexually tinged with an uncomfortable inkling of incest, suggests that Arturo is raging out of control, another urgent reason for him to get away from home.

Twisting the epic convention in which mortals and immortals, the living and the dead converse with one another, Arturo also talks to, and even has some good things to say, to books, dead authors, photographs, and the photographs of dead authors in the frontispieces to books, not to mention President Roosevelt who is "old Kid, old Pal, old Sock" (RL 44), or an old deaf man with a runny nose who is "Plato with a cold." With his floating love and hatred, he harangues the insect world, the animal world, ants, bees, crabs, crickets, and fish. He woos the vegetable world, elm trees, palm trees, and mere bushes. He confides in the mineral world of inanimate objects, both natural and man-made: fog and stoves, blood and buttons, books and cigarettes, matches and match scratches on the wall, his own knuckles and his little sister's pink sweater, which he throws out of his cell of alienation, his "private study, which was the clothes closet" (RL 18).

Arturo knows that he is out of control, and he doesn't spare himself from name-calling. He is first and foremost a fool, an idiot, a crazy liar, a monster, a Frankenstein, a fake, a coward and, like his sister, a dirty stinking Christian. Somewhat less flatteringly, he is also a beast, toad, swine, dog, jack-ass, black spider, snake, and rat. As Oscar Wilde said, "There is a luxury in self-reproach. When we blame ourselves we feel that no one else has a right to blame us. It is the confession, not the priest, that gives an absolution."[10] In his self-created alienation, Arturo talks to himself in a solipsistic luxury of self-reproach, in and out of his private study cum confessional.

Here is where Arturo keeps his icons, the naked women in "art" magazines, which he views like a monk by candle light. His unction is masturbation. "Inside was the odor of burning wax and brief passions spent on the floor" (RL 19). His trophy case of pin-up girls is as populous as Robert Herrick's mythical passions: Chloe, Elaine, Rosa, Marcella, Helen, Hazel, Tanya, Marie, Ruby, Jean, Nina and the Little Girl. Each has her virtue, some unforgettable characteristic that endears her to him, her skin, fingernails, hair, mouth, or fingers, but finally they are as unimportant to him as Briseus, the trophy Trojan slave girl Agamemnon took from Achilles. They are, however, a point of honor. The models in the "art" magazines allow him to populate the world with his dreams, but they are also the basis of his shame. To give up his vice, he abdicates his "study," which now takes on the atmosphere of a church. Briefly contrite, he destroys the girls of paper and ink, and his cell reverts to a clothes closet, where his sister's dresses once again hang "like the robes of millions and millions of dead nuns." The odor of his Onanistic passion is replaced by the "odor of rosaries and incense" and "of old women in black kneeling at mass." The darkness of his introspection becomes "the darkness of the confessional" (RL 108).

An intellectual bulimic with a binge-purge syndrome of voracious reading and promiscuous regurgitation, so that he is actually nourished by very little of what he consumes, Arturo is proof that a little education can be a dangerous thing. His egotism leaves very little room for a sense of history as he reads Strachey and Macaulay and misquotes the clichés of Marx, Krafft-Ebing, the Bible, and *Poor Richard's Almanac* almost in a single breath. He makes a mess of the philosophers, perverting Bergson's *élan vital* by using it to put down his sister for reading the popular novelist Kathleen Norris, and he blames everything from his having to support a couple of "parasitical women" to the "decline of the west" on her reading of Norris's "disgusting pig-vomit" (RL 116). It is the same reaction as that of the hated Comstock censors to his own reading material, and the violence of his reaction underscores the parody. In his dangerous half-ignorance, he worships the worst, most superficial elements of his philosophical trinity, becoming more racist than Spengler, more misogynist than Schopenhauer, and more fascist than Nietzsche. At work he reads *Zarathustra* on the toilet, "memorizing a long passage about voluptuousness" (RL 11) in hopes of seducing the svelte librarian Miss Hopkins. At home he reads Comte and Kant in the bathtub, but finds them "so dull I had to pretend they were fascinating" (RL 85) and falls asleep so that his mother has to dry him off and put him to bed like an infant.

Arturo is so obsessed with words that he often loses all sense of what he is saying. He parrots Marxist jargon, informing the girl on the arm of the cannery boss that she is "a capitalistic slut" whose time will be up "when the revolution comes" (RL 92), and telling his mother and sister that "Religion is the opium of the people" (RL 23). But words are the opium of Arturo Bandini. "I'm writing all the time. My head swims in a transvaluated phantasmagoria of phrases" (RL 99). Imagining his Nobel Prize acceptance speech, he free associates into babble:

> The hand that wrote. Me and you and my hand and Keats. John Keats and Arturo Bandini and my hand, the hand of John Keats Bandini. Wonderful. Oh hand land band stand grand land . . . Yes, I wrote it . . . Ladies and gentlemen of the committee, of the titty committee, ditty, bitty, committee, I wrote it, ladies and gentlemen, I wrote it. Yes indeed (RL 133).

Transvaluated indeed. In his reckless name-calling he mixes up his racial slurs and confuses the categories of his biases: Romero the Italian grocer has treated him with "levantine scurrilousness" (RL 27); he calls Filipinos "nigger" (RL 65) and Mexicans "Filipino" (RL 68), partly to annoy them, but one gets the sense that he really has no idea of anyone's true identity, including his own. His sister sums up his pseudo-intellectual pretensions precisely: "Mamma, listen to him! Using words without knowing what they mean." This is too much for him. "She could ridicule my beliefs and persecute me for my philosophy and I would not complain. But no one could make fun of my English" (RL 75). Throwing away his rhetoric Arturo takes up his cudgel and attacks her physically.

The odor of the fish cannery that clings to him wherever he goes is the perfect antidote to Arturo's bookish fantasies, reminding him that though he lives in parallel and contradictory worlds that vie for the status of his ontological reality, he cannot escape the workaday world by receding into his own fantastic imagination. The stench contributes to his status as a social pariah. Ashamed of his own smell, he quits going to the movies or the library. Denying his shame, he calls the stench in his clothes and hair and skin the "smell of honest labor. It's a man's smell. It's not for effetes and dilettantes. It's fish." His sister replies: "It's disgusting" (RL 74). If Arturo were honest with himself, he would agree. The odor has an emetic effect on him during his first day in the cannery and he does nothing but vomit. He tells the Mexican, Japanese and Filipino women, who are standing "ankle-deep in fish guts," that he is a great writer and blames his reaction on the "idiosyncracies of an artistic stomach." All they can do is laugh when, every few minutes, "Arturo Bandini the great writer was heaving again" (RL 58-9).

Nevertheless, Arturo keeps on writing, even if only in his head. His interests and subjects are dispersed, touching on economics, labor conditions, philosophy, painting and architecture. In his wild literary ambitions, Arturo resembles the narrator of Knut Hamsun's *Hunger*, who abandons a treatise called "Crimes of the Future" as too "elementary and simple-minded," only to embark on "a consideration in three parts of Philosophical Consciousness. Naturally I'd find a moment to break the neck of some of Kant's sophistries . . ." and is thwarted in his work because he has left his pencil in the pocket of the waistcoat he has pawned.[11] Likewise, Arturo takes "random notes for a future work on foreign trade" (RL 28); more notes on "Labor conditions in the machine age, a topic for a future work" (RL 45); and "atmospheric notes" for "a Socratic symposium on Los Angeles Harbor since the days of the Spanish Conquest" (RL 38). He plans a treatise, "A Psychological Interpretation of the Stevedore Today and Yesterday," by Arturo Gabriel Bandini," but the scope of this "magnum opus" is so daunting that he gives it up before he puts a word on paper. Figuring that "philosophy was easier," he sketches out a Nietzschean-Schopenhaurean title: "A Moral and Philosophical Dissertation on Man and Woman," by Arturo Gabriel Bandini." He soon tires of "the whole thing" and decides that, like his namesake Dante Gabriel Rossetti, "my genius lay in art." He will become a painter, but abandons this career after sketching a few cats-on-the-fence, faces and triangles, and turns to architecture as his birthright, "for my father has been a carpenter and maybe the building trade was more in keeping with my heritage" (RL 29-30). But the opus that will win him the Nobel Prize, he envisions, will be called *Colossus of Destiny* — an autobiography no doubt, although he doesn't say so — and will be on the shelf "among a few indispensible others, such as the bible and the dictionary" (RL 92).

During the course of the novel, Arturo imagines the form his biography will take perhaps a dozen times. He is economist, sociologist, historian, philosopher, philanthopist, painter, poet, architect, novelist, theologian, Casanova, athlete, tyrant. By substituting inanimate objects for family and employers, he creates an audience for his fantasies, shaping the world into his vision of how it should be. But by turning humans into animals and by personifying things, he loosens his grip on reality and ultimately degrades himself by denying his own humanity, becoming a spider, a monster, a Frankenstein.

To the Crab People he massacres under the bridge he becomes the Black Killer of the Pacific Coast, and "If they wrote history I would get a lot of space in their records . . . Some day I would become a legend in their world . . . They would make me a god" (RL 36).

With the pin-up women it's the same, each with a story of Bandini the conquerer, but he had to destroy them as well and then flush them down the drain with the bath water: "They would flow down to the sea, where the dead crabs lay. The souls of the dead women would talk to the souls of the dead crabs, and they would talk only of me. My fame would increase. Crabs and women would arrive at one inevitable conclusion: that I was a terror, the Black Killer of the Pacific Coast, yet a terror respected by all, crabs and women alike: a cruel hero, but a hero nevertheless" (RL 77). Comparing his old report cards to his "God-intoxicated" sister's, he is amused to note that she could never beat him at Religion or English: "A great piece of anecdote for the biographers of Arturo Bandini. God's worst enemy making higher marks in religion than God's best friend, and both in the same family. A great irony. What a biography that would be! Ah Lord, to be alive and read it!" (RL 158)

The dreadful story he does actually write is about Arthur Banning, a rich playboy and man of the world. It swells to the size (though not the shape) of a novel, and is pure wish-fulfillment, from the Anglicized name of his alter ego to his realized sexual conquests. The writing of it is a form of revenge on a world that does not recognize or reward Arturo's worth, or the potential of his genius. Arturo is, after all, aware that he has not actualized his potential, and that such bad writing (he is also aware that the Arthur Banning story is awful) is his self-indulgent way of getting even, compensation for his own impotence.

One night he follows a woman, imagining a brilliant seduction, only to run away when the moment offers itself. Even as he is running away, however, he is still writing, turning his escape into yet another form of biographical discourse, the sports commentary. Now he is an Olympic track star, "the greatest half-miler in the history of the American track and field annals," but especially "popular among the feminine fans" (RL 125). His self-conscious on-the-scene commentary, borrowed from the narrative of radio sports broadcasters, compensates for his impotence in reality.

This penultimate scene of flight is crucial to the book as a whole, which is the story of Arturo Bandini's escape from the dreary confinement of everyday reality. He flees all forms of engagement and connection — family, heritage, religion, employers, and now lovers — toward an absolute intellectual freedom. The absurdity of his flight is shown in the disproportion between his efforts and his aim. All that adolescent emotion, undisciplined verbal vigor, and intellectual energy are expended to bring him to one relatively simple gesture: stealing the wedding ring that his mother has kept out of devotion to her dead husband, pawning it, and using the money to buy a ticket to Los Angeles. In the final scene we see Arturo waiting for the midnight train to take him over the twelve miles of road that stand between him and Los Angeles, but we cannot be sure that he actually boards it.

What Arturo still has to learn in his destined struggle to become a writer in Los Angeles, however, is that flight — physical, intellectual, or emotional — cannot establish one's identity. Nay-saying and name-calling is no substitute for action. Even when that name is earned, as for Tennyson's Ulysses, who complains, "I have become a name," the hero must still be "strong in will / To strive, to seek, to find, and not to yield." Identity is achieved through action, the creative act, which is ultimately an act of love. But this is something that the innocent and ignorant Arturo, who is both picaro and hero, has yet to learn through experience.

Like Achilles too, who finally "begins to break out at last from the prison of self-absorbed, godlike passion,"[12] Arturo has for too long postponed his entry into the battle for fame and fortune that he imagines raging in Los Angeles.

When in *Ask the Dust* Arturo is next described as a "nobody," he is in Los Angeles and has learned from his experience. Vera Rivken's description of Arturo and his laughable passions — "the pity of it all, the stupidity of it all, the absurdity of a hopelessly bad writer . . . buried in a cheap hotel in Los Angeles, California, of all places, writing banal things the world would never read and never get a chance to forget" — may humiliate him, but he accepts it because she too is a nobody and knows what she is talking about. Her put-down of Arturo's pretensions of creating literature echoes Agamemnon's put-down of Achilles' pride: "You are nobody and—" she adds, "I might have been somebody, and the road to each of us is love" (AD 81). This sibylline pronouncement finally inspires Arturo to get out of himself, to write about her life instead of his own, in a creative act of sympathy.

Just as Arturo's insults and name-calling could not define others, and only began to help him to define himself, flight is only a negation that takes him out of one place, but not yet into another. In his desire to be an artist on the model of James Joyce's, godlike and removed, Arturo envisions himself as a hero. But Stephen Hero was changed to the maze-wanderer Stephen Dedalus because Joyce understood that the hero must fail for a human epiphany to occur. In the same way, Fante transformed the Arturo of *The Road to Los Angeles* into the more sympathetic Arturo of *Ask the Dust*, who can say, with Vera Rivken, "the road to each of us is love."

> The heroes are godlike in their passionate self-esteem. But they are not gods, not immortal. They are subject, like the rest of us, to failure, above all to the irremediable failure of death. And sooner or later, in suffering, in disaster, they come to realize their limits, accept mortality and establish (or rees-

tablish) a human relationship with their fellowmen. This pattern, recurrent in the myths of the Greeks and later to be the model for some of the greatest Athenian tragedies, is first given artistic form in the *Iliad*.[13]

This same pattern of the epiphany of human failure in the face of suffering and death, recurrent in Fante's works and later developed in the tragic novels of Fante's maturity, beginning with *Wait Until Spring, Bandini* and *Ask the Dust*, is first given artistic form in *The Road to Los Angeles*.

CHAPTER 6

BANDINI'S HUNGER

ASK THE DUST
AND DREAMS FROM BUNKER HILL

> ... just leave me awhile to myself, to hunger and dream with
> eyes awake.
>
> Arturo Bandini in *Ask the Dust*

1. A Lover of Man and Beast Alike: *Ask the Dust*

It would be difficult to overestimate the importance of the
Norwegian novelist Knut Hamsun to the work of John
Fante. Hamsun's first novel, *Hunger* (1890), was to Arturo
Bandini, "a treasured piece, constantly with me since the
day I stole it from the Boulder library. I had read it so many
times I could recite it" (DB 146). According to his daughter,
Fante kept his personal copy of Hamsun's novel under lock
and key. She and her brothers knew what it was because
they heard their father talk about it, but it was a household
taboo, not to be read by anyone, nor even to be touched by
any but their father's hands.[1]

Fante was not alone in his generation's appreciation
for Hamsun. Isaac Bashevis Singer has dubbed Hamsun
"the father of the modern school of fiction in his every

aspect," pointing to Hamsun's "subjectiveness, his fragmentariness, his use of flashbacks, his lyricism. The whole modern school of fiction in the twentieth century stems from Hamsun, just as Russian literature in the nineteenth century 'came out of Gogol's greatcoat.'"[2] Singer lists Thomas Mann, Arthur Schnitzler, Gabriel D'Annunzio, Fitzgerald and Hemingway among "Hamsun's disciples," and we can add to this list Henry Miller and Charles Bukowski. Yet none comes closer to the Norwegian Nobelist, in style or spirit, than John Fante.

Interestingly enough, it was perhaps Hamsun's time spent as a laborer in America (two periods of two years each) that gave to his prose the modern edge it is known for, and which in turn influenced so many American writers of the twentieth-century. "Sigurd Hoel said he thought the excitability, the constant slang, and the sarcasm of American talk had a lot to do with *Hunger's* style."[3]

Fante was attracted not only to Hamsun's style, an ironic lyricism that exposes the absurdities of his nameless autobiographical narrator, but also to Hamsun's view of the relationship between truth and fiction. In *The Cultural Life of Modern America*, Hamsun stated: "'Truth telling does not involve seeing both sides or objectivity; truth telling is unselfish inwardness' *(uegennyttige Subjectivitet)*."[4]

Reason might suggest that this "unselfish subjectivity" would result in a self-indulgent solipsism, but as we have seen in *The Road to Los Angeles*, it actually amounts to a ruthless exposure of the self and its delusions that connects the inward truth of the teller with that of readers, who may not be willing or able to express such truths on their own, inhibited by the strictures of objectivity, and may be unwilling to admit to them when they see them in print. For a fiction writer, such a stance implies a refusal to compromise with reality or the expectations of any single listener or potential audience, and can result in prose that is both lyrical when it follows those delusions faithfully, and analytical when it observes the psyche's obsessions with sometimes frightening detachment and clarity.

So far, most studies of *Ask the Dust* have concentrated on its importance as a novel of place. Carey McWilliams compared it to Nathanael West's *The Day of the Locust* as one of the few novels that told what Southern California was really like. Tom Clark ranked it, along with West's book, among the four American classics about the "downside of the California dream" published in 1939, the other two being Steinbeck's *The Grapes of Wrath* and Chandler's *The Big Sleep*; but "it is Fante's book (and literary reputation) that has the most catching up to do."[5]

Other critics have focused more specifically on Bandini's love affair with Los Angeles. Will Balliet, for example, implies that Bandini's Los Angeles is a projection of his own character when he describes the city in the novel in terms that could be applied to Arturo himself, "touchingly naive and guilelessly ruthless," and claims that the city is the true protagonist of *Ask the Dust*."[6]

Along the same lines, Stephen Cooper writes: "If it is about anything, in fact, *Ask the Dust* is about desire, and as before [in *The Road to Los Angeles*] the external city again comes to be linked with Bandini's innermost impulses."[7] David Fine has called Fante's work "a regional fiction obsessively concerned with puncturing the bloated image of Southern California."[8] In answer to Fine's observation, Cooper comments: "True, Fante's work skewers the polished surface of pretense and illusion endemic to the city, but it also celebrates, even exalts the rough substance of life as he finds it in the rented rooms and sooty streets of L.A."[9]

But if we are to give the novel its due as a great work of literature, we should be able to go beyond such localizing tendencies and examine it in terms that have less to do with the setting and more to do with the unique sensibility that reacts to it. It could be argued that Bandini could have been conceived in no other city, and certainly the specificity of Arturo's experience of the Southern California landscape, from the tenderloin to the outlying foothills and desert valleys, is crucial to who Arturo Bandini is. The chemistry between his own contradictions and those of Los Angeles, his own sensitivity to the sensuous surfaces of the city, with its high rises and fishermen's shacks, its concrete and dust, its damp coast and dry inland deserts, reflects his own state of mind to an extraordinary degree. But it could also be argued that Arturo Bandini would have sprung to life in the mind of his creator no matter where Fante had been placed through the accidents of fate and finances, Chicago, Oslo, Paris or Rome. Such speculations are, however, pointless, since Bandini will forever be associated with Los Angeles. And rightly so.

But *Ask the Dust* is more than a novel of place, just as it is more than a novel about prejudice. It is true that Bandini suffers from the same kind of self-lacerating prejudice that caused Jimmy Toscana to batter his own corpse in "The Odyssey of a Wop," and that the roll call of minorities in the novel makes this an important element. But Bandini's aspirations to conquer the city on its own terms are not unusual, and neither are his reactions to being a minority among minorities. More importantly, he is an artist in the land of kitsch, who finds his place in Los Angeles as a misfit among misfits.

What is unusual, what makes Bandini *Bandini*, is his peculiar sympathy with everything around him. The Bandini of *The Road to Los Angeles* had this quality of sympathy too, but his expression of it was unsympathetic. The early rejection of the book by publishers convinced Fante that honesty was not enough to make a novel succeed with the public, and may have convinced him that it was not enough to make it succeed as art. Readers, like lovers, need to be seduced, but the Bandini of the early novel wants to be loved in spite of himself, with all his faults exposed, accepted even when he is unaccepting of others, without giving an inch, without compromise and, more importantly, without sympathy for others. Whatever feeling or understanding he has for others — and there is much, even for the inanimate world — is expressed in rage; yet he expects others to view his adolescent wrath with sympathy. Arturo would like his quarrels with humanity to be seen on an epic scale, in Homeric terms, as the wrath of Arturo, despite the picayune and egotistical nature of his quarrels.

In *Ask the Dust*, however, Arturo Bandini has undergone a change. He is still brash and full of himself, and his head is still full of wild schemes for unwritten books and ungarnered glories, but he is also full of sympathy. By the end of the book, this sympathy allows him to develop as a character who is not only sympathetic to others, but one with whom we can sympathize. His relationships with Camilla Lopez and Vera Rivken begin with insults because they are minorities or madwomen but end with him nursing one through a nervous breakdown and writing a book about the other. His relationship with Sammy Wiggins, who is neither a minority nor a woman, is especially important in the way Arturo's feelings of superiority over the bartender and author of pulp westerns are transformed into a kinship of doom.

I would like, then, to argue that the essential characteristic of *Ask the Dust* is its treatment not of place or prejudice, but the extraordinary sympathy that informs the book.
Of course, a similar sympathy informs Fante's other early
books, but it is overshadowed by Arturo's egotistical rage in
The Road to Los Angeles, and by his often sentimental retro-
spection in *Wait Until Spring, Bandini* and *Dago Red.* Here
that sympathy finds its first full expression. As Charles
Bukowski said, *Ask the Dust* was "my favorite because it was
my first discovery of the magic" (AD 6). It was also the novel
in which Fante found the first full expression of the magic of
sympathy. This is why, I think, it is *Ask the Dust* that is
generally considered to be Fante's masterpiece.

Sympathy, as distinct from empathy, is an imaginative
entering into the consciousness or sensorium of another
without necessarily implying understanding. Bandini does
not always understand why he does what he does or feels
what he feels, and he is even less capable of understanding
the thoughts or feelings of others. But he does feel for them,
often to an almost hallucinatory degree. Bandini is a sponge,
soaking up the sensory stimuli of Los Angeles, and commis-
erating with the misfits of the city, and not only the minorities with whom he identifies, but with all the down and
outers who populate the city, especially "down in the very
middle of Los Angeles" where the book opens.

Bandini also soaks up books. But here again, the Bandini of *Ask the Dust* is more sympathetic than the Bandini of
The Road to Los Angeles, because he is able to act on sentiment
despite his cynical intellectual understandings. He admits,
for example, that he has "not read Lenin" but he has "heard
him quoted" and that although he has read Nietzsche and
believes in "the transvaluation of values, Sir," and echoes
Mencken on the Church as "the haven of the booboisie,"

Bandini nevertheless enters the Church of Our Lady for what he transparently calls "sentimental reasons" (AD 22). The Bandini of *The Road to Los Angeles*, of course, would never be caught dead in a Church, much less admitting to not having read Lenin or any other writer he had ever heard of, and thus leaves us with no moment of vulnerability in which to enter into his experience with our own sympathetic reaction.

Fante's adaptation of Hamsun's *Hunger* into the texture, structure and events of *Ask the Dust* is an example of a sympathetic absorption of a book. Bandini might be accused of plagiarism when he tries to pass off one of Dowson's poems as his own, and reacts with indignation when Camilla tears up "my sonnet by Dowson" (AD 115), but even though he writes the poem out from memory, it is sincerely offered and appropriate in mood and theme. In short, Bandini sympathizes so much with Dowson's sentiment that he considers it his own, but he obviously does not understand it in any objective sense, since Dowson's poem is not a sonnet. On the other hand, Fante sympathizes so fully with Hamsun's *Hunger* that he goes beyond simple appropriation to create a work so infused with the spirit of the original, and yet so original in itself, that it might well be called a radical translation, not from one language to another, but from one time and place to another, transcending simple identification to become the paradoxical sympathetic expression of truth that is implied by Hamsun's concept of "unselfish subjectivity."

Two passages, one from *Hunger* and one from *Ask the Dust*, suggest the many parallels between Hamsun's narrator and Fante's. Both passages are from the opening chapters, and each show the narrator at work, with the rent due, writing under the gun. First Hamsun:

I wrote 1848 twenty times, wrote it crossways and intersecting and every possible way, waiting for a usable idea to come. A swarm of vague thoughts were battling about in my brain. The mood of the approaching dusk made me despondent and sentimental. Fall was here and had already begun to put everything in a deep sleep — the flies and small creatures had received their first shock; high in trees and down near the earth you could hear the sounds of a laboring life, breathing, restless, and rustling, struggling not to die. The whole community of insects would rouse themselves one more time, poke their yellow heads up out of the moss, lift their legs, put out expeditions, feeling with their long antennae, and then suddenly collapse, roll over, and turn their stomachs to the sky. Every plant had received the mark — the delicate breath of the first frost had passed over it. Grass stems held themselves stiffly up toward the sun, and the fallen leaves slipped across the ground with a sound like that of traveling silkworms. It was the hour of fall, well into the festival of what is not eternal. The roses have taken on a fever, their blood-red leaves have a strange unnatural flush . . . I myself felt like an insect about to go under, attacked by annihilation in this world ready to go to sleep. I jumped up, laboring with profound terrors, and took three or four long steps up the path. No! I cried, and clenched both fists, this has to end! And I sat down again, brought out the pencil and paper in order to grapple with the article. When the rent was right before my eyes, it would never do to give up.[10]

Notice the sympathy of the narrator's reaction to the natural world, which is not the romantic projection of his own feelings onto the world (empathy, or the pathetic fallacy), but rather an absorption of the world into his own identity.

In Fante, the sympathetic absorption of the world, especially the plant and insect world, is narrated by Bandini in the third person, as though he is watching himself struggle in the same way that he observes the natural stoicism of the palm tree and the carousing industry of the ants.

The lean days of determination. That was the word for it, determination: Arturo Bandini in front of his typewriter two full days in succession, determined to succeed; but it didn't work, the longest siege of hard and fast determination in his life, and not one line done, only two words written over and over across the page, up and down, the same words: palm tree, palm tree, palm tree, a battle to the death between the palm tree and me, and the palm tree won: see it out there swaying in the blue air, creaking sweetly in the blue air. The palm tree won after two fighting days, and I crawled out of the window and sat at the foot of the tree. Time passed, a moment or two, and I slept, little brown ants carousing in the hair on my legs (AD 17).

Fante's version is perhaps less "poetic" than Hamsun's, with a sardonic touch at the end that implies a satirical view of his own presence in nature, like that of Gulliver in Lilliput, looming and unconscious.

Ask the Dust begins where the last story in *Dago Red* left off. A writer is sitting in a cheap Bunker Hill hotel room wondering how he is going to pay the rent to the landlady who is slipping notes under his door. It is Arturo Bandini. His mood is mellow and understated compared to the manic Bandini of *The Road to Los Angeles*, but you can tell it is Arturo because as soon as he hits the street he "stood before an imaginary pitcher, and swatted a home run over the fence" (AD 11). He wanders the streets around Bunker Hill, along Olive Street past the Philharmonic Auditorium, letting his senses spur his memory and his desire, until he sees a beautiful woman in a silver fox fur get out of a long black car and enter the Biltmore Hotel, and "she was a song across the sidewalk" (AD 12). He stands in front of a pipe shop and in the window's reflection he sees himself as "a great author with that natty Italian briar, and a cane, stepping out of a big black car, and she was there too, proud as hell of me, the lady in the silver fox fur" (13).

Then comes the most famous paragraph in the book, Fante's love poem in prose to Los Angeles: "Los Angeles, give me some of you! Los Angeles come to me the way I came to you, my feet over your streets, you pretty town I loved you so much, you sad flower in the sand, you pretty town" (AD 13). Fante's apostrophe to Los Angeles sums up Arturo Bandini's love affair with the city of palm trees and dust. A year or two older than the Arturo who boarded the bus in Wilmington, this Arturo has been shorn of some of the bristling arrogance that turned all his ambition into insults. "I am twenty," he says. "I have reached the age of reason" (AD 19). He still talks to inanimate objects, but his eloquence has turned from insults to apostrophes sweetly lyrical with melancholy. "I had a philosophy in those days," says Bandini. "I was a lover of man and beast alike" (AD 16).

Arturo's relationship with the city is not, however, all sweetness and sunlight. Like the protagonist of Hamsun's *Hunger*, Arturo is desperately poor and impulsive and has delusions of grandeur. He lives in the Alta Loma Hotel, which is built upside down on a hillside, "so that the main floor was on the level with the street but the tenth floor was downstairs ten levels" (AD 15). His room is "down on the sixth floor, room 678, up near the front of the hill, so that my window was on a level with the green hillside and there was no need for a key, for the window was always open." Outside the window is the palm tree that he struggles and identifies with, and that reminds him of Palm Sunday and Cleopatra, "but the palm was blackish at its branches, stained by carbon monoxide coming out of the Third Street Tunnel, its crusted trunk choked with dust and sand that blew in from the Mojave and Santa Ana deserts" (AD 16).

When he returns to his room, after bumping "accidentally on purpose" into "Aztec princesses and Mayan princesses" in the Grand Central Market and in the Church of Our Lady, he carries the memory back to his room, "where dust gathered upon my typewriter and Pedro the mouse sat in his hole, his black eyes watching me through that time of dream and reverie" (AD 15).

So far, Arturo has published only one story, "The Little Dog Laughed," and he shows to anyone and everyone, including his landlady, who doesn't read it but is sufficiently impressed not to throw him out into the California heat when he doesn't pay his rent on time. Only four people really appreciate the story: the editor who published it, J. C. Hackmuth, whose initials suggest that he is Bandini's savior; "a great Italian critic" named Leonardo, who is not really a critic but just a man who lives in West Virginia; a little girl named Judy Palmer, who lives in the Alta Loma Hotel; and Bandini himself. Nevertheless, Arturo is sure that someday he'll see his books "in the library with the big boys on the shelves, old Dreiser, old Mencken, all the boys down there, and I went to see them, Hya Dreiser, Hya Mencken" (AD 13). His slot is right there next to Arnold Bennett: "not much that Arnold Bennett, but I'd be there to sort of bolster up the B's, old Arturo Bandini, one of the boys" (AD 13). The title of Bandini's story, like the one he publishes later called "The Long Lost Hills," indicates nothing about its subject matter or theme. Neither title hints that it bears any relation to the religious and ethnic flavor that distinguished Fante's own first stories, like "Altar Boy" or "The Odyssey of a Wop."

Bandini has faith in his ability to write, but he uses his faith like a bank account (or credit card) on which he keeps drawing advances. He lies to his landlady that a check is in the mail, which, he reasons, "wasn't really a lie; it was a wish, not a lie, and maybe it wasn't even a wish, maybe it was a fact, and the only way to find out was watch the mailman." But the mailman always has the same answer when Bandini asks if he has any mail: "no, three million times; yes, once." When he feels that "the old zip is gone and I can't write anymore," Bandini writes to Hackmuth, just as Fante wrote to Mencken, asking for advice (Could it be the climate?) and praise (Do I write as well as Faulkner?), and telling lies (How the blonde girl tumbled in the park!). It is all exaggeration and prevarication, but it keeps him in the story-telling frame of mind.

Having left his family back in Boulder, Arturo is determined to make it as an American writer, and to fit into the California dream, which is the American dream in Technicolor. Upon his arrival in Los Angeles by bus, "dusty to the skin" like all the other "uprooted ones, the empty sad folks" who were "the new Californians," he takes a room at the Alta Loma Hotel. The first thing he has to do is to enter into the prejudices of his landlady, who informs him that neither Mexicans nor Jews are allowed in her hotel. Full of his recent success as author of "The Little Dog Laughed," Bandini is oblivious to the injustice of her prejudice. He is an American, he boasts, denying his connection to these other immigrants and outsiders. He is more concerned with making sure that his signature is suitably "intricate, oriental, illegible, with a mighty slashing underscore, a signature more complex than that of the great Hackmuth. After the signature I wrote, 'Boulder, Colorado'" (AD 49). The landlady, whose prejudice is matched only by her ignorance, regards him coldly and announces, "Boulder is *not* in Colorado."

She and her husband, she says, "went through Boulder, Nebraska, thirty years ago, on our way out here. You will kindly change that, please." He tries to argue, but finally gives in. In effect, her ultimatum is that he must accept her prejudice and her ignorance, or go. He tries to argue, but finally gives in, since her ignorance is just as absurd as her prejudice, which he has already accepted. In fact, Arturo is only too willing to accept the prejudice and ignorance around him, if only others will overlook the fact that "I am poor, and my name ends in a soft vowel" (AD 47).

This early acquiescence in the injustice around him takes on new meaning later, when he falls in love with a Mexican and loses his virginity to a Jew, literally embracing the outsiders that his landlady excludes from her topsy-turvy hotel, and thus learning how to embrace his own status as an alien and an outsider. By accepting Camilla Lopez and Vera Rivken, he comes to accept himself. He also begins to order his priorities in favor of human beings over his own art. In the beginning he overlooked the landlady's injustice because he was only interested in his own story, and in perfecting his signature; in the end, he casts his recently published novel about Vera Rivken into the desert in the direction where the mad Camilla has disappeared. For Arturo, Vera and Camilla have one and the same significance, indicated by his ironic "launch" of "the story of Vera Rivken, a slice out of life," that is inscribed "To Camilla, with love, Arturo."

When he meets Camilla Lopez at the Columbia Buffet (called the Liberty Buffet in the *Prologue to Ask the Dust*), where she works as a waitress, he calls her "a filthy little Greaser," while he is "an American and goddamn proud of it" (AD 44). The problem, of course, is that Arturo identifies too closely with her racial type, which is, if anything, closer to the Italian type than that of the Filipinos, for whom Fante said that he had developed a special sympathy because their tradition was, like his, Latin (SL 175). Camilla, for her part, sometimes uses the name Lombard (after Carole Lombard, but the name is Italian in origin), "professionally." But Arturo feels the sting of his injustice to her, and to himself: "Ah, Camilla! When I was a kid back home in Colorado it was Smith and Parker and Jones who hurt me with their hideous names, called me Wop and Dago and Greaser, and their children hurt me, just as I hurt you tonight . . . and when I say Greaser to you it is not my heart that speaks, but the quivering of an old wound, and I am ashamed of the terrible thing I have done" (AD 46-7). Both Arturo and Camilla are trying hard to be Americans, but like the landlady, they have a hard time knowing what it means to be an American if they can't exclude someone from the charmed circle of racial chauvinism. Even Camilla objects to Arturo playing with "Japs" when they go to Terminal Island.

It is, however, precisely Camilla's "racial type" that Arturo falls in love with (AD 39). In the *Prologue to Ask the Dust*, the prose sketch that formed the basis of the novel, Fante stated his intention in this way: "He couldn't bear her because she was simply Mexican to him and he was an American and she was beneath him, and that is the story — the Ramona theme, only this time it is an Italian-American telling it, and he, Bandini, is sympathetic with the girl because he understands this business of social prejudice." He romanticizes Camilla, turning her into a Ramona, or a Mayan princess, just as Hamsun's narrator in *Hunger* falls in love with the exotic Princess Ylayali of his imagination. As the symbol of Camilla's racial type, Bandini almost comes to fetishize her huaraches, which he both insults and worships. Coming to accept her for herself, as an individual beyond her racial difference, Arturo scolds her for not taking more pride in her heritage: "If I were a Mexican I'd knock your head off. You're a disgrace to your people" (AD 122). Yet he too is a traitor to his people, and by scolding Camilla he is scolding himself, just as when he insulted her he was insulting himself.

Through Camilla, Arturo meets Sammy Wiggins, the bartender at the Columbia Buffet, who is a writer of pulp westerns. Dying of tuberculosis, Sammy wants to finish his novel more than anything else in life, and spurns Camilla. Camilla, however, thrives on this abuse, and enlists Arturo to help Sammy by offering his expert criticism of Sammy's writing. Arturo jumps at the chance to get back at Sammy for taking his place in Camilla's affections. He writes out a scathing critique, but cannot bring himself to mail it. Later, he visits Sammy in his shack in the Mojave Desert, and they talk about writing. Sammy is interested "in the financial side of writing more than in writing itself" and is "convinced that only by favoritism were stories sold." Arturo listens and listens, with perhaps more patience than we have ever seen him display before, and does not argue with the embittered writer: "It was useless to try to dissuade him, and I didn't try, because I knew that his kind of rationalizing was necessary in view of his sheer inability to write" (AD 138).

In the end, through his encounters with other outsiders like Sammy Wiggins, Arturo ceases to feel like an outsider himself. Not only is his novel accepted, which gives him the confidence of a substantial success, but he has also learned that he is not the only misfit in the world, and indeed the vast majority of those around him would never be able to fit in at all. "I looked at the faces around me, and I knew mine was like theirs" (AD 160-1). He and they would never really becomes insiders, not in Los Angeles, not in California, not in America, not in the world. One only accepts the condition of being an outsider among other outsiders, which is the human condition. It is not that Arturo feels any more or less American, only that he feels just as human.

This leveling theme is found in the dust that is everywhere, and is the controlling image of the novel. Dust represents all that is entropic, inevitable, ontologically democratic. It is the dust on the shoes of the dust bowl migrants, whose dreams turn to dust in the California sun. In Los Angeles it is the dust of the once chic Bunker Hill neighborhoods decaying into dust. In Long Beach dust is stirred up by the earthquake as a reminder of Arturo's mortality. It is the prayer that turns to dust in Arturo's mouth (AD 99). Dust blows in from the desert on the hot Santa Ana winds to settle on the palm trees and to gather on Arturo Bandini's typewriter, jamming the keys and covering his paper. Dust is what death returns us to.

Fante's working title for the novel was "Ask the dust on the road," a phrase lifted from Hamsun's novel, *Pan*. It is also the opening sentence of *Prologue to Ask the Dust*, in which Fante acknowledges the novel's debt to Hamsun more openly than anywhere else, describing the novel he is planning to write as: "Hamsun's *Hunger*, but this is hunger for living in a land of dust, hunger for seeing and doing. Yes, Hamsun's *Hunger*"). As though in answer to Arturo's questioning of the dust on the road, Vera Rivken speaks the key line of the novel: "Does it matter? You are nobody, and I might have been somebody, and the road to each of us is love" (AD 81). We are not told the title of Arturo's novel, but it is, in a way, *Ask the Dust*, Bandini's *Hunger*, which he commits back to the dust of the Mojave desert. The Prologue began: "Ask the dust on the road! Ask the Joshua trees standing alone where the Mojave begins. Ask them about Camilla Lopez, and they will whisper her name." We are never really told the question that the name of Camilla is the answer to, either. But as Vera Rivken would ask, "Does it matter?"

2. How To Write a Screen Play: *Dreams from Bunker Hill*

Even before *Ask the Dust* was reissued in 1980, Fante had begun the novel that was to become *Dreams from Bunker Hill.* Its working title was "How to Write a Screen Play," and it would be a kind of revision of Fante's own best novel, just as *Ask the Dust* had been a kind of adaptation of Hamsun's *Hunger.*

Dreams from Bunker Hill and *Ask the Dust* cover much of the same ground in Arturo Bandini's history. Arturo is twenty-one (or twenty), living in the Alta Vista (or Alta Loma) Hotel on Bunker Hill, admires the great editor Heinrich Muller (or J. C. Hackmuth), who publishes his first story. Arturo goes on a shopping spree at the Goodwill (or May Company), has an affair with an older woman named Mrs. Helen Brownell (or Vera Rivken). Arturo smokes marijuana with Frank Edgington in a house in the Hollywood Hills (or with Camilla in a Temple Street apartment), and rents a fisherman's shack on Terminal Island (or a beach house in Laguna) to write. Arturo savagely critiques the romantic western fiction of Jennifer Lovelace (or the pulp western of Sammy Wiggins) and feels ashamed for having done so. There are other points of comparison, too numerous to enumerate, such as their plagiarism of poems by Rupert Brooke (or Ernest Dowson) to impress the Duke of Sardinia (or Camilla). The two books overlap, and inevitably contradict one another in some details.

Both Bandinis share the same goal, to write a novel, but each takes a different course to do so. The early Bandini takes the low road of poverty, the direct route along which he must beg, borrow and steal — but he finishes the novel. The later Bandini takes the high road of easy Hollywood money, a detour along which he lives well, but in the end the novel remains unwritten. The curious thing is that the book Bandini finishes in the earlier novel, the story of Vera Rivken may be the same story that is told in *Dreams from Bunker Hill* while the novel still to be written by the later Bandini seems to be the already written *Ask the Dust* in which Arturo said, "Oh that Helen — but not here" (AD 12). At the end of *Dreams from Bunker Hill,* we see Bandini in a hotel room with only his typewriter, an urge to write an "autobiographical novel" based on his experience on Bunker Hill, and a copy of Knut Hamsun's *Hunger* for inspiration. In other words, he is about to begin *Ask the Dust.* It is the kind of metapoeic autobiographical reference that Fante had used before by placing "Hail Mary" at the end of *Dago Red,* which ends where *Ask the Dust* begins.

Dreams from Bunker Hill begins: "My first collision with fame was hardly memorable" (BH 9), and ends: "a man had to start someplace" (BH 147). Between these two ironic columns, Fante fits the story of Arturo Bandini's bohemian beginnings not as he had told it in *Ask the Dust,* "the way it should have happened" (AD 70), but more in line with the way it actually happened. For one thing, Fante could speak more openly about sexual matters, using the array of obscenities that came naturally to him in his letters, and exploring the fact that Arturo Bandini was a "skilled ass man," which becomes a major motif in the later book. Composing the book at his Malibu home between 1978 and 1982, Fante revisited his old stomping grounds in his memory. But in the forty years that had passed since Fante had conceived Arturo Bandini on Bunker Hill, Fante had gone through enormous changes in his life. He had married his wife Joyce in 1937 — and ten years later could still say, "I'm nuts about that broad. I think she's 43 or 44 but she's got a lovely ass still and is stacked just right" (SL 260) — raised a family, built a home, made a small fortune in the movies, and lost his father, his eyesight and his legs to diabetes. Yet Fante was as full of life and ambition as ever, and still hungry for success as a writer.

Fante's illness had thrown him into a depression and Joyce decided that the only thing that might keep him alive was for him to continue writing, so she took down what he dictated, read it back, and typed it up and sent it off to his publisher. "It's difficult for me," Fante said of writing by dictation. "I have to keep everything in my head. I've never been so finicky as I am now. With my blindness has come a certain determination to become much more accurate."[11] No matter how much Fante had changed, the facts of his life had not, and neither had Arturo Bandini. It is Fante's desire to be more accurate that distinguishes this book from the other Bandini novels. In fact, had Fante been more famous, *Dreams from Bunker Hill* is the kind of book a publisher might ask him to use his own name in, as he did in *Full in Life* less justification.

But Fante was not famous, and the book was written for himself. The trouble with writing screenplays, said Fante, had always been that "you have to be aware of the audience because they participate. With a novel you're on your own."[12] This is Arturo Bandini's trouble in the novel, because in learning "how to write a screen play," he must give up his dreams of writing his own work. He is as incorrigible as ever, having refused to grow up or old, or to settle down. Fante's greatest strength as a writer had always been his distinctive narrative voice, the deceptively simple, lyrical, mostly first-person accounts of the conflict between community values and individual aspirations, and the superiority of emotional over intellectual rewards. It was a conflict made for Bandini's antagonistic idealism. No wonder that when Fante had to begin all over again in the new medium of dictation, he should hear the voice of Arturo Bandini above the others, clamoring for recognition of the original artistic vision in what Fante must have known would be his last novel. In *Dreams from Bunker Hill* John Fante and Arturo Bandini, the man and the myth, merge for the last time.

Dreams from Bunker Hill can be divided into five parts, each part showing Arturo in a new line of literary work, and often in a new residence. In part one, Chapters 1-5, he is living on Bunker Hill and working for Gustave Du Mont's literary agency, where he learns "the art of literary revision." In part two, Chapters 6-12, he gets a job as a studio hack, a back-up man for revising B-movie scripts. In part three, Chapters 13-15, he has moved from Bunker Hill into the Hollywood Hills and collaborates on a screenplay with an experienced writer. In part four, Chapters 16-20, he moves to Terminal Island and tries to work on his own fiction, but has a side-line as a love-poetry hack. And in part five, Chapters 21-26, he moves back to downtown Los Angeles and tries to rev himself up to write the long-put-off novel.

Arturo Bandini has two interests: words and derrieres. The two are linked throughout the novel, an odd and original juxtaposition, the significance of which becomes clear through the course of the novel. Arturo also has a Chandler-like flair for metaphor that enables him to capture the latter more often in words than in life. In the first six chapters, we meet six women of Arturo's acquaintance, with whom he associates books and backsides. The derriere of Jennifer

Lovelace, a writer of pioneer romances, fills a chair "like a lovely satin pillow" (DB 16), "like a lovely egg in a nest" (DB 25). That of the whore who lives across the hall, and who reads Zola's *Nana* while practicing her craft, "hung there like an orphan child" DB 19). The "hint of a nice ass" (DB 32) possessed by his fifty-five year old landlady, Mrs. Helen Brownell, justifies Arturo's having an affair with her, in spite of the fact that she is "bored" by his short story in *The American Phoenix*. The main attribute of the Main Street stripper Ginger Britton is a work of art, "her ass a perfect Rubens"; a prodigy of nature, "the ass of a young colt," altogether an "absolutely world-champion ass, incomparable, her skin glowing like the meat of a honeydew melon" (DB 31), which her vulgar audience cannot appreciate, so Arturo returns home and writes a love letter to the "dear lady of the Follies" (DB 32). The secretary of movie director Harry Schindler at Columbia Pictures is reading a novel when Arturo first sets eyes on "her sensational ass, a Hollywood perfecto" (DB 43). And finally, Jenny Palladino, the girlfriend of the Duke of Sardinia for whom Arturo composes love poetry, has an "ass from heaven" (DB 120).

Of course, it is Arturo who is an ass. His sensitivity to that part of their anatomy suggests a cinematic perspective, a dog's eye view of the world of a man down on his luck and down on himself. And in almost every case, Arturo's obsession with derrieres gets him in trouble, often causing him to lose his various literary jobs. His first job is at Du Mont's literary agency, where he learns "the art of literary revision" (DB 13) by working on such manuscripts as Jennifer Lovelace's "Passion at Dawn." When he first meets Jennifer Lovelace in the cat-infested office, Arturo gets down on his knees to brush the cat hair off "her glorious buttocks, feeling the taut muscled thighs, the roundness of her effulgent rear"

(DB 16). While he is on the floor, he peers through the keyhole at her as she examines his "savage editing" of her story of "six school teachers riding in a covered wagon across the plains, having skirmishes with Indians and outlaws" (DB 15). He is ashamed, not so much for having ruthlessly revised her manuscript, but for not working on his own material. "Why should I work on somebody else's product? Why wasn't I in my room writing my own stuff? What would Heinrich Muller do in a case like this? Surely I was a fool" (DB 13). And later, "I wondered what Heinrich Muller would say about my integrity. Integrity! I laughed. Integrity — balls. I was a nothing, a zero" (DB 17).

Arturo tries to make amends to her by offering to let her read his single published short story, and by telling her that he was in the confessional of the non-existent Church of Saint Mary of Guadalupe that very morning to ask the priest whether he had "committed a mortal sin" by desecrating her "artistic achievement" (DB 26). At her beach house she is making salad, wearing only "a cocktail apron over her sleek black bathing suit," and suddenly Arturo is again on his knees and flinging his arms around her waist. "She screamed when I bit her ass" (DB 28). Both he and the copy of *The American Phoenix* with his story in it are covered in mayonnaise, olive oil and vegetables. Fleeing this scene of ignominy, Arturo seeks the comfort of the whore across the hall, whose "bottom hung there like an orphan child," and who is still reading Zola's *Nana*, when he comes in and says, "Let's fuck" (DB 29).

When Arturo loses his job with de Kolty for working on his own manuscripts, Arturo gets another job working on other people's material at Columbia Pictures, this time through the auspices of Heinrich Muller himself. In the office of the director Harry Schindler Arturo meets another "sensational ass, a Hollywood perfecto. She moved like a snake, a large snake, a lustful boa constrictor" (DB 43). Like the Zola-reading whore, Thelma Farber is reading a novel as she works, a prostitute of another, slightly higher order, but with a lesser literary taste. The whore had offered Arturo an apple to eat while she read, but "the undulations of the boa constrictor in the green velvet dress" (DB 44) offer the more dangerous temptation. By moving across town, Arturo will become a literate prostitute himself by working for the movie industry, giving up the dreams of Bunker Hill for those of Hollywood.

Arturo begins to move in "the land of Oz" (a phrase he used to describe Jennifer Lovelace's white Victorian house in Santa Monica). Hollywood, he finds, is full of asses of another sort. On the surface, everything looks wonderful, the names on the doors of the offices next to his are Ben Hecht, Tess Slessinger, Dalton Trumbo, Nat West, Horace McCoy, Abem Candel; he is making $300 a week for not writing a line, and "the lustful boa constrictor" turns out to be his secretary. But when he meets Sinclair Lewis, he discovers that Hollywood can turn even "a giant among American writers" into "an ill-mannered boor" (DB 52). Arturo sees Lewis in Chasen's restaurant with two starlets on his arms, and introduces himself, only to be stared down by the great writer's cold blue eyes. As he had with Ginger Britton, Arturo responds with a note, this time the opposite of a fan letter, telling Lewis that he was "once a god, but now you are a swine," and adding "P.S. I hope you choke on your steak" (DB 52).[13]

Here again, Arturo is being paid to work on other people's material, although he actually ends up doing very little work at all. His boss specializes in gangster films and "all of his scripts were essentially the same, the same plot, the same characters, the same morality" (DB 45). While the same could be said of many great writers, including John Fante, the fact remains that the work is not that of Arturo Bandini. In Frank Edgington he meets a kindred soul, "a pinball addict" who hates "the madhouse" of the studio and the soul-numbing work, avoiding the work by playing pick-up-sticks, Chinese checkers, Parcheesi and old maid, and finding solace in getting drunk in Musso-Frank's, or in dives more off the beaten path. Together they explore "the flip side of Hollywood, the bars, the mean streets angling off Hollywood Boulevard to the south," and farther afield in "the Los Angeles basin, the deserts, the foothills, the outlying towns, the harbor." In the Japanese and Filipino neighborhoods around the canneries on Terminal Island, Arturo sees himself in one of the weather-beaten shacks with his typewriter, doing his own work (DB 46-8).

Alone in his office, Arturo does no writing but sits "hungering for Thelma Farber," who is "impregnable" (DB 48). When he begs to be given an assignment, like a bench-warmer on a baseball team, Arturo is told: "You're doing fine. I need you in case of emergency. I got to have a backup man, someone with talent. Don't worry about it. You're doing a great job. Keep up the good work. Cash the check and have fun" (DB 48). Bandini weeps with frustration. "I didn't want charity. I wanted to be brilliant on paper, to turn fine phrases and dig up emotional gems" (DB 48). Edgington tells him to wise up, take the money and "laugh all the way to the bank" like the other studio writers with more talent than Bandini: "Your trouble is that you're a fucking peasant. If there's so much you don't like about this town, stop jerking off and go back to that dago village your people came from" (DB 49). They begin to laugh, and like a father confessor, Edgington tells Arturo: "Go and sin no more" (DB

49). Arturo cashes his check and buys a second-hand Plymouth. "I was a new person, a successful Hollywood writer, without even writing a line. The future was limitless" (DB 49).

Having succumbed to the first temptation, Arturo is now a bonafide studio prostitute. But Edgington's comments have reminded him of where he came from, his humble beginnings, "born in a basement apartment of a macaroni factory in North Denver" (DB 55). In Chapter Nine, Arturo gives a character sketch of his life story, including his first confession at nine years old, four years after watching his cousin Catherine standing in front of a mirror combing her long red hair. "She was stark naked except for her mother's high-heeled shoes, a full-fledged woman of eight years. I did not understand the ecstasy that boiled up in me, the confusion of my cousin's electric beauty pouring into me. I stood there and masturbated. I was five years old and the world had a new and staggering dimension" (DB 55). The stripper Ginger Britton, too, had long red hair that hung to her hips and wore high-heeled shoes, and Arturo thought the vulgarity of the cheering audience was "sacrilegious" (DB 31).

The convergence of his having cashed the check and Edgington's mock absolution, seems to have brought on this memory, and how he felt "like a criminal, a skulking, snotnosed, freckle-faced, inscrutable criminal for four years thereafter, until sagging beneath the weight of my cross, I dragged myself into my first confession and told the priest the truth of my bestial life. He gave me absolution and I flung away the heavy cross and walked out into the sunlight, a free soul again" (DB 55). Arturo will not be free, however, until he is able to write novel about such experiences, instead of formulaic gangster films, westerns or, worse, warming the bench for the other writers with these assignments. This chapter of recollection ends with Arturo finding Sherwood Anderson in the library. His world "turns over" as he discovers his desire to write: "I was heartsick and lonely and in love with a book, many books, until it came naturally, and I sat there with a pencil and a long tablet, and tried to write" (DB 57).

Arturo's autobiographical flashback reminds us that this is John Fante speaking, not only here but throughout the novel.

All of the writing that occurs in the novel, however, is problematic. From Arturo's notes to Ginger Britton and Sinclair Lewis, to the letters from his mother, with their awkward phrasing that "fluttered in my head like trapped birds" (DB 59), writing is an occasion for agony. Arturo gives up his short-lived job practicing "the art of literary revision" for Du Mont, only to sit around in his office all day and not write for the moving pictures. He is making more money, but accomplishing even less.

When he experiences a lull in his affair with Mrs. Brownell, Arturo realizes that he can move on to starlets, "maybe even a star. All I had to do was apply myself" (DB 61). He denies that screen writing is bad for him, telling himself: "I loved it all. I was born to it. Maybe I wasn't writing a line, but I had found my station. I was making good money and the future was limitless" (DB 62). Here, as elsewhere, Arturo deludes himself into believing that his creative frustration is actually sexual in origin. A change of bed-partner, or a change of residence would do the trick. After all, "Bunker Hill was not forever. A man had to move on" (DB 61). And besides, Mrs. Brownell is, he notes, "five years older than my own mother," and her "buttocks [are] too small" (DB 61). "I needed a bright and lovely creature

familiar with the arts, steeped in literature, someone who
loved Keats and Rupert Brooke and Ernest Dowson. Not a
woman who got her literary inspiration from her hometown
Kansas newspaper" (DB 62). Inevitably, they have an argument and Arturo leaves, after throwing a shoe which "hit
her in the ass" (DB 66).

Even before leaving his room on Bunker Hill, Arturo
knows he will miss it and the life he has led there.

> The room spoke to me, and implored me to stay — the
> Maxfield Parrish picture on the wall, the typewriter on the
> table, my bed, my marvellous bed, the window overlooking
> the hill, the source of so many dreams, so many thoughts, a
> part of myself, the echo of myself pleading with me to stay.
> I didn't want to go but there was no denying it, I had
> somehow blundered and kicked myself out, and there was
> no turning back. Good-bye to Bunker Hill (DB 67).

Bandini moves in with Edgington, and for a while they live
"the glamorous, romantic, enthralling life in Hollywood,
beginning with a game of ping pong in the garage," and
moving on to darts, bingo and tiddlywinks (DB 69). Bandini
is still not allowed to work, feeling like "an orphan, a pariah,
non-productive, unknown and exiled" (DB 70). Then one
day Schindler says that Bandini might get to work on an
adaptation of Theodore Dreiser's *The Genius*, Arturo gets
right to work, producing stacks of notes, and even tries to go
to confession to seal the deal, but all he can think of is
Thelma Farber, his secretary, the boa: "Hail Mary full of
grace and Thelma Farber naked in my arms. Holy Mary,
Mother of God, kissing Thelma Farber's breasts, groping at
her body and running my hands along her thighs. Pray for
us sinners now and at the hour of our death and my lips
moved to Thelma's loins and I kissed her ecstatically. I was
lost, writhing. I felt my body kneeling there, the hardness in

my loins, the fullness of an erection, the absurdity of it, the maddening dichotomy" (DB 72). Ironically, Arturo doesn't get the Dreiser assignment, but he does get Thelma Farber — or almost.

After calling Schindler a bastard for not giving him anything to write, Arturo leaves his office weeping, and is comforted by Thelma, who slips off her panties and spreads out on the floor. But just as Thelma is helping Arturo to insert his "shooter," Schindler walks in and interrupts them. Arturo gallantly begs Schindler not to fire her. "Listen, kid," Schindler explains. "She eats writers alive. I mean big writers, Pulitzer prize winners, academy award writers, $3,000-a-week writers. That's what I don't understand. You! You don't even have a screen credit!" The scene, which is structured like a joke, ends with a punch line. Schindler is firing Arturo, not Thelma. "I want her around so I can keep an eye on her, but I'll tell you this — if it happens again I'll divorce her" (DB 74-5).

Through Edgington's agent, Arturo gets his next writing job as a collaborator on a western with Velda van der Zee,[14] a rich "dingbat" who lives "in a world of names, not bodies, not human beings, but famous names" (DB 81). All she does is talk, "dreaming the absurd, invoking the glamour of enchanting lies and impossible worlds she had made for herself," which makes Arturo want to leap in his car and drive "back to the reality of Bunker Hill" (DB 85). Arturo decides that they will never get anything done, so he decides to write the screenplay himself. It's difficult, until he gets a "fresh" idea "made up of film fragments I remembered from boyhood" (DB 88). He is on the right track, but he is no match for Velda van der Zee, whose mindless "revision" of his work is just what the producers — and the public — want. Arturo feels that he has "been had" and demands that his name be taken off the screenplay. He and Edgington celebrate by smoking marijuana and pissing on "the whole dirty business" of the screenplay as it burns in the fireplace. By now, Edgington has come to represent everything that Arturo hates most about Hollywood. He tears up one of Edgington's stories in an old copy of the *New Yorker*, and punches his friend in the mouth as he is moving out, burning another bridge behind him.

Missing his old life on Bunker Hill, Arturo drives in the rain and parks in the old neighborhood. Almost as soon as he parks he has "a dream, a beautiful dream of a novel" about Helen Brownell and himself. "All at once the self pity drained from me. There was life still, there was a typewriter and paper and eyes to see them," a line that is particularly poignant if we consider the blind Fante dictating these words. "I sat in my car at the top of Bunker Hill in the rain and the dream enfolded me, and I knew what I would do" (DB 98). What he plans to do is to rent a shack on Terminal Island at twenty-five dollars a month, figuring he has enough money saved to live there for the next ten years. "I would spend months in that shack, piling up the pages while I smoked a Meerschaum pipe and became a writer once more in the world" (DB 98). He rents the shack a mile or so from the canneries (where "he" worked in *The Road to Los Angeles*), but what he actually does is read Dostoyevsky, Flaubert and Dickens, loaf on the beach, learn how to bow from his Japanese landlady, and wonder "what had happened to the writer who had come there. Had I written something and left the place?" (DB 102).

Then one day the Duke of Sardinia pulls up next door in "a long red Marmon touring car," and Arturo is offered his fourth writing job in Los Angeles, this time as a love-poetry hack. Mario, a champion wrestler whose father happens to be the prince of Sardinia and who has come to Terminal Island to train, sees Arturo writing a letter to his mother, and asks, "How much for one poetry?" Arturo tells him a dollar a line and produces a ten-line sample that includes such gems as "My heart lusts for fin de siècle" and "Want not, oh love! Look to the bastions!" The Duke says, "She'sa beautiful," buys it, and sends it off to his girlfriend, Jenny Palladino. Arturo's second lyric begins with even better gibberish: "O tumbrels in the night past the lugubrious sea . . ."; but then stalls and ends on rhetorical questions: "Where are the children? / What happened to the children? / . . . / What has happened here?" The Duke is doubtful and tries to get a discount. But when he pays up, Arturo decides to give him a bonus, his favorite Rupert Brooke sonnet, "The Hill." Whether because he doesn't like sentimental poetry ("Steenk!"), or because he recognizes the plagiarism ("Nobody cheat Duke of Sardinia. *Capeesh?*"), the Duke is no dummy. Before he left Mrs. Brownell, Arturo thought he needed "someone who loved Keats and Rupert Brooke and Ernest Dowson." In the Duke of Sardinia, he may have found that someone.

The reference to Keats and Dowson reminds us that Arturo is not doing his own work. In *Ask the Dust*, for example, he tries to pass off Dowson's "Non Sum Qualis Eram Bonae Sub Regno Cynarae" for his own by substituting Camilla's name for Cynara's. No doubt Arturo's feeling for the poem was sincere, despite the fact that it is plagiarized, and the feelings of hunger and passion that it expresses are appropriate, since that poem ends:

> And I am desolate and sick of an old passion,
> Yea, hungry for the lips of my desire:
> I have been faithful to thee, Cynara! In my fashion.

And Arturo may even have been faithful to Camilla, in his fashion. But Fante's return to Dowson in this novel is his way of talking about the difficulty of originality and inspiration in comic fashion. The addition of Keats may seem out of place, unless we remember that it was Keats who is plagiarized by another writer-lover-fool who tries to pass off "An Ode to a Nightingale" as his own in his plagiaristic seduction of a mortuary beautician, in Evelyn Waugh's *The Loved One*.

When Arturo goes to the Olympic Auditorium to see the Duke in action, Arturo begins to identify with the Duke, despite the difference in their physique, not just because they are both Italian and so hated by the Mexicans, blacks and gringos in the crowd, but because Arturo discovers that in the ring, the Duke has his script written for him. "The drama was clear. The Duke could not win in this ring. He would dish out a lot of punishment, for he was the devil, but Richard Lionheart, blessed with purity, would conquer him in the end. It was what the crowd came to see and paid its money for" (DB 114). When the Duke wins the first fall, Lionheart is unable to go on, and the referee calls it a draw. A riot breaks out, not because of the unfairness of the call, but because Lionheart was not declared the winner. As with Arturo's screen writing, it is the audience who determines the plot the Duke must follow, not the skill of the wrestler or writer.

Then Jenny Palladino shows up in a model-A Ford. When Arturo looks up from his Melville, the first thing he notices is: "Her ass was from heaven" (DB 120). He invites her in for coffee, supposedly without a thought of making a pass at her, "only a wish to tumble about with her in the manner of kittens" (DB 121). Soon he is down on his knees, waxing poetic: "Bless you, lovely maiden, in the curvature of your sculptured neck" (DB 121). Like Roxanne realizing that it was Cyrano and not Christian who has been courting her all this time, Jenny Palladino says, "So you're the one!" Like Cyrano, Arturo keeps it up: "Bring her to me, oh wandering birds, suffer her not to flee in fear," which, unlike Roxanne, is exactly what Jenny Palladino does, calling for the Duke.

By the time the Duke arrives, Arturo has moved out of his Island retreat and is back on the road to Los Angeles.

Predictably, it is to Bunker Hill where Arturo goes, like "a homing bird." The hotel looks the same, but Helen Brownell's hair has turned white and she wants no part of him. He takes a room above a Filipino restaurant at Temple and Figueroa and wonders, what now? "I looked at my hands. They were soft writer's hands, the hands of a writer peasant, not suited for hard work, not equal to making phrases." He prays on his knees for "the chance to write": "Bring me peace, oh Lord. Shape me into something worthwhile. Make the typewriter sing" (DB 125). But even this old ploy, as old as Fante's story "Hail Mary," doesn't work. He goes to the cinema to see *Sin City*, written and directed by Velda van der Zee, and laughs all through the opening credits, in which his name does not appear. In fact, the only contributions by Arturo Bandini to the dialogue that sound remotely familiar are "Whoa!" and "Giddyup!" "Whoa and giddyup — my fulfillment as a screenwriter" (DB 127). When the audience seems bored by the picture, Arturo feels vindicated, "a better writer" for refusing the credit; but by the time he gets back to his room he knows he has been deluding himself: "In truth, I felt sorry for her, for all writers, for the misery of the craft" (DB 127).

In an antistrophe to Bandini's prose love poem to Los Angeles in *Ask the Dust* — that began "Los Angeles, give me some of you!" — Bandini decides that Los Angeles is no place for him: "So fuck you, Los Angeles, fuck your palm trees, and your highassed women, and your fancy streets, for I am going home, back to Colorado, back to the best damned town in the USA — Boulder, Colorado" (DB 132).

Predictably, home is not what Bandini remembers it to be. He looked forward to getting out of the heat of L.A., but when he arrives it is snowing flakes as big as dollars and he stands there "blinking at my home town. Where the hell was it?" (DB 133). His father asks him why he left his "job in pitchers" and flatly informs him: "There's nothing for you here" (DB 134). For a while Arturo, "the prodigal son," revels in the former sites of "Christmases and baseball and first communion," in the home-cooked food and warmth of family, who "did not regard me as a failure. I was a hero, a conqueror back from distant battlefields" (DB 135-6). When his little brother Tom asks how tall Hedy Lamarr is, and Arturo says, "A lot taller than you," Tom retorts: "Smart ass" (DB 137).

After the warm welcome home, Arturo wanders the streets, visiting old haunts, including the library, where he finds again "the books that changed my life: Sherwood Anderson, Jack London, Knut Hamsun, Dostoevsky, D'Annunzio, Pirandello, Flaubert, de Maupassant. The welcome they gave me was much warmer than the cold curiosity I met in the town" (DB 139). He is interviewed by an old school and baseball buddy for the local paper, and is invited to a party by Agnes Lawson, a member of the church literary society (called the Red Pencil, reminiscent of Arturo's job with Du Mont, providing "Expert literary supervision"). The party is held in a house from which he was always excluded in the past, and his feelings of inferiority resurface, causing him to brag that he is the best screenwriter in Hollywood and has just sold a poem to the *New Yorker*. And to drink too much. Soon he is starting to sound like Velda van der Zee, talking about "the ravishing figures" of all the actresses he knows. "I've dined with them, danced with them, made love with them, and I'll tell you this — I never disappointed any of them . . . I play by day, I fuck in the twilight, and I work by night. I swim with Johnny Weismuller and Esther Williams and Buster Crabbe. Everybody loves me. Understand? Everybody" (DB 142). At which point he falls, dead drunk, on his face. When someone helps him up, he throws a wild punch, only to get poked in the nose himself, and the fight is over before it begins. He sneaks out of town before his parents wake up to see his bloody nose, back on the bus to Los Angeles.

After the fiasco of his homecoming, he returns to the Bunker Hill hotel and to Mrs. Brownell intending to start anew in a "Kansas type" house in Woodland Hills. On his return, however, he discovers that she has died of a stroke.[15] The only thing left for Arturo Bandini to do is to write the novel at long last. The book that he goes to for solace and inspiration is, once again, Knut Hamsun's *Hunger*, the story of a starving scribbler who, like Arturo, is precociously talented and grandiosely deluded, painfully idealistic and embarrassingly incapable of living up to his own self-image. Starting over again with "Seventeen dollars and the fear of writing," Arturo invokes the muse of Hamsun: "Please God, please Knut Hamsun, don't desert me now" (147). What he begins to write are not his own words, nor even those of Hamsun, but some nonsense verse from Lewis Carroll:

> "The time has come," the Walrus said,
>   "To talk of many things:
> Of shoes — and ships — and sealing wax —
>   Of cabbages — and kings —"

It is not only nonsense verse, it is plagiarized nonsense verse. At least it is not the "miserable poetry" he wrote in high school, nor the dreadful love poems he wrote for the Duke of Sardinia. Nor is it "the art of literary revision" that he learned from Du Mont, nor the Hollywood nonsense of celluloid rewrites, adaptations and collaborations. "I looked at it and wet my lips," says Arturo in the closing paragraph of the novel. "It wasn't mine, but what the hell, a man had to start someplace" (DB 147). Bandini's displaced plagiarism suggests that the first novel he is sitting down to write is *Ask the Dust,* modeled on Hamsun's first novel about a starving scribbler. *Dreams from Bunker Hill* is a revision of his own past, a rewrite of his own work, a collaboration with Hamsun and his former self, and an adaptation of *Hunger* and *Ask the Dust.* These were, after all, the very skills and literary forms that Bandini had acquired in learning how to write a screenplay.

CHAPTER 7

HOLLYWOOD HOKUM

1941-1952

> It doesn't take any brains to compose a movie. Any idiot can do it, and there are a terrible lot of fools in this town getting rich turning out junk . . .
>
> John Fante in 1934

If the 1930s were Fante's decade of bohemian beginnings on Bunker Hill, the 1940s were his decade of being caught up in the temptations of Hollywood profligacy and affluence. While writing the fiction that by 1940 established his reputation, Fante had kept his roles as novelist and movie hack, at least in his own conscience, separate and distinct. He was devoted to fiction; he flirted with films. But during the 1940s and 1950s, except for *Full of Life* and a few bursts of work on the ill-fated Filipino novel, Fante the novelist fell silent.

During this period he wrote his weakest novel and his worst stories, slick, sentimental pieces that he regarded as "money-getters" from the magazines that paid top dollar. He became, as he defined the modern short story writer, "a pimp of the advertisers" (SL 133) and a prostitute of the Hollywood producers. At the same time the delicate balance that Fante had sustained between his serious writing, especially the novels, and his writing for money tipped in favor of screen writing, primarily because he could get more money turning out what he called "movie hokum" (SL 83).

Fante's attitude toward the movies, making them or watching them, can be summed up in a few lines written to his mother in 1935. "I don't like the movies, I have never liked them, and I shall never like them. But I *do* like the salaries they pay" (SL 96). There is no evidence that Fante spent much time in darkened theaters after his childhood. He claimed he had never seen several films he had worked on, including *My Six Loves* (Paramount, 1963) and *Maya* (MGM, 1963). The only project he seems proud to have been connected with was *It's All True* with Orson Welles in 1941, but even this story of his parents' courtship gave him little pleasure, and in any case it was never produced. Having viewed the business of film from the inside, Fante had no illusions about its artistic pretensions — "It doesn't take any brains to write a movie. Any idiot can do it" (SL 80) — and no interest at all in its aesthetics.

Fante was a story man. He could get excited about movie plots, character development, and snappy dialogue, but once it all came to production, he went cold.

Fiction was the only art form Fante cared anything about. The difference between Hollywood hokum and "straight literary production," he said, was that producers were interested only in "an idea" and not the "writing values" that made creating fiction worthwhile (SL 77). Collaboration and the work of committees doomed movies to appealing to the least common denominator and stifled any individual expression. The writer of movies had to give undue attention to his audience, had to in fact become the audience — "you have to think of the motion picture machine, as though you were sitting in the audience" (SL 78) — rather than being the fountainhead of inspiration.

Fante began his long and lucrative career in Hollywood by pitching original stories, but like all initiates in the trade he was soon earning his keep by patching up the B-movie scripts of others. Eventually he sold his own ideas, sharing his first screen credits with Frank Fenton for *Dinky* (Warner Brothers, 1935) and Ross Wills for *East of the River* (Warner Brothers, 1940). From 1940 to 1952 he worked on a number of films (and turned down work on a number of others), but would receive credit for only three, none of them remarkable: *The Golden Fleecing* (MGM, 1940), *Youth Runs Wild* (RKO, 1944), and *My Man and I* (MGM, 1952).

His greatest success in Hollywood came in the years after the war, partly because he was temperamentally allergic to politics, and so avoided the blacklists of the McCarthy era. Perhaps the best of Fante's films is *Full of Life* (Columbia, 1956), a charming comedy adapted from his own novel.[1] Fante collaborated with two of the most successful screenwriters of the time, Daniel Fuchs and Sonya Levien on *Jeanne Eagels* (Columbia, 1957), a biography of the 1920s film star, that critics and audiences found almost as dull to watch as Fante did to write. In 1962, two films appeared that may mark the height of Fante's creative (and earning) power in Hollywood, *The Reluctant Saint* (Dmytryk-Weiler), which took Fante to Italy to work on this biography of Joseph of Cupertino, a moody film that makes use of Fante's ability to juggle laughter and tears; and *Walk on the Wild Side* (Columbia), written with Edmund Morris, and based on Nelson Algren's novel about low-life in New Orleans, a city that Fante never visited but felt he would have liked to know.[2] Along with these mostly forgettable films that Fante worked on in his most prosperous period, many other projects were canceled in one stage of development or another for which he received credit only in the form of dollars.

Fante's last major screen credit was for a television play, *Something for a Lonely Man* (Universal Television, 1967), but he prided himself on not having to sink so low as to churn out scripts for television series. In 1965 he wrote: "I am still writing movies. I have escaped TV, but all my friends have been flushed down, including Fenton, who actually sits down dead drunk at his machine and grinds the stuff out" (SL 288).

Yet as early as 1935 Fante was saying, "I have been in pictures too long. I have gone stale," and "the movies are so different in every way from straight prose writing that I might as well have been doing nothing" (SL 95). He continued to express such misgivings for the rest of his Hollywood career. Film critic David Thomson has suggested that with the exception of *Full of Life*, based on his own novel, there is very little of John Fante in the films on which he squandered his ink and imagination. "He was prosperous, but I doubt if anyone ever heard him in those pictures, or if Fante didn't regard it all as a practicality and a mistake."[3]

Even if there is little of Fante in the films he worked on, his work on films inevitably entered into his fiction, if only because he was an autobiographical novelist who happened to be a screenwriter. Almost all of his protagonist-narrators from 1952 onward are studio hacks. A case could be made that Fante's characterization in his fiction, as well as its sentimentality and attention to dialogue, was influenced by the B-movie formulas of the 1930s. Certainly he plays upon these formulas, either for satire or humor as part of his characters' store of dreams. At times he quite consciously plays upon the heartstrings of readers, especially in the stories of the 1940s, when he cynically began to penetrate "the female capitalistic" *Woman's Home Companion* (SL 145), in addition to *Good Housekeeping*, and *Collier's*, three markets where he published nine stories from 1938 until he virtually quit the short story form in 1952.

Formally, however, Fante rarely borrows any strictly cinematic technique in his fiction. The sole example of formal contamination may be *My Dog Stupid*, which Fante claimed "is written somewhat in the fashion of a screen play,"[4] although it is difficult to say exactly how this is so, unless we consider the short scene-like chapters and the relative lack of any extended Bandini-like flights of lyrical interior monologue.

Looking back on his time in Hollywood, Fante may well have regarded it as a waste of time and a corruption of his career as a serious writer. But in the early years he welcomed the advantages Hollywood offered: the easy money, the proximity to stardom, the drinking bouts, and the chance to meet other writers succumbing to the same temptations. Fante met F. Scott Fitzgerald at the Four Star Theater and remembered the effeminate limpness of the hand that had written *The Great Gatsby*. They played cards together at the all-night stud-poker parties at the Garden of Allah on Sunset Boulevard. Thereafter, whenever Fante found himself in Hollywood for a time, he would check in at the Garden of Allah because "Fitzgerald used to go there. It was a kind of pilgrimage to me."[5] Fante considered William Faulkner "a good friend," and they used to meet, along with A. I. Bezzerides, for drinks at Musso-Frank on Hollywood Boulevard. Fante remembered Faulkner as "a southern gentleman" with a "low-key wit," who said that back home in the kitchen in Oxford, Mississippi there was a 100-gallon barrel full of fan mail that Faulkner would dip into only when he got very drunk, and then only to pull out an envelope and peer inside to see if there was any money inside — if not, he'd just toss the letter aside.[6]

Ross Wills describes taking Fante on his first studio tour, and Fante making himself right at home there. Far from being awed by the sets or the VIPs, he glided past *Keep Out* signs unmolested, having "the rare gift of 'belonging' to virtually any situation, exploring the studio with "the insatiable unself-conscious curiosity of a healthy puppy" (SL 328). This natural ability to get along with people on their own turf came in handy when pitching a story to producers, who may have been disarmed by his disingenuousness. They may also have recognized something of themselves in this "short man, very handsome," who was, in Joyce Fante's description, "sometimes rather frightening in his aggressive ambition and charisma."[7] Later, this same naturalness would get Fante into trouble, and may explain why he didn't enjoy even greater successes in Hollywood. One acquaintance from the time said Fante had "a personality like a buzzsaw."[8] Fante was known to deal out insults rather freely, as when he complimented a colleague on his "shit-colored overcoat." According to Harry Essex, a co-writer, "If he didn't like you, he could destroy you."[9] He could reduce people to tears or delight with his ridicule, or he could alienate them forever and create dedicated enemies. And he didn't mind whether the objects of his insults were lowly screenwriters like himself or the producers who paid his salary.

Fante never bothered to disguise his disgust for his job in the movies, but as the years passed he became more difficult in a milieu that required tact. Explaining Hollywood's neglect of Fante in later years, Robert Towne has said that Fante, who was "purely an artist," was just too truthful: "No matter how good a screenwriter you are, no matter how creative and brilliant, you cannot survive if you're politically maladroit"[10] — although Fante himself

would have had another name for such bowing and ana-
tomical bussing.

Fante was a capable collaborator, a real asset in Hollywood where nothing is produced without consensus, but
his artistic temperament prevented him from taking such a
division of labor seriously. He did not like "being told what
to do, how to write a story, and having to work with other
people," Joyce Fante has said. "It wasn't his own work; it
was the product of a committee."[11] This came to bother him
more as time went on, but in the early years Fante enjoyed
collaboration, whether as a way of learning the trade from
more experienced screenwriters, or as a way of having fun
with fiction. Long before he wrote the children's book *Bravo,*
Burro! (1970) with Rudolph Borchert, he co-wrote short stories with Frank Fenton, Ross Wills and Carey McWilliams.
At least one of them, "We Snatch a Frail," published in 1936,
Fante considered "a helluva funny piece . . . a satire on the
Caldwell-Hemingway-O'Hara school of scribblers. We gave
it the works and literally rolled on the floor with laughter as
we wrote it" (SL 132). Like the screenplay collaborations,
these were hardly serious literary efforts, but that was all the
more reason to have fun with them.

Soon after Fante went to work for Warner Brothers in
1934, with an introduction from Mencken to a friend and
former writer for the *New Yorker,* Joel Sayre, Fante wrote to
his mother: "The work here is very easy. In fact, I haven't
even begun to work yet. I have been lying around here in an
office sleeping for the last three days. Real work begins
tomorrow" (SL 80). And work Fante did, turning out treatment after treatment, but the higher-ups didn't seem to
notice and he was soon fired, along with Sayre. "I had this
big pile of manuscript. I just lifted it up and threw it into the
wastebasket."[12] A description of the daily routine of the

studio writer — doing nothing and collecting fat checks — appears in *Dreams from Bunker Hill*: "Sometimes I left the office and wandered down the halls. On each office door I saw the nameplate of the famous — Ben Hecht, Tess Slessinger, Dalton Trumbo, Nat West, Horace McCoy, Abem Candel . . ." (BH 45). Other writers Fante met in Hollywood, either through Carey McWilliams or his studio connections, were Joe Pagano, Louis Adamic, Carlos Bulosan, W. R. Burnett, William Faulkner, Daniel Mainwaring, John Sanford, Matt Weinstock, and William Saroyan.

Most of the relationships Fante had with these writers were trench friendships, the transitory acquaintances of a shared experience. Many of them would rather have been elsewhere, writing something else, and most considered Hollywood nothing more than a meal ticket. But they were well paid and living in a manner, as the saying goes, to which they would like to become accustomed. As a result, many fine writers, among them Fitzgerald and Faulkner, devoted their time to drinking and bellyaching instead of intellectual or literary chit-chat.

The writers Fante later recalled with the greatest fondness were those who never made the big time, like Owen Francis, "the short story writer from the Pennsylvania coal fields," "an extreme eccentric, a brawler, and a drunk," who "once stole and drove a streetcar away from the end of the line on Vermont Avenue," who squandered his screen writing earnings "much faster than he earned them," and who died soon after of a heart attack brought on when "his doctor put him on candy rather than booze" (SL 306). Another was George Milburn, an Oklahoma writer who published in the *American Mercury* a story called "Hatrack," "a sensation in its time" (SL 306).

Bigger names made less favorable impressions. Fante's chilling encounter with Sinclair Lewis seemed to prove that Tinsel Town could turn even "a god" into a "swine" (DB 52). Lewis had been one of Fante's childhood heros, and like himself, a protégé of Mencken's, so he thought he would introduce himself. As he approached the table and held out his hand, "this gaunt, red-haired steely-blue-eyed cadaver kind of guy" just stared at the extended hand, and so did the two starlets Lewis was with. Fante retreated, and sent a note to Lewis's table: "Dear Sinclair Lewis: I happen to be a protégé of H. L. Mencken, and I was under the impression that you were too. I'm sorry I interrupted you in this way, but I want to tell you you can go fuck yourself." When Lewis read the note and got up ready for a fight, Fante panicked, left the restaurant and hid in the floorboard of a parked car, as Lewis went up and down the street, shouting "Fante! Where are you? Hey, Fante! Where are you?" Telling this story in an interview in 1979, when he was writing *Dreams from Bunker Hill*, Fante uses the names Bandini and Fante interchangeably, prompting the interviewer to ask how much of the story actually happened. "That all happened," Fante replied.[13]

Although Hollywood seemed to diminish great spirits while exalting the mediocre, William Saroyan, whom Fante came to know well, was one good writer who seemed to thrive there. With Saroyan, who was Armenian, and Carey McWilliams, Fante shared many interests, including what Gerald Haslam has called "the other California," the California of the displaced from everywhere, but particularly the California of ethnic immigrants. More than once Fante's lyric, humorous style has been compared to that of the more visible and voluble Saroyan, although the comparison breaks down upon examination and on artistic grounds always to Fante's advantage. Whereas Saroyan is prolific, gabby to the point of glibness, his structure loose, often out of control, Fante is economical, terse.

In 1940, while living in Manhattan Beach, Fante made one of his few brief attempts at keeping a diary, which came to an abrupt halt when he was in a car accident. The second entry includes this: "Saroyan told me once: write them big and often Johnnie, 'cause they forget you fast" (SL 315). True as this turned out to be, since Fante wrote them small and seldom, his braggadocio response is typical: "As if I care when they forget me! The solacing conceit of immortality has long ago left me. The last time I felt it was in my thirteenth year" (SL 315). Thirty years later, Fante criticized the bulk of James T. Farrell — "Name me one man in the world who ever read a Farrell novel from beginning to end" — and Saroyan himself for writing too much: "My friend Saroyan . . . He has published 50 books. He has diarrhea. The runs. The literary runs. It is an absurdity. No man has that much to say" (SL 294). In 1976, stuck for an idea, Fante complained: "Why fight the simple fact that one has nothing to say? Most of the shit now in print was rattled off by writers who kept writing long after they should have remained silent for a spell" (SL 301).

Fante's friendship with Saroyan was long, often ambivalent, and intermittent. Saroyan based the pinball wizard Willie in *The Time of Your Life* (1939) on John Fante, who had a weakness for the game. (Will Lee, the actor who originated the role, was even said to have resembled Fante.) The play's publisher was Stanley Rose, whose Hollywood Boulevard bookshop was next door to Musso-Frank, two favorite hang-outs for "industry" types and serious writers alike, like Faulkner and Nathanael West, who spent more than one afternoon shuttling between the bookshop and the bar, with the latter claiming the lion's share of hours.

Saroyan recalls one day when Fante stopped in at Stanley Rose's bookshop with his friend Joe Pagano, another Italian-American writer from Denver, on their way next door "for steaks or lamb chops, and good booze." Fante told a story that gives a sense of his regard for Hollywood in general and agents in particular.

> One day John Fante told the story about the writer's wife who was found by the writer half-dead from some kind of terrible sexual assault.
>   "For God's sake, honey," he said, "who did it?"
>   "Who did it?" his wife screamed. "Your fucking agent did it, that's who."
>   Whereupon the writer said, "What else did Eddie have to say?"
>   For the movie agent was indeed the party who kept the good times rolling.[14]

The good times continued to roll throughout the war years.

In 1941 Fante was working on several projects that were close to his heart. One was an adaptation of a Robert Flaherty story called "My Friend Bonito" with Norman Foster. The other was a love story based on the courtship of Fante's parents.

Both stories were for a RKO documentary entitled *It's All True* with Orson Welles.[15] "All stories we do for Welles for this picture are supposed to be true stories," Fante wrote to his parents, asking them to sign a release. "Well, my story of the Italian bricklayer isn't exactly true, but I had to tell them it was true in order to sell it" (SL 195). In a milieu that usually drew nothing but scorn from Fante, he considered Welles "the finest guy in Hollywood, and the maker of the best pictures" (SL 195). When it came time to shoot *It's All True,*

Fante went to Brazil with Welles, who was arrested during "some festivity that goes on in Brazil once a year," but the project was canceled when Welles was arrested and ordered out of the country because he had "stood at the edge of the balcony and peed on the people below . . . That was the end of that project."[16] The three movies Welles did for RKO, including *Citizen Kane* which opened in May, did not make money however, and in 1943 the director's contract with the studio was canceled.

The war years were difficult for Fante emotionally, if not financially. Aside from his publisher Stackpole Sons' skirmish with Hitler in the courts, as an Italian American Fante was embarrassed by the antics of Mussolini, which may have contributed to his silence during these years. Fante saw the war coming by 1934 and declared early that he would have no part of it. "I for one refuse to be a soldier. The only war I care to fight is the one I start myself" (SL 106). Fante was alternately blithe and biting about the coming "crack-up": "The storm is coming. Christ knows what I'll do then, but you can be sure I'll regard the safety of John Fante very highly. I'll go fascist if they leave me alone and let me write what I please. I'll go red for the same reason" (SL 135). But Fante knew his bluster was "just talk," well aware that war could only mean "suppression of speech, regimentation, censorship and mushroom Hitlerism" (SL 135). Eventually, he too felt he had to do something for the cause, although he managed to avoid stooping to soldier.

A month before Pearl Harbor Joyce Fante's mother died, leaving a legacy that included income property, so that from this time forward the couple enjoyed a considerable degree of financial freedom. Soon after Joyce Fante went to Roseville to settle the estate, her husband followed and they bought a house near Nick and Maria Fante. It seemed a good opportunity for John to work on his fiction, a welcome interval of peace in a time of war.

A new job with the Office of War Information, however, took them to San Francisco in 1942. Fante had accepted the job with enthusiasm because "I felt I had something to give my country" (SL 198). Soon, though, he was complaining that he was made to do news writing instead features, and that no one would listen to his ideas, such as "a humorous, somewhat Abbott-Costello skit between two Italians in Italy" (SL 199). These skits, he felt, could lift the usual war propaganda "out of the bog of banality and into real American humor. We are known everywhere for our humor. It is the big, important American heritage. It is Mark Twain and Josh Billings and so on. It is what is expected of Americans" (SL 199). He was also tired, he said, of "toadying to frauds" in the OWI, which he described as "a big-scale Federal Writer's Project, honey-combed with the same type of bureaucrats who have been wallowing in the public trough since the Republic first got up steam and started on its spooky and misty voyage in 1776" (SL 198-9).

For several months Fante tried to transfer to the New York office of the OWI, where he planned to study Italian on the way to North Africa, where he would "instruct the Italians in the occupied territory on American democratic principles" (SL 201). Eventually he saw himself going "up into Italy" for the same purpose. All of this, however, was contingent upon his mastering the Italian language, which he was unable to do.

As soon as Fante resigned from the OWI he returned to Hollywood for another well-paying job, so that America's entry into the war had interrupted his film work only briefly. As Fante's war work ended, so did the couple's interval of peace. According to Joyce Fante, John "started drinking heavily, and fell in with a group of professional gamblers who made their living preying upon young afflu- ent victims" (SL 203). The big money evaporated, as the marriage was beginning to do, and the Fantes, now with two children, decided to save it by returning to their house in Roseville. Soon after the birth of their second son in February, 1944, Fante received a draft notice but never had to serve, thanks, it seems, to fatherhood and a letter from his editor at Viking to the effect that the work he was doing on the phantom Filipino novel would contribute to morale.

Fante had been working on the Filipino material since 1932, when Mencken told him he was obsessed with his family and should be able to find plenty of material in California to "do some stories about other people" (FM 37). Fante answered that he was working on a story about a Filipino he had worked with at the canneries in Wilmington. Fante had developed a special sympathy for Filipinos, he said, "because I am Latin and their tradition, if any, is Span- ish and Latin too" (SL 175), a comment that may show how little he really did understand them and their complex tra- dition. In the early 1940s Fante was working with renewed vigor on *The Little Brown Brothers*, which in his more san- guine moments he thought would surpass *The Grapes of Wrath*. It was to be "a book so full of sheer story that the migratory problem of the Okies is a holiday excursion by comparison" (SL 175). The sense of rivalry with Steinbeck is obvious: "I'll write a book that will make any of Steinbeck appear small peanuts" (SL 166). Fante even warned his editor: "DON'T tell Steinbeck!" (SL 175), as though the giant of California letters might steal the idea. Steinbeck was, in fact, Fante's model: "The book will be in the general vein of Tortilla Flat, but it will be a greater book than that. It will be a swashbuckling, romantic story of a proud little people kicked up and down the state under the most vicious system of race and class taboos that ever existed" (SL 175). Fante is here pitching the idea to his editor at Viking in 1940, and the note he strikes is that of a Hollywood pitch man, which he had in part become, sketching a "high concept" story line.

This enthusiasm waxed and waned over the years until the book was rejected in 1944 with unfavorable reports that complained of "an air of condescension on the part of the author" and "lack of a true sympathy" which resulted in the book sounding "like a travesty" (SL 206-07). In this case, the editors were right. It is clear that for all Fante's sympathy for Filipinos, he had no real understanding of them, as seen in his reduction of their heritage to that of their Spanish colonization. As Joyce Fante comments, "Fante never found the key" to the book because it was "unwritable," the material "unsympathetic" and the anecdotes "gross and revolting" (SL 185). The book promised to be more *Tobacco Road* than *Tortilla Flat*. Perhaps Fante knew this, and thus put all his energy in his pitches for the book, which tend toward rhetoric, sentimentality, braggadocio and bombast, rather than actually sitting down to write the book. After the rejection, Fante never returned to the novel. He did, however, publish two stories — "Helen, Thy Beauty Is to Me —" (1941) and "The Dreamer" (1947) — about Filipino men in love with the American dream and centering on their unhappy search for an American wife, a dream denied them precisely because of who they are. These stories are important for two reasons: they show what he was working on during his relatively dry spell of the 1940s, and they show his sympathy with the plight of immigrants in America.

Fante's Filipino stories, his only non-autobiographical fiction, are crucial to his other works in how they deal with prejudice. Fante's empathetic treatment of the Filipino experience allowed him to see his own ethnic conflicts in a new light. As early as 1933, when Mencken published "The Odyssey of a Wop" in the *American Mercury*, Fante had already located the perpetuation of prejudice, if not its origin, in the low self-esteem of immigrants themselves. By emulating those now-settled immigrants called Americans, Italian immigrants hoped to assimilate themselves into the alien culture. And yet by adopting the values of the new land, they also adopted the prejudices, perversely calling themselves Dago and Wop with alternating affection and deprecation. Their sons and daughters, caught up in this confusion, continued the name-calling, perpetuating the prejudice in their eagerness to become "American."

Like Horace McCoy's *They Shoot Horses, Don't They,* "Helen, Thy Beauty Is to Me —" is set in a dance hall, where the dance is no longer a symbolic ritual of love nor a celebration of life, but merely another instance of the American commercialization of courtship. Julio Sal's taxi dancer Helen turns out to be little more than a whore.[17] The taxi dancers of the Angels' Ballroom are not free agents but employees who split the dime-a-dance fee with the management. To the girls it is all business, bartering their beauty at a minute per ticket. For the Filipinos, however, it is more than a question of business, or even sex; they are embracing the American dream every time they embrace Helen. Lined up at the wicker gates, waiting to get onto the dance floor, they represent all the faceless hordes of immigrants eager to join in the dance of America.

Although Fante's dance hall symbol does not approach the brutal allegory of McCoy's marathon, it does represent the ironic degradation of the dance into an exploitation of courtship. The management of the Angels' Ballroom capitalizes on the Filipinos' desire to be part of the

American dream, reducing the Pinoys to their economic function and value: "Julio Sal, Filipino boy, forty cents an hour, Tokyo Fish Company, Wilmington"; "Johnny Dellarosa, label machine, Van Camp's, San Pedro" (WY 251-2). Defined by their function in the American economy and tolerated only for their ability to pay, the Filipinos have only this list of characteristics — name, race, occupation, wage, employer, residence — to constitute their identity.

Helen haughtily flaunts her racial superiority, yet she too is reduced to her economic function and deprived of her human identity. Helen, of course, is not her real name but a pseudonym chosen for its marketing appeal to evoke the most notorious beauty of Western culture. Helen is only one among "forty beautiful girls" advertised like any other product in a photograph at the dance hall entrance, but her name helps her to stand out, a mythical ideal imported from the Greek agora via Madison Avenue and Hollywood to the Angels' Ballroom. To Julio Sal she is Helen of Troy as the typical American housewife. To the management she and her ancient namesake are national and natural resources to be exploited and turned to a profit. Helen of Troy has become a toy: "A small white doll — that was his Helen" (WY 252). When Julio describes her to his friends as the woman he wants to marry, they try to warn him: "Is not love. Is business" (WY 256).

But Julio Sal clings to his dream to enthrone Helen in an adman's image of domestic suburban bliss: "The blissful future revealed itself in a reverie . . . — she was frying bacon and eggs in a blue-tinted kitchen like in the movie pitch, and he came grinning from the bedroom in a green robe with a yellow sash, like in the movie pitch" (WY 253). Having embraced the myth of the American dream on the dance floor, Julio Sal aspires to rescue Helen from the Ilium of the

Angels' Ballroom, only to install her in a model American kitchen because that is what the movies and the magazines have taught him.

The immigrant is by definition a dreamer. Envisioning a new and better way of life, he goes in search of it in foreign lands. Julio Sal and Cristo Sierra, like Jimmy Toscana and Arturo Bandini, are unrepentant dreamers. Denying the appearance of reality, they transform mere appearances —the sights and even the smells and sounds around them — to fit the shape and color of their incurably optimistic vision. Returning home from a night spent in Helen's arms on the dance floor, Julio Sal does not smell "the fertilizer vats, the tar, the oil, the copra, the bananas and oranges, the bilge, the old rope, the decaying anchovies, the lumber, the rubber, the salt," but only "the vast bouquet of the harbor," for "This, too, was part of the dream. While working here at this spot, I met my love — I, Julio Sal." He ignores the fact that his apartment building resembles a row of "cell blocks," and when he hears a baby cry, it is the offspring of his dreams: "A little girl, he hoped, with the face and eyes of Mamma Helen" (WY 253-4).

With Horatio Alger diligence, Julio Sal works hard and saves his money until the day he is worthy (worth enough) to propose to Helen. Dressed "according to the pictures in Esquire," Julio is the very image of the ideal American male, "sartorially correct" (WY 260). There is one imperfection in his ensemble: his brown shoes are half-soled, a poignant reminder, like his brown skin, of his dehumanized alien status. He is, in effect, half-souled. So he buys a new pair of shoes. But he cannot so easily circumvent the California law against miscegenation between Filipino men and white women, and when he buys the engagement ring, he can feel the dream already dying.

When he sees Helen again, she has changed from an exploited doll to a platinum-blonde predator. Three months of dime-a-dance minutes have taken their toll. Her hair is bleached of its natural color and her "crimson nails" are like talons as they "tear" and "nibble" at the roll of tickets every time the bell clangs. She does not recognize him, and there is "an iciness in her blue eyes that made him suddenly conscious of his race"(WY 262). As he begins to feel the pinch of his new shoes, he takes her for a drink at the bar "beyond the wicker fence," which is as far as he gets to taking her home to Luzon. He orders bottle after bottle of exorbitantly priced champagne, not getting drunk but only "a salty satisfaction in playing the fool" (WY 265). He knows he is being tricked by her and the "Kansas-like, tough, impersonal" waiter, because Julio Sal may be a "sucker" but he is not stupid. He gives her the engagement ring anyway, telling her that it was for a girl who "just die," without elaborating, since it was only his dream of her. Helen suddenly warms to him as she slips the expensive gift on her finger and says he can take her home if he wants to, revealing herself to be the whore that his friends told him she was, now that he has found her price. He does not go home with her. After midnight, Cinderella-like, Julio Sal finds himself back in the real world, heading north on a bus for the fertile vineyards of Santa Rosa, knowing "the dream was dead" (WY 266).

Fante was introduced into the Los Angeles community of Filipino writers around 1939 by Carlos Bulosan, author of *America Is in the Heart*, a moving memoir about immigrating from the Philippines. Bulosan's communist affiliation may have had something to do with the overt critique of capitalism in Fante's Filipino stories, a hint of social consciousness absent in his other fiction. Bulosan got in trouble with the *New Yorker* for plagiarism, an issue that appears in several of

Fante's fictions, but particularly in relation to immigrants in love, both Filipino and Italian, for whom expressing the subtleties of desire in a foreign tongue is naturally problematic.

In the Filipino stories, for example, language creates a barrier between the dreamer and the object of his dream. In both stories, the dreamer employs an educated man who plagiarizes poems or love letters for a price, yet another example of the impersonal and commercial nature of American courtship. The use of a mediator to articulate one's love is, of course, right out of *Cyrano de Bergerac*. In "The Dreamer," Fante's alter ego John Lane (the name of the publisher of the 1890s journal the *Yellow Book*) writes what Cristo Sierra cannot say to his dream girl, a torch singer who "went by the name of Charleen Sharron," just as Cyrano spoke and wrote for the inarticulate Christian wooing Roxanne. Unlike Christian, Julio and Cristo are unacceptable because of their race. The language barrier is illusory, disguising the real barrier, a more basic lack of understanding due to prejudice. Cristo Sierra fails to win the torch singer because "Cristo's America was a picture-book land. His ideal American woman was a picture-book heroine." Only when he is spurned by her does he realize that "his symbols were mixed" in thinking that "she was America" (WY 245). In the end he gives up his mistaken conception of America when he recognizes in his landlady Mrs. Flores the woman who loved him all along, and whom he had overlooked because she was dark like him. Only when Mrs. Flores bleaches her hair does he realize his hypocrisy: "For me she do this. Change to blonde. Is wonderful. I am big fool. Twenty years in America. I look for wrong thing. Is not clothes. Is not yellow hair. Is love. Is here," and he taps his heart (WY 250). In his eagerness to become American, Cristo Sierra had been emulating American prejudice and thus denying his own heart, identity and intrinsic worth.

Julio Sal's Cyrano is Antonio Repollo, a college graduate who writes poetry for a paper in Manila. Repollo's letter to Helen is a model of half-literate allusion, archaic diction, and thesaurean malapropism: "Dear Miss Helen: The Immortal Bard has said, 'What's in a name?' I concur. And though I know not how you are yclept for a surname, it matters little. Oh, Miss Helen! Lugubrious is often the way of amour . . . and the aroma of devotion rises from your Humble Servant" (WY 257). Julio's critical judgment is as concise as it is correct: "Steenk!" he says. His own out-pouring in his native Tagalog, which Repollo takes down by dictation, is just as lugubrious but saved by its sincerity. Until, that is, in an effort to impress her, Julio lies that his parents are rich plantation owners. Now it is Repollo's turn to criticize: "You lie, Julio Sal. Your mamma and papa are peasants. They are poor people, Julio Sal. You betray them with such lies. You make them capitalist dogs" (WY 258).

Working alongside Japanese, Mexicans and Filipinos in the canneries and on the docks of Long Beach and Wilmington allowed Fante to step back and compare notes, so to speak, on the experience of being an ethnic minority. It allowed him to separate the issue of ethnicity from the complicated emotions he had for his family, and to turn his attention away from the specific problems of Italian Americans to the larger issue of cultural alienation. One thing he discovered was that other minorities had a far worse time of it than he did.

A story set in the San Pedro harbor of Fante's immigrant experience, "One-Play Oscar" appeared in that citadel of Norman Rockwell Americana the *Saturday Evening Post* in 1950, the year Joseph McCarthy's House Un-American Activities Committee was getting under way. An upbeat story about post-war melting-pot America, this "money-getter" shows Fante deftly defusing potentially explosive material to make it sell. Managing to include everyone and to offend no one, this story avoids the difficult issues of the Cold War by showing international tensions played out by children on the football field. The title character who brings them together is Oscar Lewis, suggesting the anthropologist of the same name, who defined the duty of his profession to be the reporting of urban and rural poverty wherever it is found. The team's name is the All-Americans, and their opponents are the Hooligans and Japanese Settlement. It is a perfect set-up for the easy moral platitudes of a TV sit-com, which the story does in fact resemble, with its successive conflicts and their neat resolutions, climaxing in The Big Game.

Here is Fante at his most Hollywood. INITIAL CONFLICT: New kid on the block tries to join the local football team, but can't kick, pass, catch or block. RESOLUTION: He has the brains and knowledge for coaching and public relations and is allowed to join the team after all. SECOND CONFLICT: The team works well together until their parents forbid them to play together because of political and cultural prejudice — Yugoslav vs. Italian, French vs. German, German vs. Jew, Pole vs. Russian, Chinese vs. Japanese, etc. "But this is America!" protests the coach, the ultimate outcast, a Jew, but the All-American team suddenly erupts into a free-for-all fist-fight parody of the Second World War and its Cold War aftermath. RESOLUTION: Enter patrolman Oscar Lewis of the Harbor Detail to quell the disturbance, who, on being told that the team they are about to play has called him a coward (a politically expedient lie devised by the coach to get Oscar on their side) talks to the parents and diplomatically gets this United Nations team back together just in time for THE BIG GAME: All-Americans trail Japanese Settlement, due to the unfair advantage of their powerhouse 38-year-old, 225-pound player, Irish Hagamoro. Enter 50-year-old, 250-pound Oscar Lewis, whose "one play" incapacitates Irish Hagamoro (and himself), enabling the All-Americans to win the game. MORAL: All Americans, of whatever national or racial origin, must band together to overcome the outside threat. This is about as political as Fante gets.

Aside from these fictional forays into social concerns, Fante seems to have turned all his attention during the 1940s to earning money in Hollywood to raise his family. Looking back on his accounts, Fante later complained that the combined revenue from his first three books, despite good reviews, "wouldn't purchase a lawnmower on today's market" (SL 296). The asset of the books was that they had established his reputation with the paying magazines and provided him with credentials for Hollywood. Good reviews don't feed a family, or pay one's golf fees. The inheritance Joyce had received in 1941, along with another in 1946, put an end to their money worries, but lack of money had been Fante's excuse not to work on his serious writing too long for him to give it up now.

Fante's silence in the 1940s can be explained only in part by the diversions of Hollywood and the war. It could be argued that Fante began to concentrate on the appreciation of life itself, instead of the art that might have been made from it. His son Danny, Fante said, was "worth at least four novels out of my life." [18] Carey McWilliams has also suggested that "John would seem to be pretty much a pre-World-War-II writer. It may have been difficult for him to cope with the kind of world that began to emerge after the war" (SL 293). Joyce Fante has a simpler explanation: "He spent literally years of his life at the golf course and the gambling table" (SL 214). John was playing hooky. After she received her 1946 legacy, "John, relieved of financial pressure, played golf every day until Joyce became pregnant in 1950" (SL 213). During this time Fante turned down work at the studios while pretending to be at work on a novel. "Golf was a vice because it took all day. Between 1946 and 1950 he left the house in the morning at the same time as the men going to work, and returned in the evening in time for dinner. He did this every day, including weekends. Occasionally he sat down at the typewriter . . . Golfing continued to be a problem, interfering with his work, until the middle 1970s, when ulcers on his feet prevented his getting around" (SL 214-15). Nights were spent at the gambling tables, often with William Saroyan, who had earlier spotted Fante's passion for pinball, and whose own gambling addiction ruined both his career and his marriage. Fante played poker often, but not well, and too often for large stakes. "It was nothing for Fante to lose $1,000 at a poker game," recalls Joyce Fante. "He spent literally years of his life at the golf course and the gambling table" (SL 214). Writing to his parents in 1948, Fante claimed to be cutting down on golf, or even quitting it altogether, because there is "no money in golf" (SL 218-19), but he never mentions the more serious gambling problem.

The root of Fante's problem, however, was deeper than these distractions. Fante was producing only a trickle of short stories, about one a year, and several aborted attempts at novels, including something "experimental," in which he claimed to be "remembering the most memorable things." He justifies his inability to put these fragments together by saying, "It is as if all life today has disintegrated into atomic fragments . . . It seemed a suitable novel for our time" (SL 217). Looking at forty, Fante felt a number of burdens descending upon him, and his malingering did not lighten them. A house they bought on Van Ness in Los Angeles had developed termites and was falling apart, a situation he uses to good symbolic effect in *Full of Life*. As in the book, Joyce announced that she wanted to be re-married in the Church and become a Catholic. Worse than this was her announcement in early 1950. As she succinctly puts it: "Fante was aghast to learn that Joyce was pregnant again." She describes what it was like living with Fante at this time:

> He raged for weeks standing over Joyce, hurling obscenities. His friends, Ross Wills and Carey McWilliams, advised an abortion, probably advised him to desert. He wanted Joyce to have an abortion. He decided to leave his family, regarding Joyce and the children as an intolerable obstacle to his success. He changed his mind and stayed, but the bitterness remained. He showed no tenderness or concern for his wife, for weeks staying out late every night, and coming home so drunk that Joyce had to almost carry him up the stairs (SL 225).

To readers of *Full of Life* this candid scene will come as a surprise. "Ironically," Joyce Fante notes, "*Full of Life* depicts a sunny domestic scene with a loving young husband and wife expecting their first baby, the polar opposite of what had really been going on in the Fante household" (SL 225). The irony is compounded by the fact that this most distorted piece of autobiographical prose was published as non-fiction, with John Fante as the protagonist. "The book is fiction, pure and simply," Fante wrote to Mencken, the book's dedicatee. "Now, by virtue of this absurd change in names, the book is no longer fiction but fact" (FM 137).

What is perhaps most striking about Joyce Fante's depiction, to any reader of Fante's work, is the resemblance of Fante's behavior to that of his father in all the fiction about his childhood. As far back as 1935 Fante described the "amusing" experience of looking in the mirror and not recognizing the person he saw there. "Until I remembered Papa without his mustache. I realized then how closely we resemble one another" (SL 93). The basic father-son conflict in all the stories and novels is precisely the denial and recognition of father-son identity. If we add to Joyce Fante's candid (but naturally biased) depiction of her husband's behavior the fact that Fante discovered his father was seriously ill in 1949, and the fact of his father's death in 1950, we may better understand Fante's behavior as a struggle with his own mortality.

In 1934 Fante wrote that marriage was "a bad environment" for a writer because "His worries increase and so do his debts" (SL 73-4). Now he was drawing on this old argument as an excuse for his inability to create, blaming his wife and children instead of himself. Time was running out and he could feel the pressure. In some ways, the most difficult work in his creative life was still to come. He must have known that until he confronted these problems in his fiction, instead of playing golf, gambling or monkeying with experimental prose, he would remain in conflict with everyone, above all himself.

But if Fante could deal with his marital problems in *Full of Life* by negating or denying them, telling the story not as it was but as it was supposed to be in the Eisenhower years, he was well aware that he could not treat his father's death so cavalierly. His father had been an irritation from the time of Fante's childhood, and the resulting boil was the most painful thing in Fante's life. The older Fante got, the more he resembled his father, which meant that dealing with his father's death would mean dealing with his own. By 1954 Fante had sketched out the novel that would do just that, though it would take him another twenty-three years to write *The Brotherhood of the Grape*. He prefaces this sketch with this reflection: "My best efforts in all my books have been directed toward my father, his problems, failures and successes. His death three years ago left a deep heart wound that will never disappear. He is in my thoughts at all times, and I want to do a book about his last days. To the very end of his life, my father was a source of constant worry, specially to my mother. He drank heavily, he gambled, he quarreled, and he had a wandering eye for the ladies right down to his last breath" (SL 231-2).

Although the wounds inflicted on Fante's marriage would never fully heal, a semblance of normality was regained as he began to work out the problems, both in his life and in his fiction. The result would be his most mature piece of fiction. He finished *The Brotherhood of the Grape* in the house he bought with the money made in Hollywood and, ironically, thanks to the enormous success of his most dishonest work, *Full of Life*.

It is perhaps appropriate that the house where he was to complete the book that dealt most directly with his mortality was in the midst of the movie colony at Malibu, on Point Dume.

CHAPTER 8

EPIPHANIES OF INCOMPETENCE

1933 WAS A BAD YEAR
AND MY DOG STUPID

Dreamers, we were a house full of dreamers.
Dominic Molise in *1933 Was a Bad Year*

It can be said of Fante, as it has of Dickens, that "once the lyrical phase is past, the great author proceeds, more cautiously, through empathy."[1] The transition from the lyrical to the empathetic sensibility is perhaps not so much a sign of the great writer's development, as it is a sign of maturity, a necessary defense in the face of failure. Fante never lost his lyrical touch; that was too integral to his style. Nor did he lose his lyrical vision, which is the source of his style. He did, however, shed the excesses of his lyricism, the romantic rancor of *The Road to Los Angeles*, for example, in which Arturo Bandini's frustrated idealism is expressed as cynicism, his fear of kitsch manifested in his rejection of all sentiment. Fante's mature vision is matched by a maturity of style, in which he is undaunted by sentimentality because he is sure of the authenticity of his sentiment. The four books of the Molise quartet show the compassionate side of John Fante, the soft underbelly of the alienated artist Arturo

Bandini when he became a family man and, more importantly, when he is unable to achieve the magnificence of his
uncensored dreams.

The Molise narrators complete the cast of Fante's narrative voices. In the Toscana stories Fante had explored the
conflicts of growing up in a Catholic Italian-American family, and in the Bandini novels he had depicted the artist at
odds with all forms of community. Each of the Molise novels
tells essentially the same story of fathers and sons in conflict
from a different perspective. The bewildered boy of *1933
Was a Bad Year* becomes the bewildered adult of *Full of Life*
and *My Dog Stupid*, who finally achieves the equipoise of a
difficult maturity in *The Brotherhood of the Grape*.

In each case the protagonist narrator gives up a personal ambition to embrace his responsibility to his family,
although it is not easy and never without some sacrifice of
freedom or compromise of ideals. In abdicating their dreams
of romantic transcendence, they inherit human understanding. In each novel the revelation is the same. The
narrator's admission of failure comes in the form of an
epiphany in which he accepts his human incompetence. In
the tragicomic novel *1933 Was a Bad Year*, the narrator
Dominic Molise is an ambitious son who betrays his father,
and is clearly of the same mold as Jimmy Toscana and the
young Arturo of *Wait Until Spring, Bandini*. In *Full of Life*, a
sweet domestic post-war romance, the narrator John Fante
is a man in transition, a son about to become a father. *My
Dog Stupid*, a screenplay-like treatment of the Sixties generation gap, is a domestic farce about the screenwriter Henry J.
Molise and his offbeat family. *The Brotherhood of the Grape*,
the final novel of the Molise quartet, and the most serious in
tone, is an elegy on the death of Henry (without the J.)
Molise's father.

All of the Molise narrators are dreamers locked in mortal combat with their families, escapists with talent (Dominic for baseball, John Fante, Henry J. and Henry Molise for writing), and all end by giving up their idealistic escape routes for the warm security of human family ties, with all its confinements and responsibilities.

Like the Saga of Arturo Bandini, the Molise family quartet begins with a novel set in Colorado, followed by three set in California, roughly giving the same proportions to the quartets as Fante's life. Although they live in three different decades spanning a half century and reflect each era's depression or affluence, the Molise families share more than the same background, Abruzzi origins, Catholic faith, or Italianate name. They share the same malaise, the Molise malaise, which cannot be reduced to socio-economic criteria, though each family is typical of its era. Theirs is the universal malaise of generations, the perpetual gap between parent and child. The child may indeed be father to the man, but that does not allow them to understand each other. In fact, it even complicates matters. A sense of identification can instill both pride and shame, rebellion and reconciliation.

This theme of father-son identity is developed in each book through similar family relationships. The tension between the father with his human faults and frailties, and the son with his still fierce idealism and ambitions, is complicated by the presence of the mother (or wife), with her heady sensuality and stubborn spirituality that sometimes unite and sometimes come between husband and son. By using a different perspective in each novel, Fante anatomizes the father-son relationship from several angles, so that when we view the novels together, we get a circumspect view of the generational conflict. The son's limited perspective in *1933 Was A Bad Year* is expanded by that of the transitional figure of *Full of Life*, a son who becomes a father. *My Dog Stupid* gives us a father beset by alienated sons, while *The Brotherhood of the Grape* shows us the son who, at the death of his own father, must finally abdicate — at the advanced age of fifty — the childish prerogatives of a son and accept the responsibilities of his role as patriarch.

Fante's anatomy of the father-son relationship through this inevitable progression balances these necessary and complementary forces: youth's uncompromising cruelty in the name of speaking the truth, and maturity's impotent wisdom in the face of youth's zealous attack on a lifetime of compromise. It is, in a sense, an internal dialogue — as though Arturo Bandini were arguing with Henry Molise — and the result is a tender and tragic portrayal of both stances of the generational struggle: the rebellious ambition of early potential set against the hard wisdom of eventual failure.

In the two Molise novels published after his death, Fante explores the father-son conflict from antipodal points of view. *1933 Was a Bad Year* is told by a son ambitious to become a baseball player against the wishes of his bricklayer father in the unpromising era of the Depression, while *My Dog Stupid* is told by a father who has fulfilled his ambition to become a screenwriter battling sons who lack any ambition except to join in the revolution of the 1960s. The young Dominic Molise may have a different name than the middle-aged Henry J. Molise (whose son is named Dominic), but they are, like the screenwriter John Fante of *Full of Life*, all avatars of the same character.

The conflict in both books is resolved by the narrator coming to terms with his responsibility and accepting his supposed adversary. The moral is clear. For Fante, the family is the personification of the limits reality places on our ideals, limits which it is impossible (or immoral) to trample in pursuit of one's dreams. The only reward is that the family reminds us that we are human. "We were a house full of dreamers," says the young Dominic Molise. But with so many dreams in one household, conflict is inevitable, and so is the abdication of dreams.

1. Stealing Home: The Moral Dimension of Baseball (*1933 Was a Bad Year*)

One of John Fante's early claims to fame was being portrayed as the pinball maniac Willie in William Saroyan's *The Time of Your Life* (1939). But long before he became a writer, gravitated to Hollywood, where he met Saroyan, and turned to more sedentary activities like pinball, gambling and golf, John Fante's first love was baseball. Growing up in Colorado, Fante attended Regis College, a Jesuit boarding school, where the priests taught ethics in the classroom and stole bases on the playground. But Colorado, with its long winters, was a bad place for a baseball player, and the young John Fante longed for Spring and enough money to take him to California for a try-out with the Chicago Cubs at their training camp on Catalina Island, so that he could follow in the footsteps of Joe DiMaggio and the other Italian-American players who had given their people pride and hope.

Fante did eventually make it to California, but the closest he came to Catalina was working in the canneries around San Pedro and loading supplies onto the boats bound for the island. In time books took the place of baseball, and Fante was dreaming of seeing his name on bestseller lists instead of on the roster of a major league team, and of winning the Nobel Prize instead of the World Series.

These early dreams and how they did not pan out became material for much of his always autobiographical fiction.

In *Ask the Dust* Arturo Bandini made it to Los Angeles and sold his first story, but he still kept up with the box scores of the American League, while "scrupulously" avoiding those of the National League, noting "with satisfaction that Joe DiMaggio was still a credit to the Italian people, because he was leading the league in batting" (AD 11)[2]. In times of stress, when the rent is due or the writing is not going well, Bandini reverts to the dream, stepping into the streets of Los Angeles and swatting home runs over an imaginary fence.

In the stories and novels about his childhood in Colorado baseball plays a more essential role. "Big Leaguer" (1933) and "The Road to Hell" (1937) began to plumb a moral dimension, linking baseball and theft, that continued to fascinate Fante well into the 1960s. In "Big Leaguer" young Jimmy Toscana is befriended by a nun named Sister Agnes who takes him under her wing, following his pitching feats and figuring out his batting average — 599, which, he notes, is "better than Rogers Hornsby" (WY 61) in the years he led the league from 1920 to 1925; in return, he steals her treasured picture of her family. In "The Road to Hell" Jimmy seems to resolve his problem of sticky fingers by resisting the temptation to steal baseballs from a sporting goods store after hearing a priest's sermon (that he claims not to believe) about a boy who stole a catcher's glove and was turned to stone.

Fante returned to this baseball-theft motif in a late story, "In the Spring," published in *Collier's* in 1952. Jake Crane is a boy from Boulder, Colorado who dreams of making headlines with no-hitters and entering the Hall of Fame, but his father is against it. Jake and his friend Burt conspire to run away to Phoenix to try out with the New York Giants. Jake steals fifteen dollars from his father's wallet, Burt steals seven, and they hitchhike through the snow as far as Fort Collins, where they mistakenly hop a freight that takes them back to Boulder. In the boxcar they lose heart, thinking that if they don't make the Giants they'll settle for room and board in the Texas League, the Southern Association, the Southeastern League, the Arizona State League, or even the Three-Eye League (WY 220-1). Jake recalls the sins of his "wasted life," like "all the money I'd stolen from my father's pants, my mother's purse, and my sister's piggy bank" (WY 222). Burt confesses to thefts of hubcaps, library books, and his father's new shoes, which he sold, condemning himself as "a no-good rat" (WY 222). The boys are picked up by the police and returned home, where Jake sobs in dread of facing up to his father, but his father forgives him.

If this story sounds flat, it is. The events unfold sketchily and the return and reconciliation with the father are bloodless. As with other stories written as "money-getters" in the 1940s and 1950s, Fante's heart just wasn't in the story. The monosyllabic Jake Crane is more monochromatic than the vowel-rich Italian Toscanas, Bandinis and Molises, the alter-egos of Fante's serious fiction in which he was not afraid to draw directly from his own experience not only for plot but for emotional texture.

Two years later, Fante was at work on expanding this story into a novel about a "boy who runs away to become a big league ballplayer" (SL 231). When he abandoned the novel in 1954, he wrote to his publisher that he still found the material to be "pretty thin" and not yet "the book I care to write." Maybe later, he quips, "the project will have more balls" (SL 231). He goes on to say that he was quitting the book for another, which would become *The Brotherhood of the Grape* (1977), because in it he could work with the death of his father. "My best efforts in all my books have been directed toward my father, his problems, failures and successes" (SL 231). When Fante returned to the baseball book, completing it sometime in the 1960s, he put this relationship at the center, calling his ballplayer Dominic Molise and drawing on his own emotional experience. This time theft plays a greater role than in "In the Spring," it has "more balls," and his heart is very much in it.

Why this obsessive return to the theft-baseball motif? In all probability there lies a kernel of guilt, an actual event in Fante's childhood that resembles or is represented by one or more of these story situations.

(The pun on "stealing" bases does not explain it; Fante was obsessional about pitching no-hitters and hitting home runs, not running bases.) Whatever the reasons for this obsessive association of baseball with theft, it is clear that it haunted Fante until he achieved a full working-out of the obsession in *1933 Was a Bad Year*.

A third element must be added to the theft-baseball motif. Each of these stories, with the exception of the secular "In the Spring," is also concerned with a boy testing the faith of his Catholic education and with his rejection of and reconciliation with his family and his Italian-American heritage. The theft only brings these conflicts to a climax, becoming the felix culpa that enables him to confess his doubt in God, family or ancestry, and so allows him to return home, contrite and absolved.

Since this theme is touched on in *Wait Until Spring, Bandini*, it is worth repeating that it was a misunderstanding about the title, which refers to baseball and not fertilizer, that led to the revival of John Fante's work in the 1980s, including *1933 Was a Bad Year*, which only appeared posthumously in 1985. In 1978 John Martin at Black Sparrow Press read in the manuscript of Charles Bukowski's novel *Women* a reference to *Wait Until Spring, Bandini*. Martin thought it was a joke about waiting until spring to put a certain well-known brand of fertilizer on the lawn. Bukowski explained that Bandini was not a fertilizer but one of the great characters in literature, Arturo Bandini, who had to "wait until spring" to play baseball, and to his father Svevo, who had to wait until spring to get back to work laying brick.

While there are other references to baseball in *Wait Until Spring, Bandini,* most of them are lyrical passages to establish the mood of the young Arturo getting through the long winter by fantasizing what he will do to impress the girls when the snow melts from the diamond, the backstop and home plate (WB 51).

One girl in particular he associates with his dreams of baseball glory, and that is Rosa Pinelli (as in Babe Pinelli, the famous ballplayer), comparing "the triumph of her tiptoed loveliness" to "a home run with the bases full" (WB 116). Aside from Rosa, the only thing that makes going to the "Sister School" tolerable, Arturo says, is baseball (WY 53). "After his twelfth year the only things in life that mattered were baseball and girls" (WB 114). One of the nuns at school, the tough Sister Celia, has a glass eye that he suspects she got when someone put her eye out with a baseball because one long afternoon when he is alone with her in detention she declares: "Football's my game . . . I hate baseball. It bores me" (WB 52).

One passage does, however, indicate the fuller reworking of the baseball material into its moral dimensions in *1933 Was a Bad Year*. During Catechism exercises, Arturo applies Church dogma to baseball. He wonders if his good-luck superstition of crossing bats with another player, a sure-fire method to get a two-base hit, is a sin, and if so, is it a venial or a mortal sin? When he skipped mass to listen to the World Series, was it a matter of breaking the first commandment: "thou shalt have no strange gods before me?" "Well," Arturo decides, "he had committed a mortal sin in missing mass, but was it another mortal sin to prefer Jimmy Foxx [the 1932 and 1933 American League MVP who led the league in batting with an average of .356, and in 1933 led both leagues in home runs and RBIs] to God Almighty during the world series?" (WB 109-110). This parody of James Joyce's angst-filled reflections *in A Portrait of the Artist as a Young Man* is only half humorous, since the Jesuit-inspired angst in both authors is real enough. Like Arturo Bandini, seventeen-year-old Dominic Molise has delusions of grandeur that involve him in moral dilemmas about the conflicts between his inherited religion and his chosen sport. But whereas Arturo alternates between seeing himself as a great writer and a great batter, Dominic focuses exclusively on baseball. When he first hears of James Joyce, Dominic says, "You mean Jim Joyce, short stop for the St. Louis Browns?" (BY 74). Dominic imagines himself pitching a no-hitter for the Cubs in the World Series, pointing to Italian-American precedents like Hall of Famers Joe DiMaggio and Tony Lazzeri, but also Babe Pinelli, Lou Fonseca, Frank Crossetti, Vic Monte, Ron Pelligrini, Sam La Torra and Boots Zarlingo. Like Bandini, Dominic sees the first step to fame as a pilgrimage west to California, the land of opportunity. His plan is simple: get to the training camp on Catalina Island, improve his fast ball, enter the Hall of Fame. Like his immigrant forefathers, he feels that if only he can escape the land of his birth and get to the land of golden opportunity, the fulfillment of his dreams is sure to follow.

We meet Dominic Molise walking home through "flames of snow" that swirl around him "like a flock of angry nuns" (BY 7), snow that will later come down in "flakes as big as eucharist wafers" (BY 44). The whirl of religious imagery foreshadows the moral blizzards to follow, as does the innocent description of Dominic's cold ears protruding "like Pinocchio's" (BY 8). But it is not Dominic's ears that will protrude as he lies, cheats and steals his way to Catalina, betraying the father who gave him life, and finally coming to appreciate the importance of home.

Wait Until Spring, Bandini opened with a similar scene, Arturo's father Svevo cursing God for the snow that keeps him from laying brick, just as his son curses it for keeping him from throwing fast balls. Like Svevo and Arturo, Dominic Molise is disgusted by his hopeless situation and plots to get out of it. And like the Bandinis who talk to God or themselves, Dominic talks to God, himself and his pitching arm, "his cunning left arm" (BY 10), *sinistra* in Italian, his Southern paw, or, as he calls it, simply The Arm.

The Arm is Dominic's confidant, his alter-ego, his best self and his worst enemy. In victory and defeat they are one, and "one day we shall die and lie side by side in the grave, Dom Molise and his beautiful arm, the sports world shocked, in mourning" (BY 13). A whiff of the Sloan's liniment that he pampers The Arm with can cheer him up and onward, reminding him who he is: "not some crumb bum nobody, but The Arm, the can-do man, the must-be man, the got-it man, not the hey-kid man, but the man with the bucket of sliders, the clutch man, Mister Hall of Fame" (BY 73). The Arm can also bring out the worst in him, like a devil "dangling limp as a serpent" from his shoulder (BY 9), competing with the nuns for Dominic's soul, urging him to give up all faith but in The Arm, even to commit crime for the sake of The Arm: "ease up, Kid, it's loneliness, you're all alone in the world; your father, your mother, your faith, they can't help you, nobody helps anybody, you only help yourself, and that's why I'm here, because we're inseparable." Dominic listens and responds. "Oh, Arm! Strong and faithful arm, talk sweetly to me now. Tell me of my future, the crowds cheering, the pitch sliding across at the knees, the batters coming up and going down, fame and fortune and victory, we shall have it all" (BY 13).

Not only the climate oppresses Dominic Molise and stands in the way of his and The Arm's dream: "Fair weather or foul, certain forces in the world were at work to destroy me" (BY 7). He feels thwarted by the circumstances of his birth. He lives at the foot of the Rocky Mountains, "bad country for a ballplayer, specially for a pitcher who hadn't thrown a ball since October" (BY 9). He is poor, too poor to finance his trip to Catalina without assistance or chicanery. The greatest obstacle is his father, an honest bricklayer from the Abruzzi, who would rather Dominic follow in his footsteps, plying the knuckle-busting family trade "planted in the blood line, blossoming with every new generation" (BY 28), until they can go into the lumber business together. "Lay brick all week long, bust my fingers, and pitch on Sundays," says Dominic with disgust. "So there it was. The whole book. The Tragic Life of Dominic Molise, written by his father. Part One: The Thrills of Bricklaying. Part Two: Fun in a Lumber Yard. Part Three: How To Let Your Father Ruin Your Life. Part Four: Here Lies Dominic Molise, Obedient Son" (BY 30-1).

This scenario bears little resemblance to the "four-part biography" by Damon Runyon that Dominic foresees in the *Saturday Evening Post*, entitled "Triumph over Adversity, the Life of Dominic Molise" (BY 13). But Dominic chooses not to fight his father at this point. "I just sat there soothing my arm, stroking it, calming it down as it whimpered like a child" (BY 31). It is The Arm, "that sweet left arm the one nearest my heart," that justifies Dominic's Machiavellian scheme to steal his father's cement mixer and sell it for the bus fare to Los Angeles.[3] As Dominic sees it, his father's attempt to thwart The Arm, a gift from God, amounts to sacrilege: "my arm, my blessed, holy arm that came from God, and if The Lord created me out of a poor bricklayer he hung me with jewels when he hinged that whizzer to my collarbone" (BY 9).

When it comes to questions of theology and meta-physics, Dominic is capable of asking the same questions that Dimitri Karamazov asked about the senselessness of poverty, disease, crippled children and death, but when his faith is shaken, he prefers to stay on the safe side of the wager, like Pascal, not to risk losing his knuckle-ball, his slider or his rhythm, and start walking batters: "The life of a pitcher was tough enough without losing his faith in God. One flash of doubt might bring a crimp in The Arm, so why muddy the water?" (BY 11).

When it comes to action, Dominic is willing to post-pone solving the mysteries of the universe and follows Dos-toyevsky's Raskolnikov. Metaphysics, existential dilemmas and morals can wait. "Plenty of time for that. Get into the minors, move up to the big time, pitch in the World Series, make the Hall of Fame. Then sit back and ask questions, ask what does God look like, and why are babies born crippled, and who made hunger and death" (BY 11). Dominic Molise has about as much chance of pitching in the World Series as he has of figuring out how many souls can fit on the button of a baseball cap. But he has learned his lessons from the

Jesuits well, mastering the knuckle-balls and sliders of casu-istry.

To get to the big leagues Dominic is willing to sell out his own father. The cement mixer is —aside from the pool cue used to earn money when he is out of work — the most valuable tool his father owns, "that tireless mixer, the Jaeger, his partner" (BY 101). Peter Molise "would never own more than the clothes on his back, his sack of mason's tools, his concrete-mixer, and his favorite pool cue" (BY 30), making his son's betrayal all the more cold-blooded. To justify his betrayal, Dominic invokes not DiMaggio but Machiavelli, explaining that the end of putting The Arm to work doing "the work of God" (BY 10) is justified by the means of stealing from his father. "Bullshit, you thief," says his friend and scrupulous co-conspirator Ken, as Dominic signs his name on the transfer-of-ownership line with the hair-split-ting comment that it is not really forgery: "Isn't my name Molise? I'm just changing my first name" (BY 110). As though to steal one's inheritance were not theft, only the claiming of "community property" (BY 105).

There is also the little matter of his having discovered lipstick on his father's collar. This echo from *Wait Until Spring, Bandini* explains why Arturo "for vague reasons he could never understand" always associated adultery with bank robbery (WB 113). Dominic's father's sin makes his own misdemeanor pale in comparison: "So it was stealing, so it was wrong. Was it as wrong as my father two-timing my mother? . . . Did he believe he could go un-punished?" (BY 108). As though the sins of the son would be looked on favorably in comparison with the sins of the father; as though the son has the divine right to punish the father. When Dominic first saw the lipstick stains, he wanted to dissociate himself entirely from his father, "to spew him, the sneak of him, the cheapness of him, the betrayal, the death in him, myself in him" (BY 32). Yet in his attempt to punish the father, he actually succeeds in cementing their identity, the "sneak" in them, the "cheapness," and the "betrayal."

Just before stealing the cement mixer, Dominic gives his father one more chance to reconsider and send him to Catalina. He begins his plea by appealing to their common Italian heritage, invoking DiMaggio, Pinelli, and the others. "People, Papa! Human beings like you and me. Sons of tailors and butchers and fishermen. Of barbers and coal miners. Italian-Americans from homes like ours, from all over the country in this land of opportunity" (BY 98). His father is not convinced; it's not that he doesn't think Dominic is "good enough" for the Cubs, but that he's "not *tough* enough." "Those men are like iron," he gently explains to his son. "They're hard, tough. They'll grind you in the dirt. They'll kill you. They'll break your heart" (BY 99). Ignoring his father's concern, Dominic is insulted: "he was telling me I was weak, my own father, and it depressed me to realize he was judging me on the basis of himself. He was a great bricklayer and a failure; I was a great ball player and I would fail too. Like father, like son. With this difference: he was from Torricella Peligna, a foreigner, and I wasn't . . . Stones, goats, bread, wine: he understood those things. Not baseball" (BY 99-100).

Having begun by appealing to their common heritage, Dominic concludes by making a cruel distinction: his father is an Italian peasant, he an American superstar. Like Peter who denied Christ the Son, Dominic the son denies Peter Molise the father. Worse than the cowardice of Peter's denial, however, was the greed of Judas's betrayal.

While committing the crime, this dawns on Dominic, but he has gone too far, he can't go back. As he hitches the cement mixer to a borrowed truck, he is observed by his Grandma Bettina, who has from the beginning of the novel been an omnipresent figure with her "fleshless" hands and "skin at her temples so pale and transparent you could almost see inside her head" (BY 16). Part wraith and part sibyl, Grandma Bettina is able to pierce his conscience with her eerie whispers. She speaks only Italian, the ancestral language, foretelling the corrupting power of "the rich promise of golden America, land of equality and brotherhood, stinking like a plague!" (BY 16). To her the Sloan's liniment on Dominic's arm reeks, the "smell of a sick country. Hear my words: one day this stench will cover all the land" (BY 17).

What she says is all oracle and insult. Part conscience and part social critic, she damns him and the American dream that has driven him to crime and, worse, to betraying his father. Watching him steal the mixer, her comment is a lament: "So this is the American way . . .To kill the soul of a man, and then chop off his hands. What will my son do without this machine?" (BY 112). But Dominic's gaze is firmly fixed and he keeps on going. "Looking straight ahead, I heard her speak of first and last things, of birth and death, of crime and damnation, of Judas and the fall of honor among sons" (BY 113). He gets past Grandma Bettina, but he is not able to get beyond his own ancestral conscience, which she and her curses represent.

On the way to sell the mixer Dominic must first drive through the cemetery where the grave of his grandfather Giovanni Molise presents a more formidable obstacle. "Had he stood there alive, I could have defied him as easily as I had his wife in our alley. But he was dead, terribly dead, and I was afraid of his helplessness" (BY 114). Confronted by his grandfather's grave, Dominic is helpless. He may be able to sell out the living, but he cannot sell out the dead. Parents are one thing, ancestors another. That his grandfather's gravestone had been fashioned by his father's hands makes it clear that to betray one is to betray all in the bloodline of the Molise generations. "The monument was my father's pride and joy. Off and on for two years he had worked on it in our shed, reducing a huge chunk of marble into the graceful cross, chipping and polishing the stone until it was as smooth as human skin" (BY 114). Dominic considers bypassing it, but he is in "a forest of monuments, and the only way around was by driving over the graves of a hundred other poor souls at peace there" (BY 114). He stops the truck, turns it around, and returns the cement mixer.

Dominic's failure of nerve in the graveyard is a moral victory. The vision of his grandfather is an epiphany about what it is to be human, to enjoy the simple pleasures, as Giovanni Molise enjoyed them: "a lover of walnuts and sunflower seeds . . . not a learned man but a scholar who smiled all the time, pleased to be just a human being in the world" (BY 114-15). In pursuit of the American dream, Dominic had almost stooped to "blight" the dream that his grandfather pursued by immigrating to America in the first place. Even The Arm rebels at this betrayal because it too is part of the grandfather: "Go back, The Arm said, turn this thing around, you fool, before I drop off; turn around and go back and forget Catalina, lay brick with your father, dig ditches, be a bum if you must, but turn away from this wickedness" (BY 115). By relenting (while not quite repenting), Dominic admits: "The lure of fame and fortune had turned me into a madman" (BY 115).

By turning back, Dominic Molise admits defeat by "forces in the world . . . trying to destroy" him. Assuming those forces to be outside himself, matters of climate, poverty and his father's opposition, he comes to realize that the most powerful forces are inside him: his conscience and the weight of his heritage.

The climax of the novel comes when he must confront his father. Dominic tries to salvage the situation with a lie: he was just going to buy some new equipment. Plucking the owner's certificate from Dominic's pocket, Peter Molise points out his son's incompetence: "You don't even know how to steal good . . . You forged my name on the wrong line" (BY 116-17). His father slaps him, challenging him to fight like a man. "If you can steal from me you can fight me" (BY 117). Dominic refuses, so his father throws the first punch and draws blood. Seeing that he has harmed his own flesh and blood, Peter Molise gasps in dismay and strikes himself on the cheek. "Mamma mia!" he says, pressing handsful of snow to his son's nose, which is bleeding and, like Pinocchio's, swollen.

The conflict having come to blows, Dominic marvels: "Maybe the bloody nose was responsible, but for once, we stopped being father and son and became friends, and I was able to tell him of my hopes and despairs, the boredom of poverty, the chance to leave home and try my hand at pro ball" (BY 118). Dominic's confession is ultimately self-serving, since it is more about his frustration than his transgression. His father, himself a gambler at cards and pool, understands the son's ambition and promises to try to come up with the money to get him to Los Angeles. Dominic drops his father off at the Onyx Bar, where we assume he is going to gamble for the fifty dollars Dominic needs for bus fare and pocket money.

Meanwhile, Dominic hurries to tell his friend Ken the good news, exulting in the "clean, sweet feeling" Fante always associates with coming out of confession (BY 120).

Not only has Dominic admitted to his father how low he was willing to stoop to realize his dream, while claiming his integrity for resisting the temptation to actually sell the mixer, but his father has wholly absolved him. Not only does he not have to say any Our Fathers, but his father has promised to get the money. But life is rarely that simple or that generous. In an ironic O. Henry twist, Peter Molise gets the money not by gambling but by selling the cement mixer himself for twenty-five dollars. Dominic's heart sinks because it's only a dollar more than the bus fare. His father's sacrifice is not enough, but Dominic figures he can count on his friend Ken for the rest.

Up until the theft Ken had been The Arm's caretaker and masseur and Dominic's fellow-dreamer, his co-conspirator in the scheme to get to "a certain tropical setting off the coast of California, owned by a chewing gum tycoon" (BY 92). Kicked out of prep school in Boston for cutting classes to go to Fenway Park, Ken keeps framed under glass, as a religious relic, an autographed band-aid "with Gehrig's dried blood and little hairs from Gehrig's thumb stuck to the adhesive" (BY 45). Ken's faith in the scheme had occasionally faltered, and stalled when it came to "borrowing" the mixer, raising a voice of reason, cowardice, sanity and conscience. When Dominic approaches him for the money, Ken has caved in to his rich Republican father's veto of the trip. "The trip was off," thinks Dominic. "No Kenny, no trip. I was too stupid to make it alone, I might go the wrong way, end up in Torricella Peligna, where I belonged" (BY 125), and where he would have to play soccer or boccie. In other words, Dominic's failure to realize his own imagined destiny threatens to reverse the real accomplishment of Giovanni Molise when he came to America.

Admitting the defeat of his dream, Dominic decides to get realistic and buy back the mixer that his father sold to finance his own less than realistic all-American dream. The Arm whimpers, "crying like a spoiled child, calling me chicken, a welcher" (BY 125), but Dominic consoles it and tells it to be patient. When Dominic gets to the service station, the mixer's engine is already dismantled and the buyer refuses to sell. All at once Dominic realizes the sacrifice Peter Molise has made by giving up his dream of going into the lumber business, and it saddles him with an intolerable burden of guilt. When his father gave him the money, Peter Molise acknowledged the strength of Dominic's left arm. Only now, seeing the dismantled mixer, does Dominic realize that the mixer was his father's right hand. All Dominic can do is weep and pay homage to the continuing sacrifice of his father for him, a prodigal son:

> I picked up the roll of money and walked back to the mixer. It was beat up and banged like my father's hands, a part of his life, so strangely ancient, as if from a far country, from Torricella Peligna. I put my arms around it and kissed it with my mouth and cried for my father and all fathers, and sons too, for being alive in that time, for myself, because I had to go to California now, I had to make good (BY 127).

At the very moment that Dominic Molise finally recognizes the error of his ways and tries to make compensation to his father, he is forced to leave the security of his family and to pursue his unrealistic dream on his own.

As we know, the John Fante who left Colorado to become a baseball player became a writer in California instead. When he returned home, it was his stories and books that he was to brag about, but his competitive edge had come from baseball. In "Home, Sweet Home" (1932), Fante's second published story, he is living the lonely life of the writer in Los Angeles, missing the warmth of his family, the affection (and food) of his mother, and the acceptance of his father. He imagines a trip home (I am tempted to say that mentally he "steals" home), where he finds his little brother bragging over spaghetti and wine about pitching a three-hit game. Fante can't resist pointing out that he would have pitched a two-hit game. "My father will not answer, for he knows I am a better pitcher than my brother, and my brother knows it too, but I have put baseball behind me now, and they know it, and they respect me, and they will not comment" (WY 154). More than anything else, Fante wanted the acceptance and respect of his father. What he could not get from baseball, he got from literature.

Baseball has been used ad nauseam as a symbol for the American dream, especially in the movies. As a screenwriter, Fante was aware of the easy scenarios; and as a writer of serious fiction, he was also aware of the power of the cliché, especially in the way it gives unrealistic hope to certain classes, like the sons of working class immigrants. Fante's contribution to the motif is to show the corrupting power of such boyish dreams, how the moral fabric and the family structure can be undermined in the pursuit of an innocent cliché. Fante deals with these serious themes with the lightest touch, with incisive humor and self-irony, and without ever putting his protagonists on the playing field.

As the girl Dominic Molise idolizes says in *1933 Was Bad Year*: "A dream is like a baseball. You have to remove the horsehide and unravel all the string before you get to the core" (BY 80). She should know, she's a psychology major at Colorado U. What she does not say is that once you've unraveled the dream to understand it, you can't play with it anymore. It's like plucking the mystery out of Hamlet. In unraveling the dream of baseball in his writing, Fante was putting his playing days behind him in order to build something that would, like his father's stone bridges and fireplaces, last. Dominic Molise doubts that Ken's autographed band-aid of Lou Gehrig will ever be worth much because "Old ball-players fade away fast" (BY 46). The work of even modest stonemasons and writers endures a little longer.

2. Walter Mitty in Malibu: *My Dog Stupid*

In the Molise chronology, *My Dog Stupid* comes after *Full of Life*. But like *1933 Was a Bad Year* this brilliant short novel was written in the 1960s, deals with the theme of an attempted betrayal that results in an epiphany of incompetence, and climaxes in a gas station.

In *My Dog Stupid* Fante examines the conflicts of family life from an entirely new perspective, the father's. Always before he had written from the point of view of the ambitious son, who could see only the human frailty and failure of his father.

Even *Full of Life* brings us only to the moment when the son becomes a father; it does not explore the difficulties of fatherhood itself. The third person narrative of *Wait Until Spring, Bandini* had, to some extent, allowed Svevo Bandini's side of the story to be told, but the narrative is still closer to Arturo and his perspective on the father's infidelity. It is curious, however, that in both *Wait Until Spring, Bandini* and *My Dog Stupid*, the catalyst for the domestic reconciliation is a dog. In each case, a dog reminds the man of the house of his identity as the man of the house, and of his own humanity. [4]

The most striking similarities, though, are between *My Dog Stupid* and *1933 Was a Bad Year*. Both the size of a novella, they are meditative in tone, frank in diction that reflects the decade in which they were written, parallel in several elements of plot, and similar in their themes of a dream deferred. In both novels, the father gives up his dream for his incorrigible son Dominic, though Dominic is the narrator in only one. Chronologically, Dominic of the earlier novel should be Henry J. Molise of the later novel, but by naming both sons Dominic, Fante suggests the perpetual nature of the struggle between fathers and sons. Although the relationship between Henry J. Molise and his own father does not enter into the novel until the last few pages, it is clear that he is getting back from his son Dominic, "the family's prime screwball," whatever hell he may have given his father when he was a Dominic-like son himself in the 1930s.

The time and place have changed, as has the economic standing of the Molise family, but they have not left their problems behind. They have made the symbolic journey from Colorado to California, and have risen out of the poverty of the Depression to the affluence of the 1960s, but the Molise malaise is still the long and difficult process of coming to grips with the discrepancy between the spiritual ideals and material aspirations of youth on the one hand, and the absurdly inadequate compromises of adulthood. *My Dog Stupid* shows Henry J. Molise first denying and then accepting the inevitability of the nature of compromise.

Henry J. Molise is an unemployed but prosperous writer of "cop-out scenarios for fifteen hundred a week (when employed!)" (WR 109). He has provided well for his family, who don't understand him and even blame him for selling out. They live in a "Y-shaped so-called rancho" house in Malibu, which is paid for, and he drives a 1967 Porsche 356, which is not. Competent at providing for his family, he is less able to take care of his own dreams, for which he has somehow lost the fervor along the way. His Porsche is the symbol of his independence, but this is in danger of being repossessed, since he is four payments behind on it. He is also prone to getting lost in his own neighborhood, unable to find his way home in the rain without calling his wife. He lives on "a thrust of land jutting into the sea like a tit in a porno movie, the northern tip of the crescent that forms Santa Monica Bay" (WR 9) called Point Dume, an appropriate name for the point to which Henry J. Molise has come in his emotional life.

Molise is the Rodney Dangerfield of his own household. He gets no respect from his children who despise him for selling out to Hollywood but nonetheless enjoy the affluence of his prostitution. His wife, too, tends to berate him. To escape these ungrateful burdens, Molise decides to sell his Porsche in exchange for a ticket on Al Italia to Rome, "with seventy thousand bucks in my jeans and a new life on the Piazza Navonne, with a brunette for a change" (WR 11).

In the Old Country of his ancestors, he fantasizes, he will live a life of leisure, sipping cappuccino and writing what he wants to write, instead of the pablum he has had to turn out for Hollywood to support his family. In the end, however, he realizes that he can do so only at the expense of giving up everything he loves. Only by betraying his wife and children can he escape his adult responsibilities and replenish the romantic dreams of his youth.

The novel opens with Henry J. Molise driving home in his Porsche on a dark and stormy night from a studio conference with a producer who wants him to write, on speculation, "a film about the Tate Murders 'in the manner of *Bonnie and Clyde,* with wit and style.'" He gets lost in the neighborhood he has lived in for twenty years only a couple

of blocks from home, and has to call his wife from a telephone booth, asking her "to come and show me the way
home" (WR 9). When she arrives to fetch him, she brings
along a .22 pistol because there is "something terrible in the
yard" (WR 10). In the rain and the dark, Molise and his wife
mistake the "dark piled-up mass" for a bear, a burro, a sheep,
a lion, or "one of the kids," but on closer examination they
discover that it is "just a dog" (WR 11). As it turns out, it is
not just a dog, it is the catalyst that brings the absurdity of
Henry J. Molise's existence into focus. The family adopts the
dog, in spite of its antisocial antics, and Molise reluctantly
assents. As the dog's antisocial behavior escalates, complicating his life, his affection for the stray dog that appeared,
like a brute changeling on his lawn, grows and eventually
replaces his estranged family in his affections. Stupid has a
will of iron and a hard-on to match, humping all the wrong
objects of desire and complicating Molise's life. Yet Molise
comes to identify with the dog and calls it Stupid. In the end,
it is his dog Stupid who becomes his center of meaning and
causes him to give up his idea of Rome, restoring him to his
family, and to himself.

Henry J. Molise is an existential anti-hero, common to
the 1960s, whose domestic angst is played out in an atmosphere of farce. Having lost the meaning of his existence, he
seems to have two alternatives, neither of which appeals to
him. He can retreat to the romanticism of his youth by
fleeing to Rome, or he can live a life of quiet desperation in
the lukewarm embrace of his family. Like other Fante protagonists, Molise has striven to overthrow the superstition
of his mother's religion and his father's ancestry. He has
succeeded in rejecting the Old World values and in embracing the American dream of material success. When this
dream dissolves, however, he has nothing left to put in place

of the Old World values, except the relativism he has absorbed in Hollywood. And he feels the abyss. His fantasy of going to Rome, in fact, underscores his nostalgia for the Old World values.

In America, land of upward (and in Fante's case) westward mobility, a man's essence — his success and freedom — is symbolized by the car he drives. Automobiles always play an important role in Fante's fiction. In America, land of upward (and in Fante's case) westward mobility, a man's essence — his success and freedom — is symbolized by the car he drives. In "The Orgy," for example, published posthumously with *My Dog Stupid* in *West of Rome*, the black hod-carrier Speed Blivin's success in his sideline as stock market investor is evidenced by the "snazzy yellow Marmon touring car" he drives to the work site to quit his job (WR 157). Speed's parting gift to Nick is a gold mine called Yellow Belly, as a reminder of the yellow Marmon. Nick brings his crony Frank Gagliano into the deal because he owns an old Reo truck, "a bone-rattling machine with solid rubber tires and chain-driven wheels" (WR 165). Nick's wife, who is sensitive to the power of automobiles, refuses to ride in Gagliano's truck: "'An atheist's car!' she said. 'I'd rather walk.'" Nick ridicules her superstition: "You think the car don't believe in God, either?" (WR 165). But he is just as superstitious as she. Seeing only cowardice in the mine's name of "Yellow Belly," he and Gagliano change its name to "Old Red Devil," unwittingly showing that the mine's true purpose is not to strike it rich but to serve as an excuse to indulge their weekend independence by drinking and entertaining the woman who arrives at the mine in a car that fits her character: an old black Cadillac with too many miles on the odometer.

In the Bandini books Arturo is impressed when he sees his father Svevo riding in a rich widow's car. Everyone Arturo knows drives beat up rattletraps with busted fenders and no tops, like Camilla with her "1929 Ford roadster with horsehair bursting from upholstery, battered fenders and no top" (AD 62). When Arturo publishes his novel, he buys a 1929 Ford with no top that goes like the wind (AD 152). Only the inaccessible rich drive dream cars, like the woman who gets out of a black automobile in front of the Biltmore, or the actors and actresses Bandini brags about knowing, who drive Dusenbergs, LaSalles and Marmons. So when Henry J. Molise drives up in a Porsche 356, we know Arturo would have been impressed.

In *My Dog Stupid*, vehicles are the stuff of dreams fulfilled: powerful Porsches, classic Packards, vogue T-Birds, rare Avantis, and sporty MGs. As a true Californian ("true" meaning transplanted), Henry J. Molise sees his his car as a symbol for all that he has become and all that he would like to be. His Porsche (an import — never mind that it is not paid for) is a two-seater. His son Dominic, on the other hand, drives a 1940 Packard, a big, expensive-to-maintain classic, with plenty of room for back-seat pleasures; the car reeks of marijuana smoke and is littered with panties. The father-son conflict is expressed here through the automobiles they drive. The vehicular conflict that began in the 1930s with the sale of a cement mixer so that the young Dominic could get rich and win a girl like Dorothy Parrish who drove a LaSalle, continues in the 1960s with a young Dominic who has wrecked Henry J. Molise's previous classics, a T-Bird and an Avanti.

For the true Californian like Henry J. Molise, a car is not just a mode of transport, it is a vehicle of transcendence, not just a way of going "varoom varoom" to the Safeway, but a way out of his humdrum existence into a Walter Mitty world of imaginary satisfactions. His Porsche 356 is one aspect of his identity that he has been able to buy with the lucre of his screen writing hack work, and so become the image of the "wild carefree author." The two-seater has room for a woman or his dog, but not children, parents, furniture or other domestic baggage. For maximum driving pleasure it must be driven alone. There is some pleasure in the fleeting glances of a pedestrian audience (of which he, the son of a bricklayer viewing his own success, is one). Its value is based on its powerful forward gears (not the single reverse gear of a retrospective past) taking him glamorously into the future, his personal status machine and time-traveling capsule. In moments of cynicism Henry J. Molise would gladly exchange his four children "for a new Porsche, or even an MG GT '70" (WR 11), not only because cars are more responsive, but because they symbolize a freedom and independence he does not have.

> . . . varoom varoom up the highway, roaring past a surf creamy as enzyme detergent, the wild carefree author, filling his days with exquisite sensuality. But the wind in my face brought back the only reality and I choked over an ever-returning memory of Rome, a cup of cappuccino at the little table on the Piazza Navonne, a raven-haired girl at my side, eating watermelon and laughing as she spat the seeds to the pigeons (WR 34).

But when he actually sells the Porsche, trading this tangible symbol in for a real ticket to Rome, he gives up "the only reality" he has, his family, for the phantom and unrealistic fantasy of a faceless brunette. In doing so, he not only betrays his family, he abdicates the vehicle of his independence. When he backs out of the trip, he loses both his dream car and his dream escape.

He also gains a firmer grip on "the only reality" of his life as a family man, realizing that he has after all given up only symbols, fantasies and an imaginary identity. What he is left with in the end, like all of Fante's characters, is a poignant reminder of his mortality and the bitter-sweet recognition that he is — like his parents, wife, children, *pets*, and even his idols the great writers —only human. Watching an old movie on television, he feels vague intimations of his own mortality: "The movie gave me a clue. It was literally a film about the dead. It starred Carole Lombard, who was dead. So were the others in the cast, John Barrymore, Lionel Barrymore, Eugene Palette and the supporting players. There they were, moving on film, now rotting in their graves, poor, lovely, beautiful creatures, and it was very sad" (WR 101).

1933 Was a Bad Year concluded with the disassembled concrete mixer held hostage by the owner of a gas station who refused to sell it back. *My Dog Stupid* concludes with the owner of a gas station holding Stupid hostage. Molise offers a twenty-five dollar reward, the same amount Dominic offered for the cement mixer, but the owner holds out for $300 because Stupid is an Akita, an expensive breed, even if he is a foundling bastard without papers. Unlike Dominic, Henry J. Molise is affluent enough to pay the ransom but only because he still has the cash from selling the Porsche. "What's Rome if you have to live with the betrayal of your own son? . . . My duty is clear. God knows I have my faults, but I won't stand accused of disloyalty to my children" (WR 135). Like Dominic's father in *1933 Was a Bad Year*, Henry J. Molise (who is, after all, Dominic's father in this book, too) is willing to give up his dream trip to Rome, not as he says for his son Jamie, but for himself and the Stupid in himself. In doing so, he fulfills the promise of the young Dominic at the end of *1933 Was a Bad Year* to "make good" and pay back his father, at least in spirit.

The ransom of Stupid turns out to have one more catch. While at Griswold's Auto Repair, Stupid has fallen in love with a pig. Not wanting to break up the happy couple, Molise pays another $300 for the pig, whom he names Mary after his mother. "The smiling pig never took her eyes off me and I knew we were going to make out fine . . . She gave off comfortable bourgeois vibrations of stability and faith in the Holy Ghost. She was my mother all over again" (142). The typical Fante Holy Family is complete. Stupid is as stubborn and randy as his father, and Mary the pig is as earthy and ethereal as his mother. In *1933 Was a Bad Year* Dominic Molise is told by his grandmother that his mother is "a donkey, a cow, a pig, a chicken, a she-goat" (BY 17). When Molise takes the pig and Stupid into his comfortable American home to care for them, he is embracing the values of his lost past. In the end, Henry realizes that Stupid fills an emotional gap in his life, the result of his modernization, his Americanization. When he felt this alienation most, he thought of escape to the Old Country (even if it is the modern city of Rome and not the village in the Abruzzi where his family came from). But by accepting Stupid, and Stupid's new love, Molise accepts the memory of his father and mother, just as he wishes his own son could accept him. With the remaining $800 he got for the Porsche, Molise builds the weird couple a home of their own in his back yard.

Having come to grips with his origins, Molise is better equipped to handle his own less than ideal life in the present, including the demands of his own family. He has had an epiphany of his own incompetence, trading in his delusions of grandeur for "the only reality." His epiphany cuts through his own limited failures, exposing those of his ancestors, his parents, and his progeny. The vision of human incompetence is summed up in the pig's eyes, which throb "with pity, confusion and hopelessness" (WR 142). This epiphany is cathartic in its acceptance of absurdity, because there is so much tenderness in Molise's identification with the brute wisdom of the pig, the brute will of the dog, and his own imprisonment in brute circumstance.

In echo of Nick Carraway at the end of the pier in *The Great Gatsby*, Molise stares off from Point Dume on the western shore of the New World, reflecting on its promise as well as what was left behind in the Old World, and realizes through his own experience the loss that has occurred:

> I stared beyond the house to the horizon of the blue bay. Glinting in the sunlight, a 747 droned remotely as it made the wide circle over the sea and looped back to the mainland, heading east for Chicago, New York or even Rome. My gaze dropped to the white roof of the Y-shaped house, past the organdie curtains of Tina's window to the branches of a big ponderosa that still held the remnants of a tree-house Dominic had built when he was a boy, and then my eyes shifted to the rusted bumper of Denny's car protruding from the garage, and above that to the tattered net of Jamie's basketball hoop... Suddenly I began to cry (WR 142-3).

Not all of the questions raised in "the Y-shaped house" have been answered, nor have all the conflicts been resolved. But there has been a renewal of faith in "the only reality" of family and home. It has come at the expense of his dream of rising phoenix-like in an Al Italia 747 above and beyond his children, but he can now support his own children's more down to earth aspirations of building tree houses and slam-dunking basketballs. His tears are therefore not so

much for the death of his dreams, as for the possibilities of
his children's.

Chapter 9

Home Is Where the Hearth Is

Full of Life
and The Brotherhood of the Grape

Novel-writing is like building a house. If you do a bad job in
the slightest detail the error is enough to ruin the whole.

John Fante in 1936

1. The Child Between: *Full of Life*

The two novels in the Molise quartet about the epiphany of
failure, *1933 Was a Bad Year* and *My Dog Stupid*, themselves
failed to find publishers. The other Molise novels, *Full of Life*
and *The Brotherhood of the Grape*, although they too are concerned with failure, were Fante's greatest publishing successes. Separated by a quarter century, this pair of novels
about the birth of a son and the death of a father share the
central motif of building — a hearth in *Full of Life* and a
smokehouse in *The Brotherhood of the Grape* — as a way of
cementing relationships within the family, especially between fathers and sons.

    Full of Life is a sweet domestic comedy portraying the
simple pleasures of life in an urban setting during the post-
war baby boom. While the Fante family in the book resembles the Toscanas and Bandinis of the earlier books, they

seem somewhat reduced to quotidian proportions, less mythically alive. A series of sit-com squabbles with a large element of slapstick, the plot proceeds smoothly from conflict to resolution with only a hint here and there of the deeper tragic undertones that the Fante family was experiencing in real life. Still, these hints of an underlying clash between husband and wife, and between father and son, give the book a poignant quality that it might not otherwise have had.

The narrator is John Fante, who bears a striking resemblance to Jimmy Toscana and Arturo Bandini, although now he is Gianni the deferential son and uxorious husband, and battles termites instead of crabs. A screenwriter who would like to be a novelist again, he is having difficulty facing up to the fact that he is going to be a father. His expectant wife Joyce, who is the only new character, is planning to convert to the Catholic faith. Life becomes complicated for the young couple when the kitchen floor of their big house collapses under the weight of their "big plans" (FL 9). When they discover they have termites, they decide that they cannot really afford to pay for the repairs, so John goes to San Juan (Roseville) to ask his father, who is a builder, for his help. Old Nick Fante has other ideas. He is set on building a house for his daughter-in-law and grandson-to-be on a nearby piece of fertile ground which a paisano has promised to sell to him cheap. Nick Fante may be older now, but is just as stubborn as Guido Toscana or Svevo Bandini, and more sentimental. John finally convinces his father that he has a life of his own in Los Angeles, and Nick gives up his dream of building a house for his son's family, but not without a fight and not without uttering a prophecy: "Some day you'll have sons — thirty-five years from now, forty. You remem-

ber what your Papa said tonight: they hurt you every time"
(FL 58).

John Fante has already felt a foreshadowing of this
sorrow in the way his wife has been treating him lately.
Before her pregnancy, she would help him through the
birth pangs of writing, taking his manuscripts to bed with
her and spending hours "pruning and fixing and making
marginal notes," giving his work "a beginning and a middle
and an end," and "at first I couldn't have done it alone" (FL
16). But now she spills coffee on his manuscripts and regards
him "with coldness —the ignorant one, the fool who had
passed by in the night, a person no more, malefic, absurd"
(FL 9). Now she no longer wants to read anything he has
written, but only Dr. Arnold Gesell's *Infant and Child in the
Culture of Today*. She refuses to sleep with him, and he
contemplates either having an affair or leaving her. "But I
didn't leave. You can't leave them when they are in that
condition. It requires great tact. Nor should you make rash
statements. It requires great forbearance, but you can't
leave" (FL 124). Just as Joyce helped him through the birth
pangs of writing, John will have to help her through her
pregnancy.

Still, it is not easy, and their relationship suffers. "Like
a stone," says John, "the child got between us" (FL 16). Other
elements symbolized by stone also come between them,
including Joyce's newfound faith in the Church of St. Peter
(founded on *petrus*), and the fireplace that Nick (whose
middle name is Peter) decides to build for his grandchild
instead of repairing the floor, as he had promised.

After spending weeks sitting around the house, drinking wine and thinking and making John write down the
story of his Uncle Mingo, Nick Fante decides (two-thirds of
the way through the book) that what his grandchild needs

is a big stone hearth of Arizona flagstone. As for the kitchen floor, "That's no job for me," says the diminutive patriarch. "Get a carpenter" (FL 119). Nicholas Peter Fante is a stonemason, not a carpenter, and it is characteristic of the old man that he disdains repair as menial labor. Such patchwork is not for him. A dreamer in the true Toscana-Bandini-Molise mold, Nick must have something to build from the bottom up, and on a grand scale. Joyce, pregnant and prospective, enthusiastically falls in with Nick's plans, forming an alliance with her father-in-law, to the exclusion of the father of the child and the supposed master of the house. "They were ranged against me, and a wall separated us, a fireplace" (FL 121). Despite her husband's worries about her advanced condition, she shovels sand, mixes mortar, breaks the beautiful black stone with a hammer in the front yard and drags it into the house, where Nick practices the trade he brought with him from the Abruzzi.

The novel, as the title suggests, is as much the story of Nick Fante and his fireplace as it is of Joyce Fante and her pregnancy. Baby and fireplace become the central figures in the book, along with the collusion between the father-in-law and daughter-in-law who conceive them. She is big with child, he with his own creation, and both are "full of life." The hearth, which is the heart of the book, looms large as a symbol of domestic warmth, huge and indestructible. Joyce enthusiastically supports the project: "We'll be so warm and cozy," she says. As John points out, the great hearth is excessive, if not useless, in the California climate, especially "when the temperature drops to twenty-five below zero, and eighteen feet of snow paralyzes traffic on Wilshire Boulevard" (FL 118). But everything Nick Fante does is excessive. The opening of the novel announced, "It was a large house because we were people with big plans"

(FL 9), and Nick Fante's addition is suitably "massive," twice the size of the one he tears out of the wall because his grandson "don't want no Los Angeles fireplace. He wants a fireplace his Grandpa built" (FL 118). Only a furnace will suffice to show that it was built by Nick Fante.

John's call for economy and common sense at a time of affluence and big plans sounds cynical to his expansive father and to his expanding wife. Practically, a kitchen floor would better serve the young family's immediate needs. But Nick Fante is no pragmatist, despite his peasant habits of thrift when it comes to food, clothing and transportation. Proud, stubborn and sentimental, not unlike Joyce in her present state, Nick has decided that a sturdy hearth (or heart) will keep a family together far better and longer than the mere shell of a house, no matter how structurally sound. It is a view that John considers "superstitious and ignorant," but it is also unassailable. The present requires a kitchen floor, but the future demands a fireplace. Stone is something a man can count on, says Nick, just as his wife counted on the rock of the Church to get them through the trials of their life together, even more than on her husband. While child and fireplace symbolize the future life of the family, Joyce herself is preparing for even more distant eventualities.

As the child grows in her womb, so does Joyce's faith, no longer "a whim" or "passing fancy" (FL 99), and so does his father's fireplace. All three now come between Joyce and John, but she is sure that all three promise to bind and sustain them in the future. While Joyce and the fireplace grow sturdier, Fante himself is falling apart, like the worm-eaten and walked-on kitchen floor. When Joyce explains that she wants their marriage to be sanctified in the Church, John says, "You mean — we've been living in adultery all these years?" She ignores his objection, and says, "You won't be able to divorce me, ever" (FL 104).

First, though, she has to be baptized and he has to reaffirm his faith. But while John admires "the beauty of her effort," he cannot bring himself to pray: "my own lips dry for lack of words, I, the phrasemaker, and the pages of my soul were blank and unlettered" (FL 136). Her devotion endears her anew to Nick, who tries to convince his son to get into the confession box for the sake of the baby. John refuses, and Nick tries to force him in physically. When John repels his father's attack by clinging to a church pew, Nick enters the confessional himself to make his first confession in fifty-five years, as an example to his wayward son. Nick is heard shouting his confession in Italian and arguing with the priest, but he comes out subdued and reflective. [1]

During her pregnancy, Joyce has been studying theology as earnestly as books on child care. After John's unsuccessful confession, however, she forgives him because of something she has found in Emerson: "'I appeal to your customs. I must be myself. I cannot break myself any longer for you or you. If you can love me for what I am, we shall be the happier. If you cannot I will seek to deserve that you should. I will not hide my tastes or aversions'" (FL 143). Through this text on tolerance, which is more literate than the others Joyce has been immersed in, they find their way back to each other. [2]

One of the things that keeps John from the Church is that he has too many unanswered questions, or, as Nick puts it, "The kid reads too much" (FL 107). In "The Wrath of God," Jimmy Toscana found his way back into the confessional through the tolerance of the well-read priest, Father Driscoll. But the priest who tries to convince John to return to his faith has no such saving grace. Even Joyce admits that

Father John, who is preparing her for her conversion, has his theology mixed up, that he's really a Calvinist, and she tries to put him straight. In John's discussion with the priest about a number of points of Church dogma, it becomes clear that Father John's theology is all tautology. "So you want to know if the Bishop of Rome is really infallible in matters of faith and morals. Fante, I shall clear that up for you at once: he is." He gives equally illuminating answers to such conundrums as the immaculate conception, consecration, resurrection and original sin. As for birth control, "There ain't any" (FL 108).

On the issue of birth control, however, Nick has something to say, and takes over the discussion:

> "I told him, Father, I said, 'I don't like that stuff.' It's not the girl's fault, Father. She's a Protestant. She don't know no better. But him: he told me. 'I like to control my family,' he told me that, coupla days ago. Me, his own father."
>
> "I did say something like that," I admitted. "But what I meant was this. Father, my income . . ."
>
> "You see?" Papa interrupted. "Nearly four years, they been married. Plenty time for two, a little boy and a little girl. My grandchildren. But are they here, Father? Go upstairs. Look in all the rooms, under the beds, in the closets. You won't find them. Little Nicky and little Philomela. Nicky, he'd be about three now, talking to his Grandpa. The little girl, she'd be just walking. You see them around, Father? Go out in the back yard; look in the garage. No, you won't find them, because they ain't here. And it's his fault!" (FL 108)

Nick grows more maudlin as he describes the phantom children, feeling sorry for himself because he can't buy his namesake an ice cream cone: "There's two I'll never see, but they're here, someplace, and their Grandpa's not feeling so good, because he can't buy them ice cream cones" (FL 109). At first, Joyce is reasonable and tries to calm him down, but then she too is caught up in Nick's sentimental hallucination. [3]

Only after the birth of the child does John enter the hospital chapel and reconcile himself to his faith. But first he must reconcile himself to becoming a father. After Joyce is taken to the delivery room, John spends a night alone, grappling with the problem of fatherhood: "I began to cry because I didn't want to be a father, or a husband, or even a man, I wanted to be six or seven again, asleep in my mother's arms, and then I fell asleep, dreaming of my mother" (FL 154). He is awakened by his father, who tells him he has a phone call. "The baby's coming." At the hospital he tries to comfort her in her labor, but "I could not find the words of consolation, only the clichés, the adumbrations and traps of futile language, the miserable inadequacies" (FL 155). He suffers sympathetic labor pains with her, so that she has to offer him a glass of water and wants to call the doctor for him. Soon he is unable to take it any longer and leaves to undergo his own difficulties. Walking on the hospital grounds, he sees a small Gothic chapel: "It was the hospital chapel. Suddenly, inexplicably, I began to cry, for here was the Thing I sought, the end of the desert, my house upon the earth." Kneeling in the small chapel, while his wife is giving birth to his son, John transcends the "futile language" of consolation and confession, and returns to his faith without it: "I knelt as a tide of contrition engulfed me, a thundering cataract that roared in my ears. There was no need to pray, to beg forgiveness. My whole being lost itself in the deep drift, like waves returning to the shore. I was there for nearly an hour, and full of laughter as I rose to go. For it was a time for laughter, a time for great joy" (FL 159).

In the end the couple still have a termite-infested floor, but also a beautiful stone fireplace of Arizona flagstone, a renewed faith, and a child. It is suggested that all three will last at least a lifetime, just as Fante had earlier envisioned the fireplace as lasting a millennium (or a decade, which is the same thing in the temporary landscape of Los Angeles), a sort of Stonehenge to the Fante spirit in the midst of parking lots: "I pictured the scene, not a thousand years hence, but only ten or fifteen, when our house would doubtless be torn down to make room for a parking lot, cars driving in and out, but always around Papa's indestructible fireplace, because it defied all efforts to tear it down" (FL 118-19). Before the proud new grandfather leaves after the birth of his grandson, he observes his handiwork: "Plenty room for Santa Claus to come down the chimney" (FL 161), a hint that his contribution to the household will always be his privileged entry into the life of the new family, as though he were the jolly, hoary figure of Babbo Natale, or Old Saint Nick.

The unrelenting sweetness and light infusing the book would cloy if not for the Fante charm, here at its most domestic and optimistic. Fante is a great comic writer, who exploits his talent to the full in this book to catch the wave of middle-class American optimism in the 1950s. As the narrator of *Full of Life*, a screenwriter, cynically comments, "If you have what they want at the moment they pay you, and pay you well. At that moment I had what they wanted, and every Thursday there came this big check" (FL 11). Fante puts his screen writing talents to work here in hilarious pathos, as in the scene where Nick wonders where his phantom grandchildren are, and physical comedy, as when Nick tries to force his son into the confessional. In striving for full comic effect, Fante even stoops for the first time to caricaturing Italian-American speech, using Nick's broken English for comic effect: "What's these termites doing in your house?" (FL 59); and "Don't call me ignorance. I'm your Papa" (FL 46). But the Fante eye for the epiphanic details of character and situation are here in force.

We need to remember that *Full of Life* is a book very much of its time, published at the height of the post-war baby boom. In it, Fante reflects the tenor of his time as faithfully as he did the Depression in *1933 Was a Bad Year*, or the silly side of the 1960s in *My Dog Stupid*.

A book about hope and all that is promised by biological birth and spiritual rebirth, *Full of Life* is a serenade to a wife's pregnancy and faith, and a memorial to a father's lust for building things that last. It is also an appreciation of the domestic virtues by a man coming to terms with becoming a father, who in the process makes progress toward coming to terms with his own father.

It is a truism, of course, that comedy, and especially farce, is often written out of a great despair. What informs the sunny quality of this book are the clouds of tragedy out of which it was written. Joyce Fante has commented that the domestic scene depicted in *Full of Life* was "the polar opposite of what had really been going on in the Fante household" (SL 225). When we consider, too, that Fante's father had recently died and that Fante himself would soon discover that he too suffered from diabetes, the irony of the novel's "sunny" depiction makes the autobiographical distortion less a lie than a wish-fulfillment. That the book was so popular with its audience may indicate that American society in the 1950s was itself putting on a brave face of optimism at a time when war was still fresh in the public memory and the chill of a new kind of war was being felt both in Korea and in Congress with the HUAC investigations. Perhaps America itself welcomed the book because it was suffering under the same contradiction.

2. Prodigal Father: *The Brotherhood of the Grape*

While working on a new novel about a would-be prodigal son in 1954, Fante felt dissatisfied with the material of a boy who sells his father's cement mixer to run away to become a big league ballplayer because the story, he felt, was "not important." Worse, since *Full of Life* was not important either but had "a wonderful urgency behind the writing," the new story seemed to lack not only "urgency" but also "personal significance." Thus Fante dropped what was later to become *1933 Was a Bad Year*. His work on it was not wasted, however, for "in writing out all those unsatisfactory pages, something new was added, and it has gripped me with wonderful enthusiasm — an 'important' idea, and one that I am very keen to begin at once" (SL 231). In the same letter to his publisher, Fante goes on to give a detailed synopsis of the new story, that in the completeness of its vision resembles the "prologue" to *Ask the Dust*. He begins by explaining the importance of his father to his work: "My best efforts in all my books have been directed toward my father, his problems, failures and successes. His death three years ago left a deep heart wound that will never disappear. He is in my thoughts at all times, and I want to do a book about his last days" (SL 231). Nevertheless, the extreme importance, urgency and personal significance of the new material proved so difficult to handle that *The Brotherhood of the Grape* would take Fante another twenty years to finish.

The Brotherhood of the Grape is Fante's most sober novel. Whatever there is of the absurd in the events surrounding the last years of Nick Molise, they have to do with the frailty of specific human beings caught up in forces larger than themselves, and the result, for once, is not farce but tragedy.

As the only Fante novel with death as its central concern, there is a sense of the inevitable in Nick Molise's demise that strikes a classically tragic note. When Nick Molise, at seventy-six, is accused of adultery by his wife, the resulting explosion draws the whole family into the ridiculous final act of a lifetime of drama. Henry Molise, the one son who has moved away from the family to achieve a modicum of success on his own, has gained a more mature perspective on his erratic parents than his brothers, who either ignore or despise them, their father in particular. "But what they failed to see was that I understood two old people savoring the richness of human experience again, in the violent disguise of infidelity, which did not and could not actually exist" (SL 235). Henry Molise sees, as they cannot, that his siblings are torn between dependence on one another and their need for independent accomplishment outside the family circle, and are thus blinded to the human motivations of their parents, who have never ceased being distant and dehumanized figures of authority.

The book begins with the ominous sign of red stains on Nick Molise's underwear. His wife Maria, however, reads this sign not for what it is (blood in the urine of a diabetic), but as "circumstantial evidence" of her husband's infidelity. What she imagines is lipstick from the "kiss of some tart" (though her daughter suggests that it might be red mouthwash) is actually the kiss of death. At age seventy-six, Nick is still full of life and battling to sustain his virility, despite his diabetic condition and a tell-tale chronic bladder infection. His children interpret his crimes, "his drinking, his gambling, his wenching, and his cruelty toward our mother" (BG 5), as pathetic attempts at proving his manhood. Maria later allows that the stain might be cherry jelly dropped in his lap at breakfast. In any case, Maria's spreading his underwear "over the center of the checkered table-cloth like a shameless centerpiece" (BG 8) becomes tragically ironic.

The focus on Nick Molise's death from diabetes becomes more pivotal and more tragic when we realize that the affliction which kills him, like his father before him, also threatens Henry Molise and his own sons. As Henry has to inform his brother Mario, who thinks that diabetes is a kind of venereal disease, diabetes is not contracted but inherited. Nick, who is an "alcoholic diabetic," has worsened his condition by drinking too much wine, since, as the doctor tells Henry Molise, "wine is nothing more than grape sugar" (BG 134). In this sense, the "brotherhood of the grape" refers less to Nick's wine-drinking friends at Angelo Musso's winery in the California foothills, than to the tragic legacy passed down from father to son in the blood.[4]

For the first time in his career, Fante introduces a novel with an epigraph. Significantly, it is from a book about Italy, Eduardo Verga's *The Abruzzi:* "The brotherhood of the grape! You see them in every village, these old rascals, loafing outside the cafes, drinking wine and sighing after every passing skirt." As a member of this brotherhood, which extends from the Abruzzi to Angelo Musso's winery, Nick Molise takes on the stature of an archetype, a tragic figure who represents an entire culture and a specific stance toward life and death. Seen in this light, drinking and wenching are his due and his destiny, a shake of the fist at fate.

The portrait of Nick Molise in the novel is unsparing of his faults, which makes his son's reconciliation with him all the more difficult, but all the more moving and important. He is described as a bastard and a satyr, an Italian "in the dictator mold" (BG 26), "an Abruzzi evil goat with poised evil horns" (BG 26), and "Jehovah himself" (BG 18).[5] The comparison to Jehovah should not, of course, be taken too far, since Nick Molise is painfully mortal, an old man who "takes enemas with warm wine, and eats raw eggs in the morning" (BG 52). What power he has is bluff and bluster, and he is as harmless as his namesakes, Saint Nick and Saint Joseph. Hardly the God of the Old Testament, Nicholas Joseph Molise is more like a Greek god, whose philandering is a proof of his potency, more pathetic than despicable. Like Svevo Bandini who curses his God, Nick Molise is a power-less adversary of a higher power he does not understand.[6] It is a power he is willing to wrestle with, but only because he respects his wife's God and would like in return to be re-spected as a man.

Like Henry, Nick Molise is an artist. "The town of San Elmo was his Louvre" (BG 19). Henry recalls how Nick would sometimes in the evening take one of his sons on "the Grand Tour" of the town to view "the complete works of Nick Molise" (BG 20). The structures Nick has built house every aspect of life and death in the small community: the library with steps that "flow like water," churches, banks, theaters, the high school that has "been through four earth-quakes," the fire department, the City Hall, the Municipal Water and Power, the mortuary, and even the sidewalk linking them all. "Valhalla Cemetery was crowded with my father's white marble angels . . . hawk-faced and grim . . . like vultures protecting carrion" (BG 23). The image is disturb-ing, expressive of the man's cruelty, as well as his creativity.

His children are "bored to death with his ego trip" (BG 22), and he is disgusted with them because they thwart his dream of their carrying on the tradition: *Nick Molise and Sons, Stonemasons.* "My old man had never wanted children. He had wanted apprentice bricklayers and stonemasons," and "he tried to shape his sons into stonemasons the way he shaped stone, by whacking it. He failed, of course, for the more he hammered at us, the further he drove us from any love of the craft" (BG 25). When his son Mario had a chance to play professional baseball, Nick Molise refused to sign for him, alienating his son forever. Instead of supporting Mario's dream, as Dominic Molise's father did in *1933 Was a Bad Year*, Nick Molise adamantly clings to his own, which he claims ever afterward that Mario killed, or at least sold out, like "Judas who killed Christ" (BG 4). The truth, of course, is the opposite. At Mario's baseball games, Nick heckles his son from the grandstand, and when Mario hits a home run to win the league championship, "my enraged father rushed from the grandstand and tackled the grinning Mario as he rounded third base. The police dragged him off the field and Mario got up and trotted home with the winning run" (BG 27). Unconsciously, Mario gets his revenge by missing his father's funeral because it conflicts with a big game on television.

As a writer, Henry has come to understand his father's egocentric pride in his work, since his own sons belittle his screen writing without realizing that he had had more serious hopes for his talent before he "sold out" to support them. In Chapters 9 and 10, which make use of parts of the unpublished *Road to Los Angeles*, Henry Molise remembers his first days in Los Angeles and the jobs he had to take while trying to make it as a struggling writer. He washes and buses dishes, and drives a cab for one disastrous day, which ends with him being robbed after a long fare to San Bernardino. Penniless, he bums his way to Wilmington and works at the canneries, gathers butts at the ferry terminal, eats in the soup line at the Holy Ghost Mission on Banning Street,[7] and sleeps in a Cadillac on a used car lot until he is

rousted and moves on to a boat under a bridge near the
harbor.

Here, like Arturo Bandini, Henry Molise has a run-in
with crabs, but the differences between the two scenes
epitomize the contrast between Arturo Bandini and Henry
Molise. Bandini conquers the crabs in the broad daylight
with rocks and a BB gun; Molise is conquered by them in the
dark of night.

> Something bit me and I wakened . . . They were all over me.
> They were on my legs, under my pants, they were biting,
> crawling. I felt them at my scrotum. I pulled one out of my
> hair. I jumped up and screamed. They fell from my clothes
> .... I screamed in fear. I ran out from under the bridge and
> tore off my clothes in the daylight. I saw the traffic. I pulled
> off my pants, my shirt, my shorts. I was naked, on fire,
> rubbing sand into little bleeding holes in my body, running
> like crazy, flinging myself in weeds and sand, howling like a
> dog. I heard a siren. I saw the spinning red light (BG 69-70).

The murder of so many brave crabs by Arturo Bandini,
legendary killer in the history of the Crab People, is here
avenged. The police believe the wounds are self-inflicted,
but the doctor is not so sure, even though he does not
believe they are crab bites until a few crabs crawl out of
Molise's pants and scurry across the emergency room floor.
"I cried then. I sat up and held my knees and cried because
everybody was so fucking rotten, and the only ones coming
to my rescue were the little beasties who had caused all the
trouble in the first place, the crabs." The only thing that
keeps Molise going through the ordeal is invoking the spirit
of his father: "God keep me a man like my father!" (BG 71).

Working as a laborer in the canneries, Henry is unable
to keep up with "the wiry Filipinos, the tireless Mexicans"
and he feels like a "counterfeit" and is "ashamed" (BG 75).

He hears the echo of his father's warning: "learn a trade, be something special" (BG 66). When he loses the job, he wonders what will become of him, he remembers his grandfather, "my father's father," "an itinerant knife-sharpener in Abruzzi. Was that my destiny too? Suddenly I wanted to go home, to my father's house, to my mother's arms" (BG 76). He returns to his parents' house in San Elmo to face his father's ridicule of his failure. Recuperating from the flu, he reads Dostoyevsky, and "fending off the old man with one hand and writing with the other" he completes his first short stories about his experiences at the cannery in imitative pastiches of Jack London, Raymond Chandler, James M. Cain, Hemingway, Steinbeck and Fitzgerald. They "even showed traces," he says, "of Henry Molise" (BG 77). As the stories are returned by *The Saturday Evening Post* and *Collier's*, "The old man watched me as he would an unwanted dog . . . There was a time when he growled because I read too much. Now he snarled because I wrote too much" (BG 77). Between those first stories and the present lies the success story of Henry Molise, author and screenwriter. How he left home, published, married, raised a family, all part of the long journey begun because he would not listen to his father's advice to "learn a trade, be something special" by breaking his back carrying hod for the old man.

Looking back on it all now in his childhood home, he wonders whether he has really come so far or only full circle to what had been his destiny all along. The flashback of Chapters 9 and 10 occurs as he lies in the "cradle" of his mother's bed, waiting for the morning when he would, after all the years of avoiding his father's trade, become his father's employee: "there he was again, my tireless old man, still trying to drag me into those deadly mountains where the concrete waited and some fool wanted a smokehouse built. So it had come down to this. After thirty years I had seen the light. I was a hod carrier at long last" (BG 78). Henry tries to get out of his father's project to get him into the mountains to help him build a smokehouse, but finally gives in: "My father was entitled to this last paltry triumph, this little house of stone in the Sierras" (BG 82). Once they arrive at the site, however, and he discovers that he has to sleep with his father in the cabin, he has second thoughts. He looks at his father and sees only the "unreasonable, tyrannical, boorish, profligate wop who had trapped me on this snafu safari into the mountains, far from wife and home and work, all for his bedizened vanity, to prove to himself he was still a hotshot stonemason" (BG 104). He recalls moments from his father's "lifetime of unrepentant sensuality at the expense of his wife and family": one Fourth of July when Henry was ten, finding his father in an alley with Mrs. Lorenzo up against a telephone pole, and one Easter Sunday when he was twelve, during a softball game, leaping for a fly ball and landing on his father's "bare bottom white as a winter moon as he pumped Mrs. Santucci" on the other side of the fence (BG 106).

He recalls his father at Mrs. Santucci's picnic "with a goat's head on his plate, eating the brains and the eyes, laughing and showing off before women screaming in horror" (BG 106).[8] The image is diabolical, and it seems to confirm what Henry's wife Harriet told him before he left, that the "filthy old lecher with black Dago eyes" had made a pass at her on her wedding day by pinching her "derrière." Henry laughed. "That wasn't a pass, it was a compliment. All Italians do that. I've pinched your ass a thousand times. It's fun" (BG 15). But now he is in no mood to forgive his father.

On the way to build the smokehouse, Henry and his father stop at Angelo Musso's winery, where Nick Molise and his aging Italian cronies worship at the fountainhead of the grape. It is a pilgrimage, with the men as "monks in single file paying homage to their abbot" (BG 94). Angelo Musso is eighty-four years old, toothless and voiceless, a chain-smoker who has lost his voice box to cancer, yet for "my father and most of the old-time Italians in Placer County Angelo Musso was extra special, an ancient oracle who dispensed no wisdom, a sage who gave no advice, a prophet without predictions, and a god who fermented the most enchanting wine in the world" (BG 94). Even the bees form "a halo around Angelo's gray hair" (BG 95). Later, Henry quotes an Italian proverb: "If you see a crowd of women, the church is close at hand" (BG 138). Angelo Musso is the male Italians' alternative to their wives' priests, and the earthly bread and wine he dispenses their Communion and mysterious transubstantiation. He never preaches; the only wisdom he offers is the wisdom of silence and the brotherhood of the grape. In their old age "his wine was the milk of their second childhood" (BG 93). Even Henry is seduced by this sensuous "day in Italy, the hills of Tuscany" (BG 97) and the drone of the bees telling him "to drink beyond satiety. . . to tempt death quietly, silently, in the company of drunken old men — mama mia!" (BG 96).

Seeing Nick Molise in his own element, drinking with him at Angelo Musso's and building the smokehouse together, Henry grows closer to his father, and more like him. They work and drink together all day, and pass out side by side in bed at night. They still argue for no good reason, but now they laugh together too. One day he discovers his father telling a lie, and Henry has a revelation of his father's childhood: "he was nine years old in an impoverished Italian village, trapped by his father in some boyish fabrication" (BG 100). In that moment their roles are reversed, and Henry condescends to forgive his father's fib. Seeing his father's vulnerability, he realizes that the child which is father to the man never really abandons the body, even in "his last handful of days" (BG 99).

It is still the consolation of literature, however, that shows Henry Molise the way to understanding "that streetcorner Dago, that low-born Abruzzian wop, the yahoo peasant ginzo, that shit-kicker, that curb crawler" (BG 61), his father. In other of Fante's books, it is Sherwood Anderson or Knut Hamsun who provides the literary subtext. For Henry Molise, the writer who changed him and his attitude toward his father, so that he would "never be the same," is discovered in the library his father built:

> His name was Fyodor Mikhailovich Dostoyevsky. He knew more of fathers and sons than any man in the world, and of brothers and sisters, priests and rogues, guilt and innocence. Dostoyevsky changed me. *The Idiot, The Possessed, The Brothers Karamazov, The Gambler.* He turned me inside out. I found I could breathe, could see invisible horizons. The hatred for my father melted. I loved my father, poor, suffering, haunted wretch. I loved my mother too, and all my family. It was time to become a man, to leave San Elmo and go out into the world. I wanted to think and feel like Dostoyevsky. I wanted to write (BG 62).

Molise is reminded of this epiphany, experienced long ago, when his father disappears instead of taking his insulin. When the doctor calls, telling Henry to get his father to the hospital as soon as he can find him, Henry thinks admiringly: "My old man! What a treasure he was, what excitement he kicked up! That was his genius, a talent for shaking up the small world in which he lived." As he goes through the town, stopping in at the Onyx Bar and the Cafe Roma, his father's hangouts, he laughs, pleased with his father: "He might die, but what of that? Dostoyevsky was dead, yet very much alive in my heart. He had come to me like the grace of God, a flash of lightning that illumined my life. My father had that same iridescence, a nimbus around me, my own flesh and blood, a poet asserting his will to live" (BG 154).

After his father's death, Henry plans to take his mother "under my own roof" while his sister and brothers "worked out their own lives." But first he returns to the San Elmo Public Library, his father's library, where twenty-five years earlier he had experienced his "fragment of ecstasy," like Paul, who had his "moment of truth" before Damascus. He goes straight to *The Brothers Karamazov*. "I held it in my hands, I leafed the pages, I drew it tightly into my arms, my life, my joy, my sublime Dostoyevsky. I may have failed him in my deeds, but never in my devotion. My beloved Papa was gone, but Fyodor Mikhailovich would be with me to the end of my life" (BG 171).

The night before he left for San Elmo, Henry and Harriet had a night of "flawed love," in which she ruined the mood in the midst of love-making by trying to use the moment to convince him to visit her mother, who hates Henry as much as Harriet hates his father. In the morning he glimpses the twisted sheets on the bed, the scene of their "flawed love," and remembers "seeing them exactly that way in my parents' bedroom when I was seven, and hating my father for it, for the stale smell of his cigar, and his work pants lying grotesquely on the floor, and the desire to kill him" (BG 13). Thus the first chapter concludes by foreshadowing the father's death, as well as the heart of the narrator's conflict with his father, with its echoes of Eros and Thanatos.

When Henry falls into the arms of his father's nurse immediately after his death, he falls from the moral position of judging his father, and comes to identity with him. His moral failure enables him to forgive his father's "lifetime of unrepentant sensuality at the expense of his wife and family" (BG 107). Miss Quinlan had earlier described how another patient, a ninety-two year old man on a kidney machine, "died in my arms, with his hand in my panties" (BG 156). Unlike Harriet, who reacted to his old man's "fun" with undying hatred, Miss Quinlan is charity personified. He collapses with grief in her arms, pleading, "Oh, please, Miss Quinlan. Fuck me, please, please. Save me, fuck me!" Miss Quinlan's response is: "Well, it's possible, I guess" (BG 163). This is a vitalistic sex-as-regeneration response, like Gerald's going to Gudrun after his father's death in Lawrence's *Women in Love*.[9] But Henry is also lamenting the loss of his wife's love, having once wondered if she too had pubic hair "as blond as her shoulder-length tresses" (BG 85). It is through tears that he seduces Miss Quinlan, just as it was through tears that he won his wife. "Without tears I could never have seduced a woman, and with them I never failed" (BG 161). On the way to her apartment, they stop at a supermarket and he admires her "pomegranate" knees and "magnificent derrière" that floats past his eyes "like the grace of God, like the Holy Ghost. My old man would have loved it; he would have pinched it for sure" (BG 163-4). His wife and father, in other words, are with him throughout this escapade, which is a blow struck at his wife and for his father.

Undressed, Miss Quinlan is "not nearly as attractive as she had been in her nursing costume," her body less appealing than her role as nurse, though she still uses her "professional intonation" when she asks, "Are we all undressed?" (BG 164). As she performs the prelude of "prophylaxis" and douche with professional alacrity, Henry feels more like a boy than a man. He also feels the presence of his father. "None of this invigorated my sword, or, as my father called it, my *spada* . . . she shook it and called it a shy and naughty boy . . . The dear boy . . . He's such an angel" (BG 165). When she puts honey on the tip of his *spada*, it reacts "ready to fight," but Henry feels a twinge of shame: "What a ghastly way to honor my poor father. But I was caught up in it, I had asked Miss Quinlan for it, and there was no reason to stop now, in spite of my father, my wife, and my two sons" (BG 165).

In the final moments of their intimacy, "with a terrible beauty . . . the beauty one felt but did not see," he calls her kindness "sorcery," as she takes everything: "I felt it all going away and out of me, my sword, my glands, my heart, my lungs and my brain, a banquet for a rather elderly queen — and as the sorcery subsided she lay back on the bed, panting desperately . . . She had taken everything, and I had nothing to give in return" (BG 166). More witch now than Magdalen, she undergoes yet another transformation before he gets out the door. Just as her generous breasts turned out to be "falsies" beneath her nursing uniform, so her "lovely pile of Nordic blondness" turns out to be a wig. He glimpses "a white, bald skull," suggesting her role as the "elderly queen" of death, who has just taken his father and will soon take everything from him. On his way out he thanks her, adding, "My father thanks you too." To which she replies, "He was a dear man. I'm so glad I could help" (BG 166).

At the funeral, Henry Molise stands by the grave and realizes that he is now the next in line as the family patriarch, and next in line for death. "I was myself a father. I didn't want the role. I wanted to go back to a time when I was small and my father stood strong and noisy in the house. To hell with fatherhood. I was never born to it. I was born to be a son" (BG 173). Perhaps all fathers were born to be sons in this sense of never quite accepting the change in their role when it comes, either suddenly or gradually.

Oddly enough, for all its tragic tone and its ending with a funeral, the final novel in the Molise tetralogy is the *only one* that does not end with weeping. Instead, there is a sense of relief, even happiness, a note of lively affirmation. Maria Molise declares herself "happy" not because her husband died quickly and without suffering, but only because he is dead. "Her face was beautiful, her eyes were warm with a sense of peace" (BG 178) because for the first time in her life she does not have to worry about where her husband is: "He worried me so, all the time, from the day we were married. I never knew where he was, what he was doing, or who he was with. He wouldn't tell me anything. Every night I wondered if he'd come home again. Now it's over. I don't have to worry anymore. I know where he is. That he's all right" (BG 178). After burying her husband, Maria plans the last supper, with leg of lamb and new potatoes, before Henry returns to Southern California.

Henry Molise's last words in the novel are: "Let's go home" (BG 178). Home is the end of the odyssey for each and every Molise. Driven away from home by ambition, like the prodigal son they are driven back by nostalgia for family and tradition, and by a desire for forgiveness. What the prodigal sons learn along that road is that before forgiveness can be granted to them, they must first forgive the sins of the prodigal father. Henry Molise learned how to appreciate his father from Dostoyevsky, and that "To write well a man must have a fatal ailment. It was the only way to deal with the presence of death" (BG 62). The other Molise novels are fundamentally comic, playing their tragic elements at a hilarious pace. In *1933 Was a Bad Year* the young Dominic Molise gave his father hell. In *My Dog Stupid* Henry J. Molise gets it back from his own son. The elating experience of becoming a father in *Full of Life* turns sour for both Henry Molises as they encounter the same resistance and rebellion from their children that they put their own fathers through. *The Brotherhood of the Grape* asks: "How could a man live without his father? How could he wake up in the morning and say to himself: my father is gone forever?" (BG 136). The answer is that Henry Molise, in coming to accept his identity with his father, will always have his father with him, just as he will always have Dostoyevsky, and thus will not have to endure his loss when he is gone.

The Brotherhood of the Grape goes beyond the depiction of passionate characters trapped in an absurd comedy of errors to ask how they fit into the scheme of life and death. When Henry Molise comes to terms with his own humanity at the end of the novel, there is no sense of sentimental deus ex machina, as with other Fante characters. We feel instead that Henry Molise has worked a lifetime to accept his father as he was, and himself as he is, not as he or anyone else might wish them to be in some ideal universe of fathers and sons. This brotherhood of the grape is an earthy fraternity that must be earned.

CHAPTER 10

RANCHO FANTE, POINT DUME

1952-1983

> . . . barring death or blindness, a man can get whole warehouses of work done in twenty years . . .
>
> John Fante in 1932

The money Fante made from the enormous popular and financial success of *Full of Life* enabled him to settle into a sprawling Y-shaped house he called Rancho Fante at Point Dume in Malibu, where he lived for the last thirty years of his life. The 1950s and 1960s were a time of affluence and frustration for Fante. Professionally, he was doing well as a Hollywood writer at a time when some of his colleagues were being blacklisted by the McCarthy hearings; his screen credits were adding up, and he was even sent to work on projects in Paris and Rome. Personally, he began to sort out some of the problems in his marriage that were due to his profligate behavior. Once he accepted the fact that he was over forty, the death of his father from complications of diabetes and the onset of his own struggle with the disease reminded him that he had a family to support and work to do, if he was ever to get it done. His family took center stage, especially in the 1960s, when his teenage children's lives in that decade of seeking and universal rebellion seem to have provided him with a fascinating and distant drama that must have reminded him of his own early years, and obviously provided him with much satisfaction and amusement.

The only thing that was missing was satisfaction in his art. He never stopped working during this time, but the fine novels that date from this period, *1933 Was a Bad Year* and *My Dog Stupid,* failed to find publishers. The reprint of *Ask the Dust* in a 1954 mass-market Bantam paperback edition was encouraging, but since this was due to the success of *Full of Life* (reprinted by Bantam in 1953), it did not do much to encourage his hopes for a revival of his best work on its own merits.[1] The ebullient and confident letters of the 1950s taper off in their energy and enthusiasm so that by the end of the 1970s the voice of John Fante has taken on a more somber timbre. Even the success of *The Brotherhood of the Grape,* published in 1977, did little to lighten his spirits, as he greeted each new promise from publishers and producers with a skepticism earned through many disappointments. His health, of course, had been in decline ever since he learned that he too suffered from diabetes soon after his father's death in 1950. From 1978 to his death in 1983, his health would deteriorate even more rapidly. Yet with his children grown, and his screen writing career behind him, he began to look back on his life as a whole, especially his accomplishments in the novel, and he began once more to devote himself to his art at a time when critical recognition, and indeed what has come to be known as the Fante revival, was just around the corner.

Politically, the 1950s got off to a bad start, especially in Hollywood, although Fante himself was unscathed by the uproar. In fact, the HUAC investigations worked to his advantage. When Fante's up-beat melting-pot story "One-

Play Oscar" was published in *The Saturday Evening Post*, Joseph McCarthy's House Un-American Activities Committee was holding Congressional hearings to root out the Communist elements in Hollywood. It was a spectacle that Fante regarded as "a hideously fascinating show" and "a very cruel business" (SL 229). But he had little sympathy for either side, except when individuals he cared for, like Louis Adamic, got caught in the crossfire. To Carey McWilliams, author of *Witch Hunt: The Revival of Heresy*, published by Little, Brown in 1950, two years before they published *Full of Life*, Fante wrote in 1951: "It is not easy for me to say that the Committee was merely witch-hunting, because I think the Investigation did reveal the Communist strangle-hold on the [writers] guild, the efficient methods of a few well-organized people, their great skill at parliamentary procedure, and their infinite patience in an organization composed of notoriously impatient guys" (SL 229).

According to his own accounting as he followed the hearings, Fante figured that most of the writers called before the Committee were in fact Communists. "Is the implication too remote that, unless you carry a party card, you can't work?" (SL 229). Joyce Fante remarks that, "Fante attributed his lack of employment in film during the late 1940s to the fact that he had been 'insensitive' to left-wing causes," and that when the pendulum swung the other way in the early 1950s and it was "fashionable to be anti-communist," Fante, "to his credit . . . remained steadfastly apolitical" (SL 237). Always independent and temperamentally opposed to all forms of thought control, Fante found the left-wing extremists humorless, "surprisingly grim and determined people," and every bit as frightening as the right-wing extremists: "For the life of me, I can't understand why they embraced Communism. Where is the charm of this philosophy?

Where is the human side of it?. . . they are no different than the Nazis in their grim and moody and vengeful faith in the future" (SL 229).

Never active in union disputes or political movements, Fante himself came out of the HUAC hearings unscathed. Even had the witch-hunters taken the trouble to read his fiction or investigate his life, they would have found little in the way of suspect political ideology in either. Arturo Bandini, for all his bluster and bluff blasphemy, never expressed his metaphysical disaffection in those terms. On the contrary, Bandini was far more likely to be found clamoring to get in on the American dream than criticizing its values. But perhaps HUAC was already satisfied with the findings of the FBI, who had interrogated Fante repeatedly from 1940 to 1945, concerning his alleged association with Communists. "It was always necessary to hurdle these queries before I was permitted to take a job at MGM, RKO and Warner Brothers. The heart of the matter was always Carlos Bulosan" (SL 305).

His description of Carlos Bulosan shows what kind of man Fante was: one who did not allow politics to sour his affection for individuals. Bulosan, he says, had "a fanatical aversion to the truth . . . a plagiarist who got in trouble with the *New Yorker* . . . I liked him immensely" (SL 305). Author of *America Is in the Heart* (1946), Bulosan introduced Fante to the Filipino community of Los Angeles in 1939, "the restaurants, the nightclubs, and the pool halls of the Pinoys. Also the writers" (SL 305). Fante describes an incident at a Temple Street bistro, in which Bulosan took Joyce aside and claimed to show her his Communist party card, which in the darkness she could not see. "Both of us were convinced that it was another one of his exaggerations, mainly because we couldn't believe that Communists carried party cards on their persons in that perilous time" (SL 305). What is most notable about this incident is Fante's total lack of concern about Bulosan's political affiliations and his tolerance for his peccadillos. Typically, it was not a person's race or creed that attracted or repelled Fante, but the idiosyncrasies of character, the human qualities, the very qualities that both Communist and Nazi seemed incapable of displaying or appreciating. Neither had the charm of human warmth or tolerance, both being utopian and totalitarian ideologies. "Nor is it easy to say that, come the time for liquidations, they would shed a human tear for anyone who failed to agree with their way of running the show" (SL 229).

Fante was particularly amused, albeit cynically, that his name was used by former fellow travelers to keep the HUAC "wolves" at bay. In his testimony before the Committee, Carl Foreman declared that one of his future projects was to produce *Full of Life* by John Fante for the Stanley Kramer company. "He was the perfect example of a pinkie under pressure," Fante wrote to McWilliams, reveling in Foreman's hypocrisy. "But I suppose the virtue of being a pink is flexibility." Fante was neither flattered nor fooled by Foreman's enthusiasm for "this tale of a wife converted to Catholicism, of a priest and an old man and a faltering hero who finally returns to his native religion," but saw it for what it was. "Did this Communist buy such a novel because it appealed to his philosophy, because he found (all at once) great warmth and tenderness in a manuscript? Or did he, hearing the howling of wolves coming from behind the hills, quickly say to himself: this is the kind of material I want to be caught with, when they catch me?" (SL 229-30)

Fante's cynicism comes out most clearly, though, in his summation of the affair as having had the salutary effect of making him some fast money: "this is the most fortuitous 40 thousand a man ever made: two guys pulling and tugging on a priest's cassock, both of them trying to prove how nicely the sack-cloth fits. As you can see, Lucifer was at work throughout, and his Satanic powers were of no avail against God, who was on *my* side" (SL 230).

Thanks to Hollywood (and none to the Guggenheim Foundation), Fante took three trips to Europe in the late 1950s, finally fulfilling his dream to see Italy. None of the projects he worked on, however, saw the light of the silver screen. In the summer of 1957 Fante went to Naples with the crew of "The Roses" which was written for Harry Cohn as a vehicle for Jack Lemmon. After seven weeks, production was called off. One story has it that the director Richard Quine (who directed *Full of Life* the year before, and later *The World of Suzie Wong*) failed to report in regularly, but this story is disputed.

A fiasco professionally, Fante's first trip to Italy was personally "a very moving and important experience" (SL 260). A kind of pilgrimage, it was another stage in reconciling himself to his Italian heritage. "Somehow Italy was as I imagined in terms of climate and scenery, but I found the people simply gorgeous, curteous [sic], and refined. Even the lowest peasant in Italy is somehow born to a culture and degree of civilized living that we don't know." The culture and civilization of the Italian peasant stock of his forefathers, it seems, was a pleasant surprise, although he was troubled by "the miserable plight of the Italian writer" and "the preposterous worship by Italians of anything on celluloid." The boorishness of rich Romans, not unlike their Hollywood counterparts, gave him a superior pleasure. "I detested the rich people I met, however, the frauds in the picture business, the obscene Roman men, their bucolic city-slicker arrogance" (SL 260).

In 1959 Fante was sent for a few months to Paris to work on "The Fish Don't Bite" for Darryl F. Zanuck. At the same time William Saroyan, oppressed by gambling debts, gave Zanuck a play as a vehicle for Zanuck's French mistress Juliet Greco. Zanuck canceled Fante's project and took on Saroyan's, causing a rift in the writers' friendship.

The trip was not without its advantages, however. Aside from meeting Elvis Presley, "a nice kid" (SL 264), who was staying in the same hotel, Fante managed to squeeze in meetings with Dino De Laurentiis in Rome, which resulted in a later writing trip to Rome and indirectly to his writing *The Reluctant Saint*; and with Charles Feldman in Paris, which resulted in his doing the script for Nelson Algren's *Walk on the Wild Side*.

Fante's impressions of Paris seem somewhat superficial, perhaps because his work obliged him to view it as an extension of Hollywood. Otherwise, what he saw seems filtered through what he had read, such as Henry Miller's *Tropic of Cancer*. "Paris is the vagina of the civilized world," he wrote to his wife. "It simply reeks of sex" (SL 261). The city brought out the Bandini in him, or the young man who returned to Denver in a Harpo Marx overcoat. The night he arrived in Paris he spent $460 buying drinks "for anyone who was thirsty, boys and girls alike," and the next morning suspected he had been rolled, although he couldn't remember it. He did, however, remember to take his sugar tests for his diabetic condition (SL 262). After a couple of months he was tired of Paris, which in July was hot and "the streets empty save for Americanos carrying cameras. For me it is a deadly bore. Night comes, and there is no escape except sitting in those damn cafes, drinking tea or coffee or booze. A wretched trap" (SL 267). In the short story he wrote there, "The First Time I Saw Paris," he wanders the streets, casting a critical eye on all he sees, then "almost burst into tears for my beautiful California" (SL 326).

In 1960 Fante was back in Europe, this time to work for Dino De Laurentiis in Rome on yet another ill-fated project, although another project arranged at this time did result in a script based on the life of Joseph of Cupertino, *The Reluctant Saint*. Again Fante was complaining of the presence of other Americans, especially the "fat Catholic broads all fired up about touring the Vatican" (SL 270), which he thought over-rated and "over-sold" (SL 274). Sometimes he felt tourist overload, overwhelmed by all there was to see; he felt he was "walking through post-cards = a one dimensional contact with the past" (SL 273). Still, Rome was "almost suffocatingly beautiful" with its "gold-on-red tint implanted in buildings" (SL 271), and certainly more beautiful than Paris though without "the electricity of Paris" (SL 273). Things picked up once he was joined by his wild son Nick, who had been following in his father's footsteps by upsetting his mother by staying up all night drinking and gambling. They stayed for a while in a house where Raphael had lived near the Vatican, met an Etruscan grave robber who promised to find Nick a girl, and together sampled all the local cuisine.

A Sunday spent in East Berlin during a brief trip to Germany reinforced Fante's opinion of Communism, which had always seemed to him a particularly grim view of the world, whether in the zeal of 1930s activism, or in the more shame-faced Hollywood brand. "How dull it is — how hopeless — blocks & blocks of somber, bullet-pocked apartments, scarcely any people in the streets, seldom a car, and when one bangs past it is of a 1935 or '36 vintage. Any man who loves Communism should see East Berlin. To hell with Marxian dogma. What the eye looks upon in E. Berlin answers all the questions. You get very uneasy driving those deadly quiet streets. The air is full of fear, police. The people walk slowly, without gaiety. In all the world there is no Sunday afternoon like it" (SL 272). This made his contact with the film industry in Rome all the more annoying, since he found it filled with "Red Intelligentzia of the kind that used to prevail in Hollywood" (SL 275), sneering and mouthing Anti-American clichés, but basically "without principle, hypocritical, lost" (SL 275-76).

In spite of the city's annoyances, and his letters home full of longing to be back in Malibu, Rome worked its magic. Fante's few months there were full of small pleasures, such as finding his books in Italian translation, being interviewed by the Roman and Neapolitan newspapers, and seeing the opening of the film version of *Full of Life*. Fante also found great material there for his next novel, *My Dog Stupid*, completed in 1971, although unpublished until after his death (in *West of Rome*, 1986). In the end, this Malibu Walter Mitty gives up the dream of escaping to Rome in order to embrace the life of a man devoted to his snotty children, his bitchy wife, and his stupid dog.[2]

On his return to Rancho Fante, Fante seemed to take greater pleasure than ever in his family. The entire Molise family can be recognized in Fante's glowing letters to McWilliams about the Fante clan. James, writes Fante, is "an angel of a boy, a rosebud, a joy"; Victoria, "refreshing too but something of a spoiled princess, very demanding and emotional"; Nick, "at Santa Monica High now, a car-happy kid," as his father had been, "any car, car, car, car, morning and night, cars, this car, that car, and his world has no other features save wheels and engines"; and Danny, "a good mind but gets terrible grades . . . likes to read, likes to save money, and now and then gets into fights . . . a judo expert and too tough for me now."[3] In each child Fante, ever the proud father and always the somewhat egotistical autobiographer, chooses those elements that most resemble himself. James's childishness, Victoria's emotion, Nick's passion for cars, and Danny's anti-intellectual intelligence form a composite portrait of Fante's own character.

Unlike *Full of Life,* which had glossed over family troubles in an idyllic recital of clichés of 1950s affluence, *My Dog Stupid* was — "another boil," says Fante, "I lanced it" (SL 294) — apparently concentrated on the troubles at the expense of the overall harmony that prevailed in the Fante household during the turbulent 1960s.

Still, the Fante family reflected the changes and social pressures of the times. Danny was driving a cab in New York, a "loathsome job" in Fante's eyes: "it must be that somewhere in my genes there was a strain that drove donkeys on Abruzzian trails, and now that the donkey is being retired one moves on to taxi cabs." Nick, his grandfather's namesake, was his parents' greatest worry, "the very quintessence of today's revolution," who made "Rimbeau [sic] look like an Eagle scout." "He has a fatal fascination for black women, and what they have done to him would throw Governor Wallace into a fit of ecstasy. I tell you Carey, when Joyce and I sit down to dinner with Nick we have the feeling that our terrible white skin disgusts him . . . and his black heart . . . I am thinking of calling my house Watts By The Sea."[4]

An interesting postscript to Fante's fictional treatments of immigrants and ethnics is to be found in his own life. By the mid-1970s, however, things seem to have sorted themselves out on the home front, the family having weathered the storm of the 1960s without tragedy. Danny graduated from cab driver to Rolls-Royce rental agent, Victoria married a "Babbitt husband," and James married a Japanese bride.

The "oddball son" Nick had become "a preacher of the gospel," having been ordained by a Hungarian machinist, Fante remarks, for five bucks; "his black wife is a pretty good country-and-western singer and has signed a contract to record a couple of songs." All three of his sons married women of ethnic backgrounds, one Japanese, one Jewish, one black. Here is Fante in 1971, a grandfather gloating to Carey McWilliams with undisguised pride: "My little black and white granddaughter is now three, a very beautiful child. She was here Easter and we hid eggs all over the yard for her to find. She is an aggressive little creature and my fearless dogs run and hide in terror at the sight of her."[5] Fante's family had become a multiethnic melting-pot, not unlike the ill-assorted football team in "One-Play Oscar." Family gatherings at their home on the Pacific must have seemed like a meeting of the United Nations compared to the homogeneous Italian gatherings of John Fante's childhood in Colorado. Fante could pack all the racial slurs like loaded pistols, as in the letter to McWilliams about Italian Americans. But they are the cap pistols of the tough-kid voice that he perfected in Two-Gun Jimmy Toscana. Underneath the western cowboy toughness is the true Fante, full of an eastering hope in his own family, if not in humanity.

At the same time Fante began to feel death closing in. Diagnosed in 1955 with diabetes that would lead to blindness, he was now beginning to develop ulcers between his toes that he cursed for keeping him off the golf course, and that would lead to the amputation of one leg and then the other. No longer in need of money, he wrote his last script, a teleplay called *Something for a Lonely Man,* in 1967, and published his last short story, the powerful "My Father's God," published (not for money) in *Italian Americana* in 1975. It was a good time to devote himself to his art, even though

My Dog Stupid, in which he had had great faith, and which today appears to be one of his masterpieces, failed to find a publisher. As Neil Gordon has said, to compare Fante with Hemingway or Dos Passos does not quite yield results: "He fit better with Joyce, or Miller, or even with the writers published in the Paris of the 1950s by Maurice Girodias — Trocchi, Burroughs, Genet"[6] — which makes it all the more perplexing that Grove Press, who published several of these writers, rejected *My Dog Stupid* in 1971. When he sat down to his desk in the 1970s, Fante must have felt his time running out.

He dreamed of a Fante revival. Robert Towne's movie option of *Ask the Dust* gave Fante hope that some publisher may be interested in reprinting the book that many felt his best work, a classic about California, and a masterpiece of the American novel. Towne had read McWilliams' praise for Fante while doing research for the film *Chinatown*. In *Southern California Country: An Island on the Land* (1946) McWilliams had written that he could think of "only four novels that suggest what Southern California" was really like in the years between 1935 and 1946: Mark Lee Luther's *The Boosters,* Frank Fenton's *A Place in the Sun,* Nathanael West's *The Day of the Locust,* and John Fante's *Ask the Dust.*[7] McWilliams had also written an introduction for Carlos Bulosan's *America Is in the Heart,* which had just come out in paperback, so Fante asked his old friend to make inquiries, saying, "I would give both testicles if the editors could be persuaded to do my *Ask the Dust*" (SL 295). McWilliams suggested the idea to the University of Washington Press and Peregrine Smith, but nothing came of the plan. Despite the help of friends and the interest of would-be critics and biographers, Fante's hope for a revival of his work would have to wait.

Fante resented critics and biographers. He didn't mind their interest in his work, but he snapped when they snooped into his private life and presumed to theorize. Marilyn Murphy-Plittman, a student writing a biographical sketch of Fante, wrote Fante and McWilliams asking for biographical details to support her thesis that Fante had sold out his talent to the movies because after the death of his father he no longer had the emotional defenses "to keep from succumbing to the money temptation entirely. His defense had been his need to not please the old man who saw success in terms of money, not artistic achievement. Without that force to react against, he gave in and no longer worked at perfecting his talent . . . Another promising artist down the tubes" (SL 290).

McWilliams gently and rightly pooh-poohs Murphy-Plittman's wrong-headed theory, pointing out that John Fante simply enjoyed life too much to work himself to death for art. Unlike Arthur Miller or Matthew Josephson, who kept "a regular writing schedule day after day, week after week . . . in season and out," Fante never had to have his arm twisted to get him away from his work or onto the golf course or gaming tables. Writers like Fante have, wrote McWilliams, "a great zest for life and joy in living. These types are inclined, naturally, to play hooky whenever they can and it takes very little to tempt them from their desks" (SL 292).

Fante is harder than McWilliams on this would-be biographer and her theories. After reading a copy of McWilliams' reply to Murphy-Plittman, Fante writes: "Your letter to Ms. Murphy-Plittman of Feb. 18 [1972] is interesting, informative and possibly even truthful. I enjoyed it thoroughly. The fellow you write about is most unusual. I should like to meet him sometime, but I don't think I would

care to know him intimately" (SL 293). Fante goes on, however, to blast her theory with both barrels blazing:

> A curious fact about biographers of writers is their stubborn
> resistance to reality. I don't necessarily include yourself, but
> Murphy-Plittman is a good example of a biographer wearing
> blinkers as she gallops toward her goal. For example, I am
> always accused of forsaking my writing for the Hollywood
> glitter and gold. Nobody who writes or reflects on my life
> bothers to consider the hard fact that I had a family to
> maintain, that four children, a wife and a house were in-
> volved. That I worked as a screenwriter is treated as if I had
> had a bout with the clap. If, on the other hand, I had pumped
> gas instead, or been a brick-layer, the ensuing glamor would
> have immortalized me. But who really gives a shit? Writing
> is a disease of these times. Almost everybody is articulate
> these days and the resultant cacophony is deafening. Mur-
> phy-Plittman is a perfect example. She bores the hell out of
> me (SL 294).

If Fante seems overly defensive here, it is because Murphy-
Plittman assumed he was washed-up as an artist, instead of
blaming publishers or indeed the reading public. If his in-
vective seems excessive, it may be that Fante felt the grain of
truth in the wound. Unlike the optimistic tyro who wrote to
Mencken in 1932 that, "barring death or blindness, a man
can get whole warehouses of work done in twenty years"
(FM 26), the John Fante of 1972 knew that he had not lived
up to his braggadocio.

Fante's life-long obsession with his money problems,
which here as elsewhere he overstates, may be understood
in terms of his childhood poverty and the lean days on
Bunker Hill. But Fante too often used the lack of money as
an excuse for not writing novels, when he did not lack
money at all. Even before Joyce Fante's legacy of 1941, and
another in 1946, which assured the couple of a substantial

source of income, Fante was making a fortune in Depression terms during the mid-1930s. As Joyce Fante points out, "He wasn't strictly compelled to write screenplays."[8] Even if we consider his gambling losses during the 1940s, Fante's constant refrain of being broke or on the verge of bankruptcy is incredible, clearly an alibi for not giving more attention to his fiction.

Whether John Fante actually had more novels to write is as futile as wondering whether John Keats would have written more poems, had he lived to Fante's age. Even Joyce Fante is undecided on the question. In 1986 she stated definitively, "John wrote all the novels he had in him."[9] Yet in 1989 she makes an about-face: "I think he could have been a much greater writer than he was. He had other novels he could have written."[10] In any case, money was not the problem. In the end Joyce Fante seems to have concluded, with McWilliams, that the real reason Fante neglected his fiction was that he was more avid for life than art: "I think he put enjoyment of life above literature."[11]

On Valentine's Eve 1975, Fante wrote to McWilliams: "I have written a new novel, by far my best work" (SL 296). *The Brotherhood of the Grape* looked as though it was going to be Fante's greatest success, a blockbuster, surpassing even *Full of Life*. A movie contract was negotiated with Francis Ford Coppola and Robert Towne, who contributed a blurb printed as a foreword, before the book contract was even finalized. Serialized by Coppola's *City Magazine* in 1975 before its publication by Houghton-Mifflin in 1977, *The Brotherhood of the Grape* did in fact turn out to be a critical success, which was more satisfying still. Fante had not published a novel he really cared about since *Ask the Dust* in 1939, almost forty years earlier. The *New York Times Book Review* described the new novel as "alternately full of cleansing laughter and as comical as a toothache."

More Hollywood bad luck: the movie announced on the dust jacket of the book never materialized. It was to have been written by Robert Towne, whose most recent screenplay was Roman Polanski's *Chinatown*, which had featured the growing pains of multi-ethnic Los Angeles in the 1930s (the movie was inspired by Towne's reading of McWilliams' book, *California, The Great Exception*). Coppola was to direct it, fresh from his success with another story about Italian Americans, *The Godfather*. But Coppola's fortunes took a turn for the worse in 1978 with the financial disaster *Apocalypse Now*, and projects had to be canceled. Fante's story was one of the casualties.

The Brotherhood of the Grape returned to the subject of Fante's relationship with his father. By this time, however, Fante was himself the head of the family, similarly beset by alienated sons, and, as the years advanced, sensitive to the uncomfortable similarities between himself and old Nick Fante. Just as his father had taken pride in his work, constructing with his own hands buildings that his son could not identify with, so Fante took pride in his writing, constructing stories that his sons ignored, took for granted, or openly derided. Like his father, he had been a sinner in his time, not only against the wife he loved but against his own ideals. Most importantly, like his father, who had died in 1950 from complications with diabetes, John Fante had known since 1955 that he had inherited the disease. While writing the novel, Fante developed gangrene between his toes. Not long after the book's publication his legs had to be amputated. By 1978, a year after the book's publication, John Fante would go blind as a result of the disease. As time passed he could foresee, more clearly than ever, his own death in his father's.

Ironically, it was in the same year that the Fante revival began to take shape. There are two stories about how this occurred. The Los Angeles writer Ben Pleasants claims to have been the one to bring *Ask the Dust* to the attention of John Martin, the publisher of Black Sparrow Press.[12] Everyone else agrees that it was Bukowski's reference to Fante in the manuscript of his 1978 novel *Women*. Black Sparrow editor Julie Curtis Voss recalls that the staff thought Bandini was "a made-up name, maybe a joke, because Bandini is a brand of fertilizer. We thought, 'You wait until spring to put on your fertilizer.'" Martin called Bukowski and said, "'Bukowski, that was a great little joke you slipped in there about John Fante' and he said, 'You don't know who John Fante is?' That conversation led to Black Sparrow's decision to publish all of Fante's books."[13]

The revival began with *Ask the Dust*. In his preface Bukowski bequeathed Fante's novel to a new generation of readers, but in a deeper sense he was bequeathing a new generation of readers, readers prepared by Bukowski's own books, to John Fante. By this time Bukowski had met his idol, finding him in the Motion Picture and Television Country House in Woodland Hills, a rest home "for Hollywood people, actors, writers and so forth, and it was a nice place full of forgotten people," like "one of the original Tarzans" who "was running up and down the halls giving his calls."[14]

In his preface Bukowski mentioned that there was more to tell about the story of John Fante, "a story of terrible luck and a terrible fate," but that he felt Fante did not want the story told yet. In 1989 Bukowski wrote a brief homage to Fante for *The New Haven Advocate*, in which he describes a bedside visit to Fante, who was planning his next novel, "about a woman baseball player who made the major leagues." Meanwhile, the doctors were "chopping more and more of his legs away, a horrible and terrible way to exit." Fante told him: "The doctor came in today, told me, 'Well, we're going to have to lop off some more of you.' I like that, 'lop,' that's what he said, the bastard."[15] Perhaps because it rhymed with Wop.

Bukowski also describes a dinner at the house in Malibu, where Fante returned before he died. In a scene reminiscent of *The Brotherhood of the Grape,* in which Nick Molise spends his last hours drinking with his *paisani* at Angelo Musso's winery, Fante drank a glass of wine with his guest, though he knew it was poison in his condition. "I know that you're a drinker," Fante told Bukowski, "so I'm going to have a glass of wine with you." As the brotherhood of the grape would have said, "It is better to die of drink than to die of thirst" (BG 160). It was the last time Bukowski saw him. When the family phoned to ask Bukowski to deliver the eulogy at Fante's funeral, Bukowski said that he was "honored but that someone else should. I knew that I would cry if I did so. Tough guys don't cry."[16]

Like Jimmy Toscana who was not scared by priests and Nick Molise who would not give up without a struggle, John Fante refused to be defeated in the final debilitating years, months and days of his life. He continued to write by dictation, relying on his voice to hit all the right notes in the score of memory, just as Guido Toscana had hit all the right notes in his courtship of Maria Scarpi, whose voice was that of the little girl in the throat of Enrico Caruso. "It's difficult for me," said Fante, about the process of writing by dictation. "I have to keep everything in my head. I've never been so finicky as I am now. With my blindness has come a certain determination to become much more accurate."[17] Indeed, *Dreams from Bunker Hill*, the book he dictated in the end, revisits the old haunts of *Ask the Dust*, a more accurate remembrance of things past. The tough kid voice continued to ring true, now somewhat mellower, more meditative, more accurate, until Fante's death on May 8, 1983, at the age of seventy-four. Sometimes, if we listen, we can still hear the echo of that altar boy braggadocio.

Chapter 11

The Legacy of John Fante

To feel that you have a destiny is a nuisance.

John Fante

In 1932 H. L. Mencken published the first story of an unknown writer living in obscurity in Los Angeles named John Fante, the son of a bricklayer from the Abruzzi. Half a century later the author of "Altar Boy" had to be rediscovered by Charles Bukowski. Bukowski's preface to the 1980 reissue of *Ask the Dust* deserves credit for kick-starting the Fante revival. Recalling his own anonymous days in Los Angeles, Bukowski felt dissatisfied with the "very slick and careful Word-Culture" of the modern writers. "One had to go back to the pre-Revolution writers of Russia to find any gamble, any passion" (AD 5). Then he found a few volumes by John Fante gathering dust on the shelves of the L. A. Public Library, just where Arturo Bandini had imagined his works being someday, "to sort of bolster up the B's" (AD 13). The author of these books, said Bukowski, became "my god" and exerted "a lifetime influence on my writing."

As Bukowski pressed the book into the hands of a new generation of readers, he offered a more personal recommendation: "I finally met the author this year. There is much more to the story of John Fante. It is a story of terrible luck and a terrible fate and of a rare and natural courage. Some day it will be told but I feel that he doesn't want me to tell it here. But let me say that the way of his words and way of his way are the same: strong and good and warm. That's enough. Now this book is yours" (AD 6-7).

John Fante may be one of the few writers for whom the cliché "before his time" can be used without exaggeration. By 1940 Fante had three books — *Wait Until Spring, Bandini, Ask the Dust* and *Dago Red* — and a promising future. The problem was, the future would take a little longer to arrive than he thought. John Fante couldn't afford to wait. He cashed in on his reputation as a short story writer by going to Hollywood, where he hoped to make enough money to support his true calling as a novelist. His reputation as a novelist would have to wait a little longer. Word-of-mouth publicity and the support of a few readers with long memories kept him going.

At his death in 1983, with only a handful of books back in print, the Fante revival had just begun. But more novels were on the way: reissues of books thirty and forty years old, a new one he had dictated to his wife when he was blind and bed-ridden just before his death, and newly discovered manuscripts twenty and fifty years old that were found only after his death along with their rejection slips. The reviews were better than ever. His audience was more responsive than ever, more devoted, and ever growing. By the end of the 1980s, all eight novels were available, in addition to a collected and expanded edition of his short stories. These were followed by two volumes of letters, the first devoted to his twenty-two year correspondence with Mencken, the second to the discontinuous first-person narrative of his life as told to Carey McWilliams, his mother, and a host of other friends, supporters and family members. Never one to keep up the self-absorbed reflection of a journal, Fante preferred to unburden himself in letters to an audience of a single reader at a time who was bound to be more sympathetic to his fate than he was to himself. The letters provide an invaluable record of his life — and his voice.

Appreciations began to appear in places like *Rolling Stone, Life, Vogue, Esquire* and the *Times Literary Supplement*, with titles like "John Fante Finally Famous," "Fante Fever," "Forgotten Son of the Lost Generation," and "The Hottest Dead Man in Hollywood." Even Hollywood had come round again, this time to pay tribute to his art by optioning his novels for the movies. By 1990 *The Road to Los Angeles*, Fante's first novel to be rejected by New York publishers, was the only one not yet optioned by Hollywood. In 1940 Fante had tried, briefly and unsuccessfully, to adapt his story, "A Wife for Dino Rossi," for the stage. In 1984 the Mark Taper Forum near Bunker Hill, where Fante had spent some of his most productive and least prosperous years, produced Peter Alum's stage adaptation of *Dreams from Bunker Hill*, and the Denver Center for the Performing Arts bought the rights to its native son's *1933 Was a Bad Year*. Other theater companies followed suit. In 1987 Fante was awarded the Lifetime Achievement Award by PEN, Los Angeles Center.

John Fante's time had come. The author who had been written off as a relic of the 1930s had become a writer to be reckoned with in the 1980s and 1990s.

A new readership had been waiting in the wings of postmodernity. Since much of postmodern literature has been defined by an extension of what Bukowski called the "very slick and careful Word-Culture" of modernism, the taste for Fante might seem a nostalgic throwback to simpler times, less complicated narratives. But Bukowski speaks for the other face of postmodernism when he invokes Fante as his mentor — not the safe abstraction of academic experimentalism influenced by a self-consciousness encouraged by various schools of critical theory in and out of vogue (which Fante might have called "hokum"), nor the minimalist withdrawal inculcated in the creative writing factories throbbing dully from Iowa, the heartland of American corn, but the rude authenticity of an honest voice.

Fante's influence on contemporary writers other than Bukowski has been largely unrecognized. In France, Fante has been called the father of the Los Angeles School of fiction writers, Bukowski being its most famous son. In America, Bukowski is perhaps better known as the main exponent of Los Angeles "Gab Poetry," along with Gerald Locklin, and the influence of Fante is unmistakable in these writers, if somewhat ironic, considering Fante's lack of interest in poetry.[1] Writers of "the other California," such as Gerald Haslam and Gary Soto, have also acknowledged their interest in Fante, as have a number of Italian-American authors.[2] As a whole, though, contemporary writers have not been quick to cite Fante's work as an influence. This has led some reviewers to assume that Fante has not been influential and to overstate the contrast between Fante's work and what has been currently in fashion.[3]

Bob Shacochis, however, writing in *Vogue*, sees a number of similarities not only between Fante and his own contemporaries, but an equal number of uncited Fante influences in a variety of our contemporary writers. Echoing Bukowski's opinion that the "slick and careful Word-Culture" of the modern writers left a gap that Fante's passion fills, Shacochis writes: "By comparison, the writing of Faulkner and other luminaries in the modern pantheon seems blunted, sanitized, encased in glass, while Fante's seems immediate, active, and alive." Along with that of Chandler and Saroyan, Fante's work "deserves to be preserved among the voices of the day — for the singular flavor of the lives it speaks for, his vision of a bygone world, and that vision's influence on the here and now." Shacochis goes further, suggesting that Fante is "the bridge between the emotional recklessness of the lost generation and our currently cool, if embattled, American spirit":

> His sentences spurted with riffs of energy and lyrical passion, predating the Beats; or bit with the satirical wryness that the black humorists — Terry Southern, J. P. Donleavy, the Philip Roth of *Portnoy's Complaint* — would later adopt. Indeed, the embryo of much that we mislabel original and startling in contemporary fiction is there in Fante's work, and his legacy vibrates throughout the literature of the 1980s (Carver, Ford, Janowitz, Boyle, Mason, McInerney, Ellis, *et al.*), though you won't find his beneficiaries lining up to make a claim.[4]

Compared to the modernist writers, not to mention the ironists of postmodernism, Fante's often naked sentiment seems to verge perilously on the brink of sentimentality. (The typical Fante ending dissolves in tears.) But this is precisely what Fante's postmodern audience, the "other" postmodern audience, embraces, and it is exactly what Mencken recognized in the series of impassioned letters and stories that came to him from a twenty-three year old Italian American in California: a distinctive American voice unafraid of speaking directly from the heart about his experience, unafraid of cynicism, irony and vulgarity, and equally unafraid of sentiment. Hemingway defined courage as "grace under pressure," but Fante shows that courage is also being willing to admit to cracking under pressure, to confess what is most absurd in ourselves, and to appear ridiculous when we are ridiculous. Fante doesn't flinch from such confessions. Nor does he flinch from expressing emotion. He can draw the nihilist conclusion that life may be just "a waste of wishes" (WY 40), or assert that the "road to each of us is love" (AD 81).

Despite all the sweet nostalgia of Fante's voice, or perhaps because of it, his work strikes a chord in our era of postmodern cynicism and emotional uprootedness. His voice is, after all, a nostalgia born of brutal candor about his own failings and a spirited attack on the shams of the culture of narcissism, which was bred, if not born, in Hollywood. Because Fante's observations are ruthless, his language plain, and his conclusions so often bleak, it is difficult to begrudge him his saving graces, his fiats of love and understanding and hope. In our time, when intellectuals and artists are as powerless as priests and politicians to give us hope, what could be more refreshing and necessary than to hear one clear and honest voice expressing what in ourselves we most fear and desire: viciousness and grace.

The neglect of Fante in America — his reputation in Europe has long been established — can be blamed only in part on the publishing and academic establishments. While the vagaries of the book market have allowed other writers of Fante's stature to fall through the cracks, thanks to the rise in small press publishing and the long memories of a few admirers Fante now has good distribution and has been well reviewed. The lack of critical attention is more difficult to understand, but this too is now being rectified, thanks in part to the rise in regional, especially Western and West Coast, and multi-ethnic studies in American literature. Thus only recently has Fante begun to get the critical attention he deserves. Fante holds a special place in the history of ethnic literature in the West, and some credit must go to the journals like *The Redneck Review of Literature, Italian Americana, Voices in Italian Americana,* and *MELUS* (Multi-Ethnic Literature in the United States) for bringing Fante to the attention of a wider range of critics and granting him his rightful place as one of the few Italian-American novelists to deal with immigrant culture without once mentioning the Mafia.

Fante's only competition in this line seems to be Pietro Di Donato, whose novel *Christ in Concrete* appeared in 1939, the same year as *Ask the Dust.* After these books, both writers fell into an almost complete silence. Di Donato was basically a one-shot novelist, though he did publish two inferior sequels to *Christ in Concrete* and several non-fiction studies on Italian-American issues. Fante, on the other hand, continued to write fiction that was at least as good as *Ask the Dust,* though little of it was published during his lifetime, while devoting much of his time to a career in screen writing. While Di Donato has enjoyed more critical attention, it now seems clear that Fante was the greater artist, and the one more likely to stand the test of time.

There are several reasons for Di Donato's status as the leading example of Italian-American writing in Fante's generation, including the academic and publishing establishments. Unlike Fante, Di Donato is both tantalizingly interpretable for academic critics and an "east coast regionalist" (if such a term could exist). The polemics of Di Donato's sociology, along with a heavy-handed superstructure of myth that verges on allegory, put *Christ in Concrete* squarely in the camp of Depression-era novelists with an ideological agenda. Powerful as Di Donato's novel is emotionally, however, the book is marred artistically by being so easily dated. In contrast, Fante has no program for social change and no interest in revealing the scaffolding of religious motifs that do nevertheless inform his work. The poverty and religion in Fante's work are not specific to an era. Fante's creations are compact structures, strong and simple, like the stone hearths and smoke-houses his father built, whereas Di Donato's are more ambitious public structures, like the concrete that swallows his Christ-like protagonist.

It helps, of course, that Di Donato's work is set in New York, whereas all of Fante's works take place in Colorado or California. No one would call Di Donato a "regionalist" because of the specificity of his locale. Terms like "new regionalist" and "new ethnicist" annoyed Fante because they tend to ghettoize an artist's work according an author's background or a work's setting. Even sympathetic critics, especially Californians, still tend to read Fante's works almost entirely in the context of their setting. Naturally, this can be helpful. Gerald Locklin, for example, goes beyond comparing Fante with the usual cast of Hollywood writers (West, Chandler, Cain and Fitzgerald), to point out the often overlooked similarities between Fante and Budd Schulberg, Joan Didion, Norman Mailer, and John Gregory Dunne, as the outstanding fictional chroniclers of "the country's second most populous megalopolis."[5] But the emphasis is still on second.

Unlike so many would-be Bandinis, Bukowski included, Fante did not cultivate a pose as an alternative, counter-culture or cult writer. His ideals and ambitions for himself and for his work were all-American, sometimes embarrassingly so. He resented being kept out of the mainstream by reviewers who categorized him ethnically or located his work regionally, and he would probably have had a few choice words of irony at being made a curiosity of critical fashion today. Fante wrote to his friend Carey McWilliams, author of *The New Regionalism* (1931): "if Cooper and Washington Irving were in their own times new

Regionalists, so were Thoreau and Mark Twain and every writer, in the order of their appearance in any history of literature" (SL 50). Fante recognized, however, that authors fashionably ethnic or regional today may become the American classics of tomorrow. This may, in fact, be Fante's own fate.

East Coast parochialism, as Fante came to view the New York publishing establishment, failed to prejudice foreign publishers against him. He had no trouble finding an admiring public in Europe and South America, where his books in translation still sell more copies than in the United States. Italian translations were naturally among the first to appear, but it was in France that he was first considered a peer of Hemingway, Faulkner and Steinbeck, and dubbed by *Le Monde* "un maître américain." Like Bukowski, whose fame in America was in part a boomerang effect from Germany, Fante found his real champions in Europe.

Fante is particularly popular in the land of Knut Hamsun, where his work has been chosen for the Norwegian Book-of-the-Month Club. When we consider Fante's enormous and acknowledged debt to Hamsun, the writer he most resembles, this makes perfect sense. The starving scribbler in Hamsun's *Hunger* is, after all, the direct literary ancestor of Arturo Bandini, who is, like Hamsun's hungry narrator (here described by Isaac Bashevis Singer), "frivolous in word and deed" and "speaks to people as he would to a dog or to himself."[6] Like Hamsun, Fante is the novelist of all that is odd and lyrical and contradictory in our human responses to the most familiar situations. "His heroes are all children," writes Singer of Hamsun, "as romantic as children, as irrational, and often as savage,"[7] and the same could be said of Fante. The novelist and film critic David Thomson writes: "Fante never wrote a sentence you couldn't sing, or two in a row that don't confuse your urges to laugh and cry,"[8] and the same could be said of Hamsun.

The very different regional and ethnic identities of these like-minded writers argue against relying too much on such accidentals as where they come from. And the fact that both writers translate so well, in so many languages and over such a long period of time, attests to the universality of their literary art.[9] Hamsun's settings in Christiania (Oslo) or Fante's in Los Angeles, like the authors' Scandinavian or Mediterranean heritages, merely supply the experienced particulars of events and emotions that are, essentially, neither Norwegian nor Italian-American; they are, above all, human. Carey McWilliams, in response to a student's inquiry about the importance of Fante's ethnicity to his work, wrote: "I am aware of course that ethnicity, particularly 'the new ethnicity' which will soon become the 'new, new ethnicity,' is the current intellectual fad. All sort of problems are now being interpreted in the light of the new canon. But I have some doubts that ethnic differences and ethnic backgrounds are as important as the current fashion makes them out to be" (SL 291). McWilliams's comment, written in 1972, which certainly reflects Fante's own views on the matter, seems to have been prophetic.

What *is* essential to Fante's work is his voice and vision: his poignant portrayal of the hope of imagination that leads to the despair of thwarted ambition, and of the pleasures and small victories that are the only rewards for the agonizing compromises of everyday life. The ancient Greek dramatists, like Fante, realized that tragedy is only another form of comedy: both cut us down to size. They also realized that the weight of tragedy needs to be punctuated by comic barbs for us to recognize the full range of our emotional and intellectual reactions to our fate. The failure of our superhuman ambitions forces us to admit the ridiculous nature of our humanity, to confront and so appreciate the flawed particulars in ourselves and others that make us what we are: more mistaken than vicious, in Kenneth Burke's phrase,[10] or "not so ugly as comical," in Fante's (SL 236). Failure becomes an epiphany of incompetence, a revelation of the value of human life. The simplest human pleasure is also its greatest virtue, love. Self-love, romantic love, familial love, and the more general and spontaneous outpouring of sympathy with humanity that made Arturo Bandini a "lover of man and beast alike" (AD 76) — these are Fante's central subjects and the points of his compass in mapping out the community of which he felt himself to be a part. It is the beauty of Fante's achievement, and perhaps the lesson of the odyssey of his life, that a chronicle of the birth and death of dreams is worth the telling, and worth a life of work to capture in an art that preserves the identity of one human voice.

Notes

Chapter 1

1. Fante's autobiographical fiction shares in the modern tendency to carry a protagonist over from one novel to another in a series of sequels and prequels. Earlier examples of protean authorial alter egos include James Joyce's Stephen Dedalus, William Faulkner's Quentin Compson, and Ernest Hemingway's Nick Adams (one of Fante's titles for *The Road to Los Angeles* was "In My Time"); contemporary examples are James T. Farrell's Studs Lonigan and Henry Miller's Henry Miller; a later example is Charles Bukowski's Henry Chinaski. Fante differs from these writers in his willingness to change the details of his alter egos' life and character from book to book, almost as if to assert that Arturo Bandini and the various Molise protagonists live exclusively in the landscape of the imagination created by the individual book, where the rules of verisimilitude, so important to the realist's appeal to the reader's suspension of disbelief, are themselves suspended.

2. Some of these changes could be attributed to the discontinuous publishing history of the novels. One could argue that if Fante had been able to publish the Bandini and Molise novels in the order they were written he might have attempted to make them more consistent with one another. This seems unlikely, since Fante never envisioned an over-arching plan for either of his makeshift tetralogies, in the manner of, say, Lawrence Durrell's *Alexandria Quartet*. Fante seems to have consciously chosen to keep the identity of his protagonists fluid and the "facts" of their lives in flux.

3. In stories like "Scoundrel" (*Woman's Home Companion*, 1945), "The Dreamer" (*Woman's Home Companion*, 1947) and "In the Spring" (*Collier's*, 1952), Fante seems detached from his protagonist narrators, James Kennedy, John Lane and Jake Crane, and loses the ethnic flavor and passion of the family stories. He does better in stories about Filipino and other immigrants, such as "Helen, Thy Beauty Is to Me—" (1941) and "One-Play Oscar" (1950), both published in *The Saturday Evening Post*, the first narrated in the third-person but very close to the consciousness of Julio Sal, and the second narrated by

Anthony Campiglia, an Italian alter ego who appears nowhere else in Fante's fiction.

4. As Arturo Bandini reflects in *Ask the Dust*: "I think about a few other Italians, Casanova and Cellini, and then I think about Arturo Bandini, and I have to punch myself in the head" (90). A few pages later, he says to himself: "Maybe you did write The Little Dog Laughed, but you'll never write Casanova's Memoirs" (93).

5. Oscar Wilde, *The Picture of Dorian Gray* (Harmondsworth: Penguin, 1949), p. 109.

6. "From Oral Tradition to Written Word: Toward an Ethnographically Based Literary Criticism," in *From the Margin: Writings in Italian Americana*, ed. Anthony J. Tamburri, Paolo A. Girodano and Fred L. Gardaphé (West Lafayette, Indiana: Purdue University Press, 1991), p. 300.

7. For a number of important essays on the history of critical approaches to autobiography and its relationship to autobiographical fiction, see *Autobiography: Essays Theoretical and Critical*, ed. James Olney (Princeton: Princeton University Press, 1980). Of particular interest in relation to Fante is Stephen Spender's essay, "Confessions and Autobiography" [originally published in *The Making of a Poem* (New York: Norton, 1962)]. Spender asks why we have so many "memoirs where a self-portrait verges on fiction, and novels where fiction is really autobiography," and answers: "I think it is because the inner life is regarded by most people as so dangerous that it cannot be revealed openly and directly. An antidote that can be applied at the very moment of revelation needs to be applied to this material. The antidote was once the Church. Today it is the vast machinery of psychological analysis and explanation" (p. 122).

8. Robert Bly quotes from Hamsun's *The Cultural Life of Modern America* in his Introduction to his translation of Hamsun's *Hunger:* "Truth telling does not involve seeing both sides or objectivity; truth telling is unselfish inwardness" (New York: Farrar, Straus & Giroux, 1967), p. xiv.

9. Professor Jay Martin has discussed the influence of religion on Fante's fiction in terms of the meditation, rather than the confession. Drawing on Fante's early Jesuit schooling, in which the soul-searching literary exercise is common practice, Martin accounts for the deceptively lyrical power and immediacy of Fante's autobiographical fiction by comparing it to the methods and aims of such predecessors as John Donne and James Joyce. "John Fante: The Burden of Modernism and the Life of His Mind" in Cooper and Fine (1999).

10. Pasinetti (1952).

11. I am using the term *kitsch* as defined by Milan Kundera: "the need to gaze into the mirror of the beautifying lie and to be moved to tears of gratification at one's own reflection," *The Art of the Novel*, trans. Linda Asher (New York: Grove Press, 1988), p. 135. This notion is further developed in his fiction: "As soon as kitsch is recognized for the lie it is, it moves into the context of non-kitsch, thus losing its authoritarian power and becoming as touching as any other human weakness. For none among us is superman enough to escape kitsch completely. No matter how we scorn it, kitsch is an integral part of the human condition," *The Unbearable Lightness of Being*, trans. Michael Henry Heim (New York: Harper and Row, 1984), p. 256.

12. Joyce Fante comments: "Ironically, *Full of Life* depicts a sunny domestic scene with a loving young husband and wife expecting their first baby, the polar opposite of what had really been going on in the Fante household" (SL 225).

13. Throughout this book I discuss *Full of Life* in the context of the Molise series of novels. Neither Joyce Fante nor any of the Fante scholars I have contacted seem to recall what the original family name in the book was. It seems clear, however, that in its concern with family themes, *Full of Life* belongs to the Molise cycle and not, as some writers have claimed, to the Bandini saga.

14. Kenneth Burke, *Attitudes Toward History* (Berkeley & Los Angeles: University of California Press, 1937), pp. 41-2.

Chapter 2

1. For discussions of the hyphenate writer, see Aaron (1964) and Tamburri (1989, 1991).

2. Fante's self-description as a "little squirt," comes from the synopsis of his life in his 1932 letter to Mencken (FM 29). Other sources give the date of the move to Boulder as 1920, which would have made Fante eleven at the time. The age of seven comes from Chapter 9 of *Dreams from Bunker Hill*, in which Fante retells his life story, revising his place of birth from "in a macaroni factory" to "a basement apartment of a macaroni factory" (55). In both cases, Fante recounts his early life from birth to his discovery of Sherwood Anderson and his first attempts at writing in a few short pages that differ very little, although the later retelling is, mostly, more accurate than the 1932 letter to Mencken in which he lies about his date of birth, among other facts of his life.

3. In the *Dreams from Bunker Hill* version of his story, Fante changes the first eye-opening work of Sherwood Anderson from "I Want to Know Why" to *Winesburg, Ohio*.

4. See Donovan (1941). In the *Dreams from Bunker Hill* version of this episode, Bandini says he fell in love with a girl named Agnes who worked in a clothing store. When she moves to North Platte, Nebraska to get away from him, he follows her, she rejects him, and he returns to Boulder, where he joins other "young, unemployed men," and leans "against walls in the pool halls" (56-7).

5. Donovan (1941).

6. Pleasants (1994).

7. For the material on Fante's Long Beach years, I am indebted to Frank Gaspar's "John Fante in Long Beach," a paper delivered at the John Fante Conference, May 1995.

Chapter 3

1. Several critics have noted *Dago Red*'s generic resemblance to the novel. Marianne Hauser called the book "neither a novel nor a collection of short stories, but a freely constructed family portrait, seen impressionistically" (Hauser 1940). Jerre Mangione reviewed *Dago Red* under the title "Italian-American Novelists" (Mangione 1941). More recently, Gerald Locklin in a review of *The Wine of Youth* has characterized Fante's stories as a "disjunctive bildungsroman" (Locklin 1985).

2. I deal with most of the other stories from *Dago Red* as well as the later stories collected in *The Wine of Youth* in other chapters: the Filipino stories and "One-Play Oscar" in Chapter 7, the baseball stories in Chapter 8. See also my articles, Collins (1991) and Collins (1995). Excellent readings of "A Wife for Dino Rossi" were presented at the John Fante Conference by Louise Napolitano-Carman in "Mothers and Fathers in Fante's Stories," and Leonardo Buonomo in "Masculinity and Femininity in John Fante's 'A Wife for Dino Rossi,'" the latter printed in Cooper and Fine (1999).

3. Understandably, Fante wanted "Altar Boy" to be the opening story in *Dago Red*, but the editors wisely chose "A Kidnaping in the Family" to lead off the volume, adopting an entirely different sequence than what Fante suggested, except for the final two stories (SL 167).

4. The only reason that Fante, whose sole essay was a sketch of William Saroyan in *Common Ground* in 1941, would have resorted to non-fiction would be to imitate Mencken. Whenever Fante pitched an idea in terms of a "sociological study" (like the Filipino novel), it

was a sure sign that he was bluffing and blustering, and that the project would come to nothing.

5. In his letters, however, Fante continues to take a critical view of Italian Americans. A trip to Italy in 1957 helped to give him a new perspective. Fante was impressed by the peasants but appalled at the slick Roman counterparts of Hollywood phonies. Still, as late as 1975 Fante was capable of vituperative blasts against Italian Americans: "They don't want to be lumped with the blacks and Puerto Ricans; after all, they are white folks, proud of their race and traditions; they don't want to scream and make waves like the lowly nigger, so they do nothing except hold high their heads and eat lots of pasta and see *The Godfather* six times, because that fills them with pride, that's what it's all about: Marlon Brando, Al Pacino — their kind of people, proud, romantic, not niggers screaming for their fair share of the trough." (For a discussion of Fante's use of racial slurs, see Chapter 10.) That he refers to Italian Americans as "they" instead of "we," shows that Fante is still capable of distancing himself from his heritage, although he claims his right to call his own people Wop and Dago, now in deprecation, now in affection. He doesn't miss a chance to blame religion as part of the problem: "Of course their priests are to blame too. Proud men of Mother Church, doing nothing for the belly, but saving the soul. Oh shit! Italian-Americans are so screwed up, so hopelessly unassimilated, so stupid, so castrated by their idiotic parents who, in turn were poisoned by *their* parents, all the way back to the biggest horse's ass of all time — the Emperor Constantine" (Fante to Carey McWilliams, 13 February 1975).

6. In 1979 Fante told an interviewer that he was in Venice Beach at the time of the earthquake, staying with a woman who was the model for Vera Rivken in *Ask the Dust* (Pleasants, 1994). Claudia in "The Wrath of God," however, appears to be modeled more on Helen Purcell, also approximately "in her thirty-sixth year" (WY 159) at the time of Fante's relationship with her.

7. See Mario Praz, *The Romantic Agony*, trans. Angus Davidson (New York: Oxford University Press, 1933; 2nd ed. 1951), p. 321.

Chapter 4

1. Thomson (1989).

2. For Henry Miller's amusing comments on his own failure to receive a Guggenheim in 1941, see his "Addenda" to *The Air-Conditioned Nightmare* (New York: New Directions, 1945), pp. 289-92. Miller "culls" some twenty examples of recipients, mostly academics, and

their forgettable proposals. He does not include Carey McWilliams in the list.

3. Joyce Fante's resentment of Wills is repeatedly expressed in her commentaries in the *Selected Letters*. Commenting on an early version of this chapter in 1987, Joyce Fante wrote: "I wish you had not used the Ross Wills article as a source. John resented certain things Ross said, and it is too bad to see these inaccuracies perpetuated" (personal correspondence with the author, 22 December 1987). In the present chapter, I have taken Joyce Fante's concerns into consideration and used only that factual material that has held up under further research. I have kept some of what Wills says, however, in the interest of providing a more accurate portrait of John Fante, both how he was and how he was seen by his friends and close associates, of whom Ross Wills was one of the closest at this time. In any case, the point is now moot, since the Wills article was reprinted in the *Selected Letters* in 1991, with Joyce Fante's permission.

4. Fante dedicated *Dago Red* to "Ross Wills and Carey McWilliams — good friends, evil companions." Fante evidently borrowed the term Evil Companions from a group of Denver journalists in the early part of the century.

5. These details argue that Wills was to become, along with Joel Sayre and others, the primary model for Frank Edgington in *Dreams from Bunker Hill*.

6. Fante to Carey McWilliams, 27 July 1942.

7. Pleasants (1994).

8. Pleasants (1994).

9. From Roseville, Fante wrote to McWilliams, who had recently had lunch with Marie Baray. After saying, "I bequeath her to you," Fante says he hopes she is not bothering McWilliams, a lawyer, with any more "penny ante law suits." This is probably only in reference to Marie Baray's seeking some free legal advice, rather than to any action against Fante.

10. This undated letter has been placed at "c. summer 1933" (SL 57). It might be, however, that it dates from the summer of 1937.

11. Bruno Domercq, "Grant Him This Waltz." *Paris Vogue* (November 1989). Translated by Joyce Fante. From a typescript supplied by Catherine Kordich.

12. Fante to Carey McWilliams, 6 July 1937.

13. Domercq (1989) gives the date of the marriage as March 1937, which Joyce Fante in her translation of Domercq does not correct. It is clear, however, from Fante's letter to McWilliams, dated 6 July 1937, that the marriage had not yet taken place. Later in the article Domercq quotes Mencken's letter of "condolence" in Fante's letter

of March 1938 about his "recent" marriage. Domercq's confusion is probably due to a misunderstanding of Fante's use of the word "recent."

14. Domercq (1989).
15. Garside (1939).
16. Krist (1993).
17. Binsse (1939).
18. *New Yorker* (1938 and 1939).
19. This volume was illustrated with fourteen linoleum cuts by the artist Valenti Angelo, whose own autobiographical novel on the Italian-American experience in California, *Golden Gate* (1939), was published by Viking the year before *Dago Red*.
20. Gaston Bachelard, from the Introduction to *La Poétique de l'espace* (1958), in *Critical Theory from Plato to the Present*, rev. ed., ed. Hazard Adams (Fort Worth: Harcourt Brace Jovanovich, 1992), p. 1074. Translated by Maria Jolas.
21. Krampner (1987).
22. Krampner (1987).

Chapter 5

1. It is possible that "A Wife for Dino Rossi," published for the first time in *Dago Red*, is what is left of *Pater Dolorosa*, the novel that Fante was working on after the rejection of *The Road to Los Angeles*, the material reworked as *Wait Until Spring, Bandini*. No manuscript of *Pater Dolorosa* has ever been found. The theme of the father's infidelity is reworked later, notably in "The Orgy" and *The Brotherhood of the Grape*.

2. In Domenique de Rudierre's film, Maria Bandini is played by Ornella Muti, a beautiful young actress whose brooding sensuality makes it difficult to understand Svevo's affair with the widow Hildegarde, played by Faye Dunaway. After a screening of this film in May 1995, I asked Tom Fante, John's youngest brother, if the movie's portrayal of the family was fairly accurate. "Well, it's a movie," he said. "But yes. Except that our mother was never so young or so beautiful."

3. In the film, Faye Dunaway plays this scene to suggest that the widow Hildegarde is knowingly insulting Svevo and his son to drive him home to his wife and children. Nothing in Fante's treatment of the scene, however, justifies such an unselfish interpretation of her motives. On the contrary, it seems clear that she plays the "bitch" to Svevo's "lowdown dog."

4. Byrne (1988) discusses the novel in terms of what was being rejected by publishers prior to World War II.

5. Other possible titles included "Brief Passion," "Harbor Days," and "The Oddest Fancy," but Fante finally settled on *The Road to Los Angeles* because it had "a bulky sound I like" (SL 126).

6. This strikingly obtuse reviewer notes Arturo's rage without linking it to the *Iliad*, and the elements of picaresque without recognizing them: "Arturo does not develop, for better or worse, in any dramatic way as the story progresses. In fact, it may be said that throughout the four novels, not just *The Road to Los Angeles*, Arturo Bandini remains a static, ineffective character" (Misurella, 1990). The final sentence is, of course, indefensible, and one can only suppose that Misurella recognized himself in one of Arturo's more colorful epithets, such as "Boobus Americanus" or "bucolic rainspout."

7. Bernard Knox, Introduction, Homer, *The Iliad*, trans. Robert Fagles (New York: Viking, 1990), p. 47. All quotations from the text of the *Iliad* are from this translation.

8. Quoted by Knox, pp. 58-9.

9. Knox, p. 59.

10. *The Picture of Dorian Gray* (Harmondsworth: Penguin, 1949), p. 109.

11. Knut Hamsun, *Hunger*, trans. Robert Bly (New York: Farrar, Straus & Giroux, 1967), p. 12.

12. Knox, p. 58.

13. Knox, p. 45.

Chapter 6

1. Personal communication from Fante's daughter Victoria.

2. Isaac Bashevis Singer, "Knut Hamsun, Artist of Skepticism," in Knut Hamsun, *Hunger* (New York: Farrar, Straus & Giroux, 1967), p. ix.

3. Robert Bly, "The Art of Hunger," in Knut Hamsun, *Hunger* (New York: Farrar, Straus & Giroux, 1967), p. xx.

4. Quoted by Bly, p. xiv.

5. Clark (1989).

6. Baillet (1983), p. 60.

7. Cooper (1995).

8. Fine (1984), p. 44; quoted by Cooper (1995).

9. Cooper (1995). See also Fine (1991) and Kordich (1994).

10. Knut Hamsun, *Hunger*, trans. Robert Bly (New York: Farrar, Straus & Girous, 1967), pp. 32-3.

11. Pleasants (1979).

12. Pleasants (1979).

13. Actually, Fante's note said: "Go fuck yourself!" (Pleasants, 1994).
14. Velda van der Zee is probably based on the Russian-born Sonya Levien (1888-1960), one of the most prolific screenwriters in Hollywood. Her screen credits (mostly collaborations) number well over sixty, including *Salome of the Tenements* (Famous Players-Lasky, 1925), *Rebecca of Sunnybrook Farm* (Fox, 1932), *State Fair* (Fox, 1933), *The Hunchback of Notre Dame* (RKO, 1939), *Rhapsody in Blue* (Warner Bros., 1945), *The Great Caruso* (MGM, 1951), *Oklahoma!* (Rodgers & Hammerstein/Magna, 1955), and *Jeanne Eagels* (George Sidney Productions/ Columbia, 1957). The last title was done in collaboration with Daniel Fuchs and John Fante.
15. Ironically, it was in Woodland Hills that Fante himself died, only months after the publication of *Dreams from Bunker Hill*.

Chapter 7

1. Some writers on Fante, including Seamus Cooney in his edition of the *Selected Letters*, have mistakenly cited *Full of Life* as a nominee for an Academy Award for Best Screenplay; it was *Lust for Life*, in which Kirk Douglas plays Van Gogh, that was the year's nominee. Even Joyce Fante seems to have come to believe this legend. See Domercq (1989).
2. Andrew Horton has located the Fante touch in those scenes in which characters are revealed as most endearing when they are most foolish. "John Fante and Film: *A Walk on the Wild Side* and *The Reluctant Saint*," a paper delivered at the John Fante Conference, 1995. Edward Dmytryk, who directed both films, described Fante as having "a wonderful sense of contrast. To develop character. Not every writer has that. Most writers can write a scene, but they can't develop wonderful characters . . . I think he was a great movie writer who wasn't understood by producers." Dmytryk adds that Fante's success in Hollywood was limited because "there's no question that he was an artist. There's just no question about that. " Quoted in Gordon (1993).
3. Thomson (1986).
4. Fante to Carey McWilliams, undated letter, c. 1971.
5. Pleasants (1994).
6. Pleasants (1994).
7. Baillett (1983).
8. Correspondent quoted by Gordon (1993).
9. Spotnitz (1989).
10. Spotnitz (1989).
11. See Spotnitz (1989).

12. Pleasants (1994).

13. All quotations in the Lewis story are from Pleasants (1994). The story is corroborated in an earlier interview from almost fifty years earlier (Donovan, 1941).

14. Saroyan (1976), p. 109.

15. The original reels for *It's All True* have recently been retrieved from the archives, partially restored, and made available on video. While the "My Friend Bonito" segment has survived, it is without a soundtrack, so whatever dialogue Fante may have contributed has been lost.

16. Pleasants (1994).

17. In writing about taxi dancers, Fante may well have taken his cue from a book notice in the issue of the *American Mercury* in which "Altar Boy" appeared. The book is Paul G. Cressey's *The Taxi Dance-Hall* (Chicago: University of Chicago Press, 1932). "A taxi dance-hall is one to which only men patrons are admitted. Their female partners are all young women on the staff of the establishment. The patron pays so much a dance, usually ten cents, and the money is divided between his partner and the management. A lively girl can make $30 or $40 a week in such a place. Mr. Cressey here presents the results of an investigation made in Chicago, where there are many taxi halls. He finds that the great majority of the girls tend to go downhill. They come, in the main, from very inferior homes, and so their introduction to the dance-hall seems a step upward, but very soon they turn the other way, and many end in squalid prositution." *American Mercury* (August 1932), p. xii.

18. Fante to Carey McWilliams, 23 March 1972.

Chapter 8

1. Philip Hobsbaum, *Reader's Guide to Charles Dickens* (London, 1972), p. 16.

2. DiMaggio won the batting crown in 1939 and 1940 with averages of .381 and .352.

3. In *The Road to Los Angeles* Arturo steals his dead father's wedding ring for bus fare to Los Angeles, while in *Full of Life*, Fante tells of stealing his father's cement mixer to buy a bicycle, which may be closest to the real life theft, if any, at the bottom of Fante's obsession with theft in the interest of transportation.

4. Fante's title, if not his approach, may well have been inspired by J. R. Ackerley's *My Dog Tulip* (New York: Poseidon, 1965), a wry memoir about a man and his dog, with its own brand of humor, as seen in this passage about a visit to the vet and how Ackerley and

his bitch Tulip observe an unfortunate Spaniel in the next examining room: "He was standing quietly on a table with a thermometer sticking out of his bottom, like a cigarette. And this humiliating spectacle was rendered all the more crushing by the fact that there was no one else there. Absolutely motionless, and with an air of deep absorption, the dog was standing upon the table in an empty room with a thermometer in his bottom, almost as though he had put it there himself . . . 'Oh, Tulip!' I groaned. 'If only you were like that!'" (p. 15).

Chapter 9

1. This scene, reminiscent of "My Father's God," suggests that the story may have been written as early as 1950.
2. In the movie version of *Full of Life*, Joyce's reading material is very different. On the train with John to San Juan to bring Nick back to work on the house, she reads not books on child care or theology but Kenneth Burke's *A Rhetoric of Motives*, in the familiar blue and white University of California Press paperback. This is perhaps a sly reminder by the screenwriter John Fante that there is more to the story, and to the protagonists, than meets the eye.
3. Fante had envisioned a novel of the subject of birth control since 1936, which he was never able to bring together, partly because of the odd points of view he wanted to use (God's, for example). This scene seems to be the net result.
4. Fante himself discovered in 1955 that he, like his father, was diabetic, and complications from the disease resulted in his blindness in 1978, one year after the publication of *The Brotherhood of the Grape*.
5. In a blurb for the novel, Robert Towne called Nick Molise and Jehovah "two very powerful, very grumpy old men who won't take shit from anybody."
6. In his "prologue" to the novel, Fante uses the name Svevo Bandini for Nick Molise (SL 236).
7. Arthur Banning was, of course, the name of Arturo Bandini's rich playboy alter ego in his first dismal attempt at a novel, while Banning Park was where Arturo read Nietzsche and Spengler.
8. Fante himself was an Aries, sign of the goat; his wife Joyce took an interest in astrology, as well as theology.
9. Ken Russell's movie version of Lawrence's novel appeared while Fante was writing the novel.

Chapter 10

1. *The Brotherhood of the Grape* would also be picked up by Bantam in 1978.
2. Here is the key to Fante's tender *roman à clef, My Dog Stupid*: Harriet=Joyce; Tina=Victoria; Dominic=Nick; Dennis or Denny=Danny; Jamie=James or Jimmy; Henry J. Molise=John Fante. The adopted dog of the title bears an uncanny resemblance in bearing if not in breed to Fante's pit bull: Rocco=Stupid.
3. Fante to Carey McWilliams, 15 January 1958.
4. Fante to Carey McWilliams, 27 October 1965.
5. Fante to Carey McWilliams, 21 April 1971.
6. Gordon (1993).
7. McWilliams (1946), p. 364.
8. McQuay (1989).
9. Rolfe (1986).
10. McQuay (1989).
11. McQuay (1989).
12. This is not the only fact Pleasants gets wrong. He also mis-dates *Ask the Dust*; claims that *Dago Red* (rather than *Full of Life*) was dedicated to Mencken; and places *Wait Until Spring, Bandini, Ask the Dust, Full of Life* and *The Brotherhood of the Grape* in the same "quartet" of novels.
13. Krampner (1987).
14. Bukowski (1989).
15. Bukowski (1989).
16. Bukowski (1989).
17. Pleasants (1979).

Chapter 11

1. See Robert Peters, "Gab Poetry, Duck vs. Nightingale Music: Charles Bukowski," *Margins* 16 (January 1975), pp. 24-8. Reprinted in *The Great American Poetry Bake-Off* (Metuchen, NJ & London: Scarecrow Press, 1979; see also 2nd series, 1982); and in *Where the Bee Sucks: Workers, Drones and Queens of Contemporary American Poetry* (Santa Maria: Asylum Arts, 1994).
2. Jerre Mangione was one of the first Italian-American authors to recognize Fante in print as one of the "Italian-American Novelists" in an article of the same title in *The New Republic* 104 (6 January 1941). Others have been Helen Barolini, Felix Stefanile, Kenneth Gangemi and Pasquale Verdicchio. See the controversy over Gay Talese's

New York Times Book Review article, "Where Are the Italian-American Novelists?" (14 March 1993) in *Italian Americana* 12:1 (Fall/Winter 1993), 7-37, and in *Voices in Italian Americana* 4:1 (1993), 235-7. It should be noted that Talese delivered the Headline Address at the John Fante Conference in 1995, in which he admitted that he was a late-comer to the works of Fante, but an enthusiastic late-comer.

3. Lem Coley, for example, in a review of the reissued *Full of Life* and *The Brotherhood of the Grape*, calls Fante's work "vivid and open, in contrast to today's attenuated fiction" and finds comparison of Fante's slapstick and passion only in the films of Federico Fellini. See "California: No Remorse," *American Book Review* 11:1 (March-April 1989), p. 8.

4. Shacochis (1987). Bret Easton Ellis quotes the first paragraph of *Ask the Dust* as the epigraph to his novel *The Informers* (New York: Knopf, 1994).

5. Gerald Locklin, "Dreams from Bunker Hill: John Fante," *American Book Review* 5:2.

6. Singer, p. ix.

7. Singer, p. ix.

8. Thomson (1986).

9. Translation is especially important to writers who have small audiences, either because they write in a "minor" language, or because they appeal to a limited or non-mainstream audience. As the Czech writer Arnold Lustig has said, "All writers are international, universal. We are citizens of the world, if we are really writers. And these translations . . . are an extension of the writer." Miroslav Holub elaborates: "It's the best definition I can imagine. The implication of this definition is: it's not a copy. The translation, in the existential sense of the word, is the transfer of the writer to other people." See "A Conversation with Arnold Lustig and Miroslav Holub," *Trafika: An International Literary Review* 1 (Prague: August 1993), p. 160.

10. "The progress of humane enlightenment can go no further than in picturing people not as *vicious*, but as *mistaken*. When you add that people are *necessarily* mistaken, that all people are exposed to situations in which they must act as fools, that EVERY insight contains its own special kind of blindness, you complete the comic circle, returning again to the lesson of humility that underlies great tragedy." Kenneth Burke, *Attitudes Toward History* (Berkeley & Los Angeles: University of California Press, 1937), pp. 41-2.

BIBLIOGRAPHY

Books by John Fante

Wait Until Spring, Bandini. New York: Stackpole Sons, 1938. Santa
Barbara: Black Sparrow, 1983.

Ask the Dust. New York: Stackpole Sons, 1939. New York: Bantam, 1954.
Santa Barbara: Black Sparrow, 1980; Preface by Charles Bukowski.

Dago Red. New York: Viking, 1940. Illustrated with woodcuts by Valenti
Angelo.

Full of Life. Boston: Little, Brown, 1952. New York: Bantam, 1953. Santa
Rosa: Black Sparrow, 1987.

Bravo, Burro! (with Rudolph Borchert). New York: Hawthorn Books, 1970.
Illustrated by Marilyn Hirsch.

The Brotherhood of the Grape. Boston: Houghton Mifflin, 1977. New York:
Bantam, 1978. Santa Rosa: Black Sparrow, 1988.

Dreams from Bunker Hill. Santa Barbara: Black Sparrow, 1982.

1933 Was a Bad Year. Santa Barbara: Black Sparrow, 1985.

The Wine of Youth: Selected Stories. Santa Barbara: Black Sparrow, 1985.
Includes *Dago Red* and selected later stories.

The Road to Los Angeles. Santa Barbara: Black Sparrow, 1985.

West of Rome. Santa Rosa: Black Sparrow, 1986. Comprises "My Dog
Stupid" and "The Orgy."

*Fante/Mencken. John Fante & H. L. Mencken: A Personal Correspondence
1930-1952*. Ed. Michael Moreau. Santa Rosa: Black Sparrow, 1989.
Illustrated with 22 photographs.

Prologue to Ask the Dust. San Francisco: Magnolia Editions — Modernism,
1990. Santa Rosa: Black Sparrow, 1990. Illustrated with etchings by
John Register.

Selected Letters 1932-1981. Ed. Seamus Cooney. Santa Rosa: Black
Sparrow, 1991. Illustrated with 39 photographs.

Short Stories by John Fante

"Altar Boy." *American Mercury* 26 (August 1932): 395-404.
"Home, Sweet Home." *American Mercury* 27 (November 1932): 271-77.

"First Communion." *American Mercury* 28 (February 1933): 171-75.

"Big Leaguer." *American Mercury* 28 (March 1933): 281-86.

"The Odyssey of a Wop." *American Mercury* 30 (September 1933): 89-97.

"One of Us." *Atlantic Monthly* 154 (October 1934): 432-39.

"Washed in the Rain." *Westways* (October 1934).

"Bricklayer in the Snow." *American Mercury* 37 (January 1936): 50-55.

"A Kidnaping in the Family." *Harper's Bazaar* (June 1936).

"We Snatch a Frail" (with Frank Fenton). *The Pacific Weekly* (November 1936).

"Postman Rings and Rings." *American Mercury* (March 1937): 310-16.

"Charge It." *Scribner's* 101 (April 1937): 28-31.

"The Road to Hell." *American Mercury* 42 (October 1937): 214-19.

"None So Blind." *Woman's Home Companion* 65 (April 1938): 19-20.

"A Nun No More." *Virginia Quarterly Review* 16 (Fall 1940): 566-74.

"Helen, Thy Beauty Is to Me —." *Saturday Evening Post* 213 (1 March 1941):14-15, 76, 78, 80.

"The Taming of Valenti." *Esquire* (April 1941): 42-3, 169-71.

"That Wonderful Bird." *Good Housekeeping* 112 (May 1941): 24-5, 167-72.

"Mary Osaka, I Love You." *Good Housekeeping* 115 (October 1942): 40-41, 167-78.

"Scoundrel." *Woman's Home Companion* 72 (March 1945): 22-3.

"Papa Christmas Tree." *Woman's Home Companion* 73 (December 1946): 18-19, 72-4.

"The Dreamer." *Woman's Home Companion* 74 (June 1947): 22-3, 41-2, 44, 47.

"The Wine of Youth." *Woman's Home Companion* 75 (December 1948): 24-5, 114, 122-25.

"One-Play Oscar." *Saturday Evening Post* 223 (November 1950): 28, 109, 111-12, 114.

"In the Spring." *Collier's* 129 (15 March 1952): 21, 34, 36, 38.

"Full of Life" (excerpt). *Reader's Digest* 60 (May 1952): 131-56.

"The Big Hunger." *Collier's* 130 (2 August 1952): 58, 60-1.

"My Father's God." *Italian Americana* (Autumn 1975): 18-31.

Article by John Fante

"Bill Saroyan." *Common Ground* 1:2 (Winter 1941): 64-6.

Screenplays by John Fante

Dinky (with Frank Fenton). Warner Brothers, 1935.

East of the River (with Ross B. Wills). Warner Brothers, 1940. Directed by
 Alfred E. Green.
The Golden Fleecing (with Lynn Root & Frank Fenton). MGM, 1940.
 Directed by Leslie Fenton.
Youth Runs Wild (with Herbert Kline). RKO, 1944. Directed by Mark
 Robson.
My Man and I (with Jack Leonard). MGM, 1952. Directed by William A
 Wellman.
Full of Life. Columbia Pictures, 1956. Directed by Richard Quine.
Jeanne Eagels (with Daniel Fuchs & Sonya Levien). Columbia, 1957.
 Directed by George Sidney.
A Walk on the Wild Side (with Edmund Morris). Dmytyrk-Weiler,
 Columbia, 1962. Directed by Edward Dmytryk.
The Reluctant Saint (with Joseph Petracca). Dmytryk-Weiler, Davis-Royal
 Films International, 1962. Directed by Edward Dmytryk.
My Six Loves (with Joseph Cavelli & William Wood). Paramount, 1963.
 Directed by Gower Champion.
Maya. MGM, 1966.
Something for a Lonely Man. Universal Television, 1967.

Works Consulted

Aaron, Daniel. "The Hyphenate Writer and American Letters." *Smith
 Alumnae Quarterly* (July 1964): 213-17.
Ackerley, J. R. *My Dog Tulip.* New York: Poseidon, 1965.
Angelo, Valenti. *Golden Gate.* New York: Viking, 1939.
Anonymous. Review of *Wait Until Spring, Bandini. New Yorker* 14 (15
 October 1938): 94.
_____. Review of *Wait Until Spring, Bandini* by "W.S." "The New Books."
 Saturday Review 19 (29 October 1938), 20.
_____. Review of *Wait Until Spring, Bandini. New Republic* 97 (9 November
 1938), 28.
_____. Review of *Wait Until Spring, Bandini.*"Books in Brief." *North
 American Review* 246 (Winter 1938-39): 405-6.
_____. Review of *Ask the Dust. New Yorker* 15 (11 November 1939): 73-4.
_____. Review of *Ask the Dust* by "N.L.R." "The New Books." *Saturday
 Review* 21 (25 November 1939): 20.
_____. Review of *Ask the Dust. The Nation* 15 (20 January 1940): 80.
_____. Review of *Dago Red. Boston Transcript* (25 September 1940): 11.
_____. Review of *Dago Red. The Nation* 15 (20 September 1940): 281.
_____. Review of *Dago Red. New Yorker* 16 (28 September 1940): 62.
_____. Review of *Dago Red.* "Teller of Tales." *Time* 36 (7 October 1940): 85.

_____. Review of *Dago Red*. *Booklist* 37 (1 November 1940): 90.

_____. Review of *Full of Life*. *Kirkus* 20 (15 February 1952): 149.

_____. Review of *Full of Life*. *San Francisco Chronicle* (8 May 1952): 20.

_____. Review of *Full of Life*. *Bookmark* 11 (June 1952): 210.

_____. Review of *Full of Life*. *Springfield Republican* (29 June 1952).

_____. Review of *Brotherhood of the Grape*. *Kirkus* 44 (15 December 1976): 1316.

_____.Review of *Brotherhood of the Grape*. *Publishers Weekly* 210 (27 December 1976): 55.

_____. Review of *Brotherhood of the Grape*. *Library Journal* 102 (1 April 1977): 832.

_____. Review of *Brotherhood of the Grape*. *Booklist* 73 (1 May 1977): 1326.

_____. Review of *Ask the Dust*. *Booklist* 76 (15 May 1980): 1348.

_____. Review of *Ask the Dust*. *Kliatt Paperback Book Guide* 14 (Spring 1980): 5.

_____. "American Classic." *Life* 12:11 (October 1989). Announces film of *Wait Until Spring, Bandini*.

Bachelard, Gaston. "Introduction to *La Poétique de l'espace*" (1958), trans. Maria Jolas. In *Critical Theory from Plato to the Present*, rev. ed., ed. Hazard Adams. Fort Worth: Harcout Brace Jovanovich, 1992: 1073-81.

Baillet, Will. "Reporter." *California Historical Society* (August 1983): 60. Fante in Arturo Bandini's Los Angeles, a city "touchingly naive and guilelessly ruthless" and the true protagonist of *Ask the Dust*.

Barry, Iris. "The Raw Justice of Life." *New York Herald Tribune Books* (29 September 1940): 2. Calls "One of Us" the best story in *Dago Red*, for its unromantic child's point of view.

_____. "Behind the Orange Blossoms." *New York Herald Tribune Books* (12 November 1939): 9. Review of *Ask the Dust*.

Bellamy, Joe David. Review of *Brotherhood of the Grape*. *New York Times Book Review* (6 March 1977): 30-1. Calls the book "full of cleansing laughter and as comical as a toothache."

Béranger, Jean F. "Echoes of Protest in John Fante's Works." In Cooper and Fine (1999).

Binsse, Harry Lorin. Review of *Ask the Dust*. *The Commonweal* 31:6 (1 December 1939): 140-1. Finds Fante's "strange novel" to be "most emphatically *not* recommended for reading by the young, or even by the old who dislike sordid pictures of immorality," yet praises the work as having passages that "must particularly appeal to a Catholic reader."

Brown, Carole. "John Fante's *The Brotherhood of the Grape* and Robert Canzoneri's *A Highly Ramified Tree*." *Italian Americana* 3:2 (Spring/Summer 1977): 256-64.

Bukowski, Charles. *Women*. Santa Rosa: Black Sparrow Press, 1978. Mention of Fante that led to the Fante Revival.

_____. Preface to *Ask the Dust*. Santa Barbara: Black Sparrow, 1980: 5-7. Bukowski acknowledges his debt to Fante.

_____. "Remembering John Fante." *New Haven Advocate* (27 February 1989). The poet who delivered the eulogy at Fante's funeral recalls the last days of his hero and friend.

Bulosan, Carlos. *America Is in the Heart* (1946). Memoir by Fante's Filipino friend.

Buonomo, Leonardo. "Masculinity and Femininity in John Fante's 'A Wife for Dino Rossi.'" In Cooper and Fine (1999).

Burke, Kenneth. *Attitudes Toward History*. Berkeley and Los Angeles: University of California Press, 1937.

Byrne, Jack. Review of *The Road to Los Angeles*. *Contemporary Review of Literature* 8:1 (Spring 1988): 206-07. Discusses this posthumously published novel as evidence of Fante's promise and of what kind of writing was being rejected just prior to World War II.

Cammett, John M, ed. *The Italian-American Novel*: Proceedings of the Second Annual American Italian Historical Association Conference. Staten Island, NY: American Italian Historical Association, 1969. Includes a Panel Discussion on the Future of the Italian-American Novel, in which Jerre Mangione urges everyone to read Fante "because he writes about people who are not caught in an urban environment."

Chamberlain, John. Review of *Wait Until Spring, Bandini*. "Books." *Scribner's Magazine* (December 1938): 69-70.

Champlin, Charles. "The Paper Chaser." *Los Angeles Times*, 1 August 1975.

Christie, Tom. "Fante's Inferno." *Buzz* (October 1995). Calls Fante's gift "not the gift of Stevens, Joyce, or Dunne [sic]," and suggests that any comparison between Fante and writers like T. S. Eliot are "just a tad overwrought." Criticizes academics for taking an interest in Fante because "their reputations stand to gain by it."

Clark, Tom. "The Luck of John Fante." *Los Angeles Times Book Review* (9 April 1989): 4. Fante's career, with an emphasis on the early days in Los Angeles and the 1980s revival.

Cobb, Jane. "The Fante Family at Home." *New York Times Book Review* (15 June 1952): 15. Review of *Full of Life*.

Coley, Lem. "California: No Remorse." *American Book Review* 11:1 (March-April 1989): 8. Calls reissued *Full of Life* and *The Brotherhood of the Grape* "vivid and open, in contrast to today's attenuated fiction," and compares Fante's slapstick and passion to Fellini's.

Collins, Richard. Review of *Fante/Mencken*. *New Delta Review* 7:1 (1990): 72-5. Examines Fante's relationship to Mencken.

_____. "Of Wops, Dagos and Filipinos: John Fante and the Immigrant Experience." *Redneck Review of Literature* 21 (Fall 1991): 44-8. Focuses on Filipino short stories in relation to Fante's concern with his own ethnicity in "The Odyssey of a Wop" and *Ask the Dust*.

_____. Review of *Selected Letters: 1932-1981* and *Prologue to* Ask the Dust. *Redneck Review of Literature* 22 (Spring 1992): 57-58. Differences between the Fante biography as revealed in the letters and as fictionalized in the novels.

_____. "Stealing Home: John Fante and the Moral Dimension of Baseball." *Aethlon: The Journal of Sport Literature* 12:1 (Summer 1995): 81-91. On the motif of theft and confession in the baseball stories and *1933 Was a Bad Year*.

_____. "Fante, Family, and the Fiction of Confession." In Cooper and Fine (1999).

Cooper, Stephen. "John Fante's Eternal City." *Los Angeles in Fiction: A Collection of Essays*, rev. ed., ed. David Fine. Albuquerque: University of New Mexico Press, 1995: 83-99. Fante's love affair with the city from the point of view of Arturo Bandini in *The Road to Los Angeles* and *Ask the Dust*. This essay by the authorized biographer of Fante includes a useful bibliographical note.

Cooper, Stephen and David Fine. *John Fante: A Critical Gathering*. Madison, NJ: Fairleigh Dickinson University Press, 1999. The first collection of substantial criticism, these eleven essays are based on papers delivered at "John Fante: The First Conference," California State University, Long Beach, 1995. Essays are listed separately in this bibliography.

Cressey, Paul G. *The Taxi Dance-Hall*. Chicago: Chicago University Press, 1932. Sociological study of taxi dancers and Filipino men.

Davenport, Basil. "Toscana Saga." *Saturday Review of Literature* 22 (12 October 1940): 18. Review of *Dago Red*.

de Conde, Alexander. *Half Bitter, Half Sweet*. New York: Scribner's, 1971: 382. Mentions "Giovanni" Fante.

de Kay, Drake. Review of *Wait Until Spring, Bandini*. *New York Times Book Review* (23 October 1938): 6-7. Credits Fante's talents for narrative and characterization.

Dever, Joe. "Laughter Mixed with Woe." *The Commonweal* 56:6 (16 May 1952): 155-6. *Full of Life* avoids the "dangerous retrogression" of autobiography.

Domerq, Bruno. "Grant Him This Waltz." *Paris Vogue* (November 1989): 90 ff. Profile of Fante for French readers.

Donovan, Richard. "John Fante of Roseville." *San Francisco Chronicle* (19 March 1941): 13. Based on an interview, this vivid yet unreliable depiction of Fante's early years shows Fante's tendency to fictionalize his biography.

Farrell, James T. "Two Second-Generation Americans." *Atlantic Monthly* 163:1 (January 1939). Calls *Wait Until Spring, Bandini* "rich in its humanness."

Fine, David. "Down and Out in Los Angeles: John Fante's *Ask the Dust.*" *Californians* 9:2 (September/October 1991): 48-51.

_____. "American Short Story Writers Since World War II." *Dictionary of Literary Biography* 130. Detroit: Gale, 1993. Useful overview of the short stories.

_____. "*Ask the Dust* and the Los Angeles Novel of the Thirties." In Cooper and Fine (1999).

Gardaphé, Fred L. "From Oral Tradition to Written Word: Toward an Ethnographically Based Literary Criticism." In *From the Margin: Writings in Italian Americana.* Ed. Anthony Julian Tamburri, et al. West Lafayette: Purdue University Press, 1991, 294-306.

_____. "Left Out: Three Italian/American Writers of the Thirties — John Fante, Pietro di Donato and Jerre Mangione." In *Re-Visiting the 30s,* ed. Bill Mullen and Sherry Linkon. Champaign: University of Illinois Press, 1994.

_____. *Italian Signs, American Streets: The Evolution of Italian American Narrative.* Durham: Duke University Press, 1996. Uses Vico to classify Italian-American narrative into three "ages" or "modes": the Age of Gods (poetic mode); Age of Heroes (mythic mode); Age of Men (philosophic mode). Fante falls into Gardaphé's "early mythic mode."

_____. "Evviva John Fante!" *Dagoes Read: Tradition and the Italian/American Writer.* Toronto: Guernica Editions, 1997. Reviews of *The Road to Los Angeles* and *West of Rome* that appeared in *Fra Noi.*

_____. "John Fante's American *Fantasia.*" In Gardaphé (1996): 57-66; and in Cooper and Fine (1999).

Garside, E. B. "John Fante vs. John Selby." *Atlantic Monthly* 164:6 (December 1939). Review of *Ask the Dust.*

Gordon, Neil. "Realization and Recognition: The Art and Life of John Fante." *Boston Review* 18:5 (1993): 24-9. One of the better articles on Fante in Hollywood. Includes interviews with fellow novelists and screenwriters Harry Essex (*The Creature from the Black Lagoon*) and A. I. Bezzerides (*They Drive By Night* and *Kiss Me Deadly*); Edward Dmytryk, who directed Fante screenplays (*Walk on the Wild Side* and *The Reluctant Saint*); and Frank Spotnitz, director of an unfinished documentary on Fante.

Green, Rose Basile. *The Italian-American Novel: A Document of the Interaction of Two Cultures.* Madison, N.J.: Fairleigh Dickinson

University Press, 1974: 157-63. Locates *Dago Red*, *Wait Until Spring*, *Bandini*, and *Full of Life* in the context of "the fourth phase of the development of Italian-American fiction," the "counterrevulsion" or "back-trailing" phase that takes "another look at Italian-American life to see where it stood in the panorama of the national scene." Inexplicably, omits any discussion of *Ask the Dust*.

_____. "The Italian-American Novel in the Main Stream of American Literature." In Cammett (1969). Fante uses "psychological probings not found in previous Italian-American writers," especially "out-of-place emotionalism."

Guida, George. "Italian-American Modernism: John Fante's *Ask the Dust*." In Cooper and Fine (1999).

Guy, David. "Striking Tales from an Unsung Storyteller." *USA Today* (11 August 1989). On the Fante revival.

Hamsun, Knut. *Hunger*. Trans. Robert Bly. New York: Farrar, Straus and Giroux, 1967.

_____. *Pan*. Trans. James W. McFarlane. New York: Farrar, Straus and Giroux, 1956. The source for the title of *Ask the Dust*.

Harrison, Russell. *Against the American Dream: Essays on Charles Bukowski*. Santa Rosa: Black Sparrow, 1994. Chapter 8 considers the influence of Fante on Bukowksi. Tries to put a Marxist grid over Bukowski's fiction and a racist grid over Fante's.

Hauser, Marianne. "The Portrait of an Italian Family." *New York Times Book Review* (29 September 1940): 7. Calls *Dago Red* "neither a novel nor a collection of short stories, but a freely constructed family portrait, seen impressionistically."

Hemesath, James B. *Vintage Colorado Stories: When Past Met Present*. Niwot: University Press of Colorado, 1997: 42-56. Includes Fante's "In the Spring."

Hier, Grant. "Written Like Mad Sonnets: The Poetics of John Fante's Prose." In Cooper and Fine (1999).

Hobsbaum, Philip. *Reader's Guide to Charles Dickens*. London, 1972.

Homer. *The Iliad*. Trans. Robert Fagles. New York: Viking, 1990.

Horvath, Brooke K. Review of *Full of Life*. *Review of Contemporary Fiction* 8:3 (Fall 1988): 169. By current standards, this "small masterpiece of quiet comedy" may seem "terribly unfashionable," but proves Fante to be "more than an American P.G. Wodehouse."

Jack, Peter Monro. "A Brash Young Man in Love with Fame." *New York Times Book Review* (19 November 1939): 7.

Jackson, Joseph Henry, ed. *Continent's End: A Collection of California Writing*. New York: Whittlesey House, 1944: 5-21. Includes Fante's "Helen, Thy Beauty Is to Me —," with a concise note on the state of the Filipino in America after World War II.

Kaganoff, Penny. Review of *Fante/Mencken*. *Publisher's Weekly* (7 July 1989): 55.

Kendall, Elaine. "A Damon Runyon Story Gone West." *Los Angeles Times — View* 23 (23 March 1982): 6.

Kordich, Kate. "John Fante's *Ask the Dust*: A Border Reading." *MELUS* (forthcoming). Reads Fante's novel, using the multicultural "border theory" of D. Emily Hicks.

_____. "Mythic Los Angeles, the Metaphysical, and a Brief Exegesis on the Dust in *Ask the Dust*." In Cooper and Fine (1999).

Krampner, Jon. "A Forgotten Face from Bunker Hill: Rediscovering John Fante." *Los Angeles Downtown News* (14 September 1987): 1,6-8. The Fante revival, with an emphasis on Fante in Los Angeles, especially the Bunker Hill area in the 1930s.

Kundera, Milan. *The Art of the Novel*. Trans. Linda Asher. New York: Grove Press, 1988.

_____. *The Unbearable Lightness of Being*. Trans. Michael Henry Heim. New York: Harper and Row, 1984.

Lazar, Jerry. "Fante Fever." *California* (April 1989). Posthumous Fante in Hollywood.

Littell, Robert. Review of *Dago Red*. "Outstanding Novels." *Yale Review* 30 (Winter 1941): 12.

Locklin, Gerald. "Dreams from Bunker Hill: John Fante." *American Book Review* 5:2. Along with the usual comparisons to West, Chandler, Cain, and Fitzgerald, Fante's name is sensibly linked with Budd Schulberg, Joan Didion, Norman Mailer, John Gregory Dunne, and Bukowski as the outstanding fictional chroniclers of "the country's second most populous megalopolis."

_____. Review of *The Wine of Youth*. *Studies in Short Fiction* 22:4 (Fall 1985): 482-83. Fante's stories as a "disjunctive bildungsroman."

Luconi, Stefano. "The Protean Ethnic Identities in John Fante's Italian-American Characters." In Cooper and Fine (1999).

Mangan, Gerard. "Artist of the Fallen World." *Times Literary Supplement* 4381 (20 March 1987): 303.

Mangione, Jerre. Review of *Dago Red*. "Italian-American Novelists." *New Republic* 104 (6 January 1941): 29.

Manguel, Alberto. "Chic Bums." *Saturday Night* (May 1989): 63-65.

Martin, Jay. "John Fante: The Burden of Modernism and the Life of His Mind." In Cooper and Fine (1999).

Matuz, Roger, ed. "John Fante." *Contemporary Literary Criticism*, v. 60. Detroit: Gale, 1984: 127-36. Excerpts eighteen articles and reviews from 1938 to 1989.

McQuay, David. "John Fante Finally Famous." *Denver Post* (18 July 1989). On the Fante revival, with comments by Joyce Fante on whether

Hollywood or "enjoyment of life" kept Fante from writing more novels.

McWilliams, Carey. *Southern California Country: An Island on the Land*. New York: Duell, Sloan & Pearce, 1946. Calls *Ask the Dust* one of the four or five great novels about California in the 1930s, along with John Steinbeck's *The Grapes of Wrath*, Nathanael West's *The Day of the Locust*, and Frank Fenton's *A Place in the Sun*.

The Carey McWilliams Papers, Special Collections #1319, at the University Research Library, University of California, Los Angeles. Contains correspondence between McWilliams and Fante, most (but not all) of which is included in *Selected Letters 1932-1981*.

Miller, Henry. *The Air-Conditioned Nightmare*. New York: New Directions, 1945.

Miller, John, ed. *Los Angeles Stories: Great Writers on the City*. San Francisco: Chronicle Books, 1991: 33-9. Includes Chapter 1 of *Ask the Dust*.

Misurella, Fred. Review of *The Road to Los Angeles*. *Italian Americana* 9:1 (Fall/Winter 1991): 105-09. Pedantically contends, with Q. D. Leavis, that opera and Catholicism have encouraged Italian-American writers to tend toward "melodrama and oversimplification," and that Fante accordingly "allows no aesthetic or psychological distance for the reader."

Mullen, Bill and Sherry Linkon, eds. *Re-Visiting the 30s*. Champaign: University of Illinois Press, 1994. See Gardaphé (1994).

Mullen, Michael. "John Fante." *Dictionary of Literary Biography Yearbook*. Detroit: Bruccoli Clark, 1983: 103-106. Standard biographical entry includes bibliography and filmography.

_____. "John Fante: A Working Checklist." *Bulletin of Bibliography* 41:1 (1982): 38-41. Useful for sources to 1982.

Norklun, Kathi. "John Fante (1909-1983) and the Great L.A. Novel." *L.A. Weekly* (20-26 May, 1983). One of the better overviews of the Fante revival.

Olney, James, ed. *Autobiography: Essays Theoretical and Critical*. Princeton: Princeton University Press, 1980.

Pasinetti, P. M. "Immigrants' Children." *Saturday Review* 35:17 (26 April 1952): 17-18, 33. Review of *Full of Life* congratulates Fante on avoiding "the horrors of cuteness" in the "cliché-ridden territory" of domestic comedy.

Patti, Samuel J. "Recent Italian American Literature: The Case of John Fante." In Tamburri (1991): 329-37. Fante as a preparatory instance of post-1974 Italian American literature's coming of age in the way he addresses "the universal human condition."

Peragallo, Olga. "Fante, John Thomas." In *Italian American Authors and Their Contributions to American Literature*. New York: S. F. Vanni, 1949: 93-6. Fante as one who treats "the racial aspect of American regionalism."

Peters, Robert. "Gab Poetry, Duck vs. Nightnigale Music: Charles Bukowski." *Margins* 16 (January 1957): 24-8. Reprinted in *The Great American Poetry Bake-Off*. Metuchen, NJ & London: Scarecrow Press, 1979. Also reprinted in *Where the Bee Sucks: Workers, Drones and Queens of Contemporary American Poetry*. Santa Maria: Asylum Arts, 1994.

Pleasants, Ben. "Stories of Irony from the Hands of John Fante." *Los Angeles Times* (10 July 1979). Often misinformed comments from a friend of Fante.

____. "The Last Interview of John Fante." *Los Angeles Times Magazine* 39:2 (February 1994): 90-5.

Praz, Mario. *The Romantic Agony*. Trans. Angus Davidson. New York: Oxford University Press, 1933; 2nd ed. 1951.

Reed, Paul Richard. *Small Press Review* 12 (December 1980): 15.

Rolfe, Lionel, ed. *Literary L.A.* San Francisco: Chronicle Books, 1981.

Rolfe, Lionel. "John Fante: A Voice of Los Angeles Past is Heard Again." *California Living*, (17 August 1986). More on the Fante revival, emphasizing Fante as an ethnic writer, and additional comments by Bukowski, Gerald Locklin and Joyce Fante.

Rosengarten, Frank. "Alienation, The Quest for Identity, and Social Conflict in The Italian-American Novel." In Cammett (1969). Sees symptoms of social conflict in the aesthetic flaws of Fante's style, which "oscillates between a rather careless and even slovenly slanginess and occasional attempts at elegant, graceful English prose." Good example of how critics could miss Fante's lyric mastery even as they condescended to diagnose his social malaise.

Saroyan, William. "The Patriotic Revolutionary Big-Money Non-Writers of Hollywood." *Sons Come & Go, Mothers Hang in Forever*. New York: McGraw-Hill, 1976. Brief anecdote from an old Hollywood drinking, gambling and writing companion.

Schulberg, Budd. *The Four Seasons of Success*. Garden City: Doubleday, 1972. Hollywood milieu in which Fante moved.

See, Carolyn. Review of *Brotherhood of the Grape*. "Fante Births Another Novel about a Flawed Family." *Los Angeles Times Book Review* (3 April 1977): 3.

Shacochis, Bob. "Forgotten Son of the Lost Generation." *Vogue* (December 1987): 190 ff. Gives Fante his due as the father of the Los Angeles School of postmodern fiction.

Singer, Isaac Bashevis. "Knut Hamsun, Artist of Skepticism." In *Hamsun* (1967): v-xii.

Spencer, Joanna. Review of *Full of Life*. "Pre-Natal." *New York Herald Tribune Book Review* (27 April 1952): 9.

Spender, Stephen. "Confessions and Autobiography." In *The Making of a Poem*. New York: Norton, 1962. Also in Olney (1980): 115-22.

Spotnitz, Frank. "The Hottest Dead Man in Hollywood." *American Film* 14 (July-August 1989): 40-44, 54. Fante's love-hate relationship with Hollywood, past and present, by the maker of a documentary film on Fante.

Sylvester, Harry. Review of *Dago Red*. *The Commonweal* 37:26 (18 October 1940): 533-4.

Talese, Gay. "Where Are the Italian-American Novelists?" *New York Times Book Review* (14 March 1993): 1. Controversial article that did *not* mention Fante. Talese later delivered the Headline Address, "John Fante and the Dilemma of the Italian-American Writer" at the John Fante Conference, 1995.

Tamburri, Anthony J. "To Hyphenate or Not to Hyphenate: The Italian/American Writer and *Italianatà*." *Italian Journal* 3:5, 37-42.

_____. *To Hyphenate or Not to Hyphenate: The Italian/American Writer: An Other American*. Montreal: Guernica Editions, 1991. Expanded version of the *Italian Journal* article.

Tamburri, Anthony J., Paolo A. Giordano, Fred L. Gardaphé, eds. *From the Margin: Writings in Italian Americana*. West Lafayette: Purdue University Press, 1991. An important collection of essays, poetry and fiction, with a useful bibliography.

Thomson, David. "Los Angeles as Fante's Inferno." *Boston Sunday Globe* (5 January 1986).

Ulin, David L. "Back From the Dust." *Los Angeles Times Book Review* (14 May 1995): 9. Report on the Fante Conference in Long Beach, 1995: "Scholars seek to burnish the reputation of John Fante, the legendary Los Angeles writer."

Verdicchio, Pasquale. "Fante's Inferno." In *Devils in Paradise: Writings on Post-Emigrant Culture*. Toronto: Guernica Editions, 1997.

Veronesi, Sandro. "John Fante: la giovinezza come destino." Preface to John Fante, *Un anno terrible*, trans. Alessandra Osti. Roma: Fazi Editore, 1996: vii-xvi. This preface to the Italian edition of *1933 Was a Bad Year* locates the Fante magic, "the priceless gusto of Fante's books," which is part of "the repertoire of American miracles, such as Coca-Cola and Kim Novak" not in his *italianatà* of the "wounded Abruzzo," but in his raging "hormones, hormones everywhere." [My translation.]

Volpe, Gerald. Review of *Ask the Dust*. *MELUS* 7:2 (Summer 1980): 93-5.

Walton, Edna Lou. "Italy in Colorado." *The Nation* 148:3 (14 January 1939): 72. Compares *Wait Until Spring, Bandini* to Ignazio Silone's *Fontamara*, in conveying "the speech of a somewhat inarticulate people."

Warga, Wayne. "A Reclamation on Bunker Hill." *Los Angeles Times* (5 March 1980). Review of *Ask the Dust*.

Weber, Donald. "Shame and Self-Hatred in John Fante's Works." In Cooper and Fine (1999).

Wilde, Oscar. *The Picture of Dorian Gray*. Harmondsworth: Penguin, 1949.

Wiley, Mark. "The Italian-Catholic in America in John Fante's Fiction." Unpublished paper in the Special Collections of the Library of California State University, Long Beach. Cited by Gerald Locklin in his review of *Dreams from Bunker Hill*.

Wills, Ross B. "John Fante." *Common Ground* 1 (Spring 1941): 84-90. Amusing but unreliable caricature of Fante in the early Hollywood years. Included as an appendix to *Selected Letters 1932-1981*.

Wiloch, Thomas. "John Fante." *Contemporary Authors: New Revision Series*, v. 23. Detroit: Gale, 1984.

Young, Jeffrey. "A Conversation with Arnošt Lustig and Miroslav Holub." *Trafika* 1 (Autumn 1993): 155-69.

The John Fante Conference, 1995

"John Fante: The First Conference" took place at California State University, Long Beach, May 4-6, 1995. In addition to screenings of *Full of Life* and *Wait Until Spring, Bandini*, there was a screening and discussion of Frank Spotnitz's *John Fante: A Life* (a documentary in progress), a student panel, discussions with the Fante family and A. I. Bezzerides, and the following papers. Those preceded by an asterisk appear in Cooper and Fine (1999), some with altered titles:

*Beranger, Jean Francois. "Echoes of Protest in Fante's Works."

*Buonomo, Leonardo. "Masculinity and Femininity in Fante's 'A Wife for Dino Rossi.'"

Bush, Mary Bucci. "Possessing Women in John Fante's Fiction."

*Collins, Richard. "Fante's Families."

Cooper, Stephen. "Knut Hamsun's Influence on John Fante."

Diedrich, Rene. "John Fante: A Writer for Writers."

Dunn, Geoffrey. "Fante and the Filipino."

*Fine, David. "*Ask the Dust* as L.A. Novel."

*Gardaphé, Fred L. "John Fante's American Fantasia."

Gaspar, Frank. "The Young John Fante at Long Beach City College."

Gray, Lucy. "John Fante's Influence on Charles Bukowski."

*Guida, George. "Italian-American Modernism: John Fante's *Ask the Dust*."

Horton, Andrew. "Fante and Film: *A Walk on the Wild Side* and *The Reluctant Saint*."

*Kordich, Catherine. "Fante's Fiction as Historical Narrative."

Lim, Paulino. "Fante's Depictions of Filipino-Americans."

Locklin, Gerald. "Fante and Bukowski."

*Luconi, Stefano. "The Protean Ethnic Identities of John Fante's Characters."

*Martin, Jay. "John Fante: The Life of His Mind" (Keynote Address).

Napolitano-Carman, Louise. "Mothers and Fathers in John Fante's Short Stories."

Nericcio, Bill. "An Italian/American in the Suburbs, or, Exiles in Plasticland: Why John Fante's *My Dog Stupid* Bites."

Pompele, Giovanna. "Guilty Men: Sexuality and Catholicism in John Fante."

Talese, Gay. "John Fante and the Dilemma of the Italian-American Writer" (Headline Address).

Verdicchio, Pasquale. "Fante's Inferno." See Verdicchio (1997).

*Weber, Donald. "Shame and Self-Hatred in Fante's Early Fiction."

NOTE ON THE AUTHOR

Richard Collins was born in Oregon in 1952 and grew up in Southern California. Educated at the University of Oregon and the University of California, Irvine, he has won a number of fellowships and grants: an NEH to the School of Criticism and Theory, an NEH to study portraiture at Columbia University, a Fulbright to do research on the *fin de siècle* in London, a Leverhulme USA/Commonwealth Lectureship in American Studies at University College of Swansea, and a Fulbright Senior Lectureship in American Literature at the Universities of Bucharest and Timisoara, Romania. He has also taught at Louisiana State University and the American University in Bulgaria.

His articles and reviews on John Fante have appeared in *Aethlon: The Journal of Sport Literature, New Delta Review* and the *Redneck Review of Literature*. He has published criticism in Europe and America on a number of authors, from Hegel and Tennyson to James Merrill, Nicholson Baker and Andrei Codrescu.

His fiction, poetry and translations have appeared in *The Literary Review, The Southern Humanities Review, Fiction International, Exquisite Corpse, Asylum Annual, Negative Capability, Rosebud, Libido,* and *Yellow Silk*. His work has also been anthologized in *The Ecstatic Moment: The Best of Libido* (Dell, 1997), *Best American Erotica* (Simon & Schuster, 1999), and *Thus Spake the Corpse* (Black Sparrow, 1999). His books include a novel, *Foolscape* (1983), a chapbook of poetry, *This Degradation* (1992), and a translation of Ioan Flora's *Fifty Novels and Other Utopias* (Bucharest: Editura Eminescu, 1996).

He lives with his wife in New Orleans, where he is Associate Professor of English at Xavier University.

Printed in January 2000 by

in Longueuil, Quebec